The Politics of Money

The Fed Under Alan Greenspan

David M. Jones

New York Institute of Finance

New York London Toronto Sydney Tokyo Singapore

Library of Congress Cataloging-in-Publication Data

Jones, David M. (David Milton)
The politics of money : the Fed under Alan Greenspan / by David M. Jones.
p. cm.
Includes bibliographical references and index.
ISBN 0-13-601634-0
1. Board of Governors of the Federal Reserve System (U.S.) 2. Monetary policy—United States. 3. Greenspan, Alan, 1926– I. Title.
HG2563.J663 1991
332.1′12′0973—dc20 91–2552
CIP

Printed in the United States of America

10 9 8 7 6 5 4 3 2 1

Jacket photo credit: The Bettmann Achieve

This book is dedicated to the late Professors Charles R. Whittlesey and Sidney Weintraub, of the University of Pennsylvania, who were invaluable guides and confidants for my journey into monetary theory and policy and to Professor emeritus C. Lowell Harriss of Columbia University who authored my first college text in economics and who continues to this day to communicate through lively correspondence words of support, insight, and wisdom.

Contents

Preface

It has been said that money is the root of all evil. Certainly, as former Federal Reserve Chairman Paul Volcker, among others, has warned, the evils of accelerating inflation pressures tend, over time, to be associated with excessive money growth; in Volker's own words, "inflation cannot persist without excessive monetary growth."[1] Without doubt, this unfavorable inflationary condition weakens U.S. international competitiveness, harms economic efficiency, encourages speculative consumer and business spending, depresses savings and investment, and favors debtors over lenders.

The good news is that investors can benefit from a better understanding of Federal Reserve (Fed) procedures and techniques used to control this excessive money growth and its evils. This may actually be a force for "good," at least concerning potential investment portfolio appreciation. In a broader context, the 1980s have seen the ascendancy of independently conceived and executed monetary policy actions over cumbersome and politically blunted fiscal policy measures as an important influence on economic activity.

The Politics of Money chronicles the evolution of the modern Fed money management approach, primarily during the 1987–91 period when Alan Greenspan has been Fed Chairman. My first book, *Fed Watching and Interest Rate Projections: A Practical Guide*, chronicled mainly the evolution of Fed money management goals and techniques during the preceding 1979–87 Volcker era. During the 1987–91 period, Fed policymakers set a policy approach designed to be both countercyclical and anti-inflationary.

The central premise of this book is that (1) the ability to understand and anticipate Fed policy shifts, and (2) related interest rate movements are indispensable to successful investor portfolio adjustments. Thus, as a rule, when bond yields are rising, stock prices will decline. This is not only because the higher bond yields make bonds more attractive than stocks, but also because rising interest rates, in a more restrictive monetary policy environment, will threaten to weaken future economic activity and corporate earnings. Conversely, when bond yields decline, during a period of easier monetary conditions, stock prices typically will rise as bonds become less attractive and prospects improve for a strengthening in future economic activity and earnings.

Understanding Fed personalities is essential to understanding the monetary policy process. Indeed, strong Fed personalities have interacted with changing economic and financial circumstances to help shape the substance of the Fed's modern money management approach. During the post-World War II period and particularly since the 1951 Accord, Fed leaders have had a relatively free hand in defining policy objectives and in choosing the means to achieve them. Successful Fed Chairmen are the product of conditions in which a strong leader is challenged by a major economic or financial crisis. Their job is not easy; Fed leaders have had to cope with the cyclical extremes of depression and raging inflation. They have faced wartime financing strains, including the World War II requirement of pegged interest rates and immediate postwar political demands to continue to peg rates, despite the inevitable inflationary dangers. At other times, Fed Chairmen have faced undue political pressures. Fed leaders have also dealt with oil and food price shocks, international financial problems, stock market crashes, business bankruptcies, and bank failures.

Some modern Fed Chairmen have found it increasingly difficult to juggle economic and financial forces at the same time as withstanding intense political pressures. Critics, perhaps unfairly, have accused contemporary Fed leaders of being "flim-flam" men who practice the art of deception when it comes to hiding political motives for easing or for avoiding tightening. But, the fact remains that a good understanding of the nature and implications of largely independent Fed policy actions is crucial to profitable investment decisions.

To be successful, investors must develop a sense for the intent of Fed policymakers and follow the same monetary policy objectives, tools, and techniques. In this way, investors can better anticipate changes in monetary policy and interest rates, thereby increasing their chances of making timely and profitable adjustments in holdings of bonds, stocks, and other assets.

It is also important to recognize that the Fed's influence on economic activity in the 1990s may be lessened by several factors. Most immediately, there are hints that the federal government might increase its fiscal activism in the form of large prospective government deficit cutting measures, with corresponding pressure on the Fed to ease in order to help counter the negative economic impact of this shift toward fiscal restraint. In addition, as a result of growing international financial interdependence, the impact of Fed actions may be partly offset at times by the influence of foreign bond rates and stock market developments on the U.S. bond and stock markets.

In Part One, there is a discussion of Federal Reserve objectives, together with the tools and techniques used to try to achieve these lofty aims. The better the understanding of the basics of monetary policy, the better the success at anticipating Fed policy shifts and related movements in interest rates. In Part Two, the emphasis is on Fed leaders themselves and the importance of personal relationships in shaping monetary policy and maintaining Fed independence from undue political pressures. The discussion in Part Three centers on the extent of public confidence in the financial system and on the corporate takeover frenzy of the 1980s. In Part Four, international financial relationships are discussed, including conditions in which U.S. and foreign interest rate movements are "coupled" and when they are "decoupled." Also, international policy cooperation and coordination are examined, with special emphasis on the new central banking arrangements necessary for European monetary union.

Acknowledgments

Special thanks for insights into the financial markets and monetary policy are owed to retired Chairmen of Aubrey G. Lanston & Co. Inc., C. Richard Youngdahl, Jack Freeman, John Ford, and to the current Chairman Richard Kelly. Also offering invaluable advice on financial, banking, and economic policy matters at earlier stages in my career were the late Alan Holmes and Robert Stone, former Managers for Domestic Operations, System Open Market Account, Federal Reserve Bank of New York; George Garvy, retired Vice President, Federal Reserve Bank of New York; Wes Lindow, retired President, Charter New York Corporation; and George W. McKinney, Jr., former Chief Economist, Irving Trust Company.

Most helpful in offering perceptive and informed comments on the original manuscript of this book were Joe

Coyne, Assistant to the Board, Federal Reserve Board of Governors; Gary Stern, President, Federal Reserve Bank of Minneapolis; and Robert Parry, President, Federal Reserve Bank of San Francisco. (Needless to say, any mistakes in the text of this book are my own.)

Other Federal Reserve officials and former officials who have graciously offered wisdom on money policy over the years include Peter Sternlight, current Manager for Domestic Operations, System Open Market Account, Federal Reserve Bank of New York; Michael Prell, Director of Research, Federal Reserve Board of Governors; Robert Holland, former member of the Federal Reserve Board of Governors; Dewey Daane, former member of the Federal Reserve Board of Governors; Lyle Gramley, former member of the Federal Reserve Board of Governors; and Frank Morris, retired President, Federal Reserve Bank of Boston.

Also of great help in communicating ideas about monetary policy have been Lou Dobbs, Myron Kandel, Bill Hartley, and Stuart Varney of CNN, Robert MacNeil and Jim Lehrer of Public Television's "MacNeil/Lehrer News Hour," Charles Gibson and Joan Lunden of ABC's "Good Morning America," and Ray Brady of the "CBS Evening News."

Last but not least, special praise should be accorded my staff at Aubrey G. Lanston & Co. Inc. including my new and extremely perceptive colleague Robert Falconer, Wilson Lam, Patricia Thrapp, and Lisa Zindorf. Two people deserve special recognition because without them this project could never have been completed—Mary Cho, whose loyal and dedicated research effort was indispensible to this project, and my treasured secretary and administrative assistant Margaret Kormanik.

Introduction

The 1980s were characterized by blatant financial excess, with comparatively few real sector imbalances. For the most part, businesses kept inventory stocks in tight alignment with sales and avoided bottlenecks and undue pressures on productive capacity. In contrast, because of the 1980s' financial excesses, banks had to cope with major domestic and foreign loan problems. On top of this, in the 1980s banks faced the unfamiliar and unfavorable forces of deregulation and interest rate volatility. Perhaps as penance for the financial sins of the past decade, the banking system suffered a dramatic 34% plunge in profits in 1989 as banks wrote off a record $22.2 billion in bad assets. The unwinding of the financial excesses of the 1980s has produced a "balance sheet" recession in the early 1990s as a dangerously overleveraged economy has been brought to its knees by a bank-induced credit crunch.

Despite an absence of imbalances in the real sector, the 1980s saw financial distortions in the corporate balance sheet where there was a massive substitution of debt for equity. This reflected not merely the favorable tax treatment of debt over equity, but also a mindless flurry of speculative corporate takeover activities, including a new breed of aggressive corporate raiders and mega-sized leveraged buyouts (LBOs) spurred on by management greed and shortsightedness. In this heady environment, stock prices soared to record levels (with the rally most intense from late-1982 through the first eight months of 1987 and again during most of 1989). This soaring stock market was spurred on by both the declining supply of equities and prolonged easy money conditions that produced an abundance of liquidity. It is not coincidental that the main precursor to the October 19, 1987, stock market crash (a single day's Dow Jones, or D-J, industrials plunge of 500 points) was the Fed's discount rate hike in September 1987. Market participants nervously perceived this Fed tightening move as bringing to an end the prolonged period of monetary ease and abundant liquidity.

As the 1980s came to a close, market discipline was reasserting itself and the past decade's asset inflation (i.e., soaring prices of homes, real estate, stocks, corporate assets, etc.) was rapidly reversing itself and turning into asset deflation. Record numbers of insolvent savings and loan associations and many banks were either closed, sold, or temporarily taken over by regulators. At the same time, many debt-heavy corporations found it increasingly difficult, if not impossible, to generate the earnings necessary to service their huge debt burdens. Corporations were selling assets to pay down some of the debt, but as these assets for sale glutted the market, they had to be sold at prices far lower than originally contemplated in many takeover deals. On October 13, 1989, the stock price collapse (a single day's D-J industrials drop of 190 points), triggered by the failure of a United Airlines management and pilots' takeover plan, signaled the end of an era of financially (rather than economically) based takeover activity.

Also helping to bring speculative corporate mergers and acquisitions (M & A) activity (and especially LBOs) to an end was the drying-up of the $200 billion high yield "junk" bond market, a major source of funds for such activities. Several major junk bond borrowers, including Campeau Corp. were forced, with much public fanfare, to declare bankruptcy. Swept away with this junk bond market collapse was the up-start, but formidable investment bank, Drexel, Burnham Lambert. This firm, which dominated the junk bond market in the 1980s, was largely done in by the same "junk" at the onset of the 1990s; it was forced to declare bankruptcy in February 1990.

During the 1985–90 period, banks have seen bad loan problems arise especially in connection with corporate highly leveraged transactions (HLTs), with less developed country (LDC) debt, and in real estate in many regions, notably the Southwest and Northeast. Because of these loan difficulties together with the threat of a potential near-term weakening in economic activity, many financial institutions are increasingly favoring liquidity over new loans, or perhaps even, in some cases, favoring the contraction of asset and liability footings instead of further expansion, in order to improve capital ratios. Bank capital positions were under pressure from tougher regulator-imposed risk-based capital guidelines. Even some of the largest money center banks (including Citibank and Chase) suffered the downgrading of their debt by the credit rating agencies, and several hard-pressed regional banks (including the Bank of Boston) saw their debt downgraded all the way to junk bond status. Reflective of the disturbing state of financial affairs as the 1990s began was the tendency for credit rating agencies to reduce the credit ratings of many larger banks to levels below those of their larger potential business loan customers, thus putting these banks at a competitive cost disadvantage in raising funds to meet business loan demands.

Even more shocking was the U.S. Controller General's (head of the General Accounting Office, Congress's financial watchdog) assertion in Congressional testimony on September 11, 1990, that he feared that no fewer than 35 major banks were in immediate danger of failing and scores of others were in trouble. Almost as if on cue, Chase, the nation's second largest bank, suffered major loan and liquidity problems later in the same month, forcing it to announce layoffs of 5,000 workers and (in a heretofore unimagined action) to cut its dividends by more than half. Soon came, from the insurance industry, considered perhaps the most solid pillar of U.S. finance, Traveler's announcement that it was sharply increasing loan loss reserves to cover bad real estate loans and slashing its dividends. Even more ominously, government regulators announced during the first weekend in January 1991 that they were taking over the faltering Bank of New England ($22 billion in assets), which represented the largest bank bailout since that of First RepublicBank of Dallas ($33 billion in assets) in March 1988.

This financial tension has brought on a private or "silent" credit squeeze (bank-induced rather than Fed policy-induced) affecting certain types of borrowers in various regions who find it difficult to obtain alternative sources of credit. This unexpectedly abrupt and sudden loan stringency has been further intensified by government regulators who have moved belatedly to toughen financial institution's capital requirements. In particular, commercial banks face toughened risk-based capital requirements which call for their ratio of capital to assets to be raised to 8% by December 1992. Moreover, the Bush Administration's massive thrift assistance plan of 1989 (initially estimated to cost $257 billion over 30 years but with subsequent estimates as high as $500 billion) has dramatically toughened capital requirements for savings and loan associations while at the same time resulting in the government's amassing of a huge quantity of unsold real estate overhanging the market. Initially, this tightening in capital requirements, especially in loan limits for single borrowers, had the effect of completely cutting off credit to many local builders and developers, and it was extremely difficult, if not impossible, for these local borrowers to promptly find alternative financial sources. As a result, housing activity nose-dived in 1990 to levels not seen since the recession of 1981–82.

The implication for the early 1990s of this potentially widespread loan stringency is clearly deflationary. Inevitably asset deflation will bring about a contraction in wealth which, in turn, will tend to depress the rate of increase in consumer spending. As increasing lender caution in the early 1990s operates to wring out the financial excesses of the 1980s, the threat is that the debt-heavy economy could be pushed over the edge into a deep recession. Indeed, the current recession, which apparently began in August 1990, is primarily attributable to this unusual bank credit "drought." Increasing numbers of banks, hard-pressed for profits and facing a prohibitive cost of capital, favor the down-sizing of their balance sheets, with an attendant cut off in most new loan activity.

The current recession is a "balance sheet" recession rather than one stemming primarily from real sector imbalances. The current recession grows mainly out of a clash between an overleveraged economy and a growing reluctance of financially burdened banks to make new loans. Moreover, rather than affecting primarily the goods' producing sector, as in the case of past recessions, the current recession appears to be spreading to the service sector with major job losses in banking, real estate, insurance, retail establishments, and transportation. These forces could prolong the recession and make recovery difficult.

A growing concern with unusual lender caution was largely responsible for a Fed easing step on July 13, 1990. In addition the Fed had under consideration beginning in the summer of 1990 a move to cut bank reserve requirements in order to improve bank profitability and help counter the bank-induced credit squeeze. On December 4, 1990, the Fed Board announced that it was eliminating the 3% reserve requirement for nonpersonal time deposit maturing within 18 months. Other Fed easing steps were taken as well in the second half of 1990 and early 1991 to help counter growing signs of an economic downturn.

Suddenly adding to fears of slumping economic activity and to at least a temporary 1990 spurt in inflation (SLUMP-FLATION) was another oil price shock in August 1990 (just as jolting but not as threatening as the ones in 1973 and 1979). This latest oil price shock stemmed from Iraq's sudden invasion and occupation of Kuwait on August 2, 1990. In the following days, oil prices soared, bond rates rocketed upward, and stock prices plummeted. For instance, on the first two days following the Iraqi invasion and occupation of Kuwait in 1990, the Dow-Jones industrial average fell a total of 148 points. During the tumultuous month of August 1990, the Dow-Jones Industrial Average was down in one instance by a whopping 422 points, before recovering some of this lost ground later in the month. The 30-year Treasury bond yield spurted to above 9⅛% from 8½%, before easing back to below 9% by month's end. And oil prices, the primary cause of all this financial instability, soared at one point during August to $32 per barrel (West Texas Crude) from a pre-oil price shock (early July) level of about $18 a barrel, before ending the month at about $27 per barrel.

Subsequently, in early October, renewed fears of Middle East military hostilities involving a possible related interruption of oil supplies from that region pushed oil prices still higher to more than $40 per barrel. However, oil prices eased lower again in November and December 1990 on news of increased OPEC (Organization of Petroleum Exporting Countries) oil supplies, moderating demands, and mounting hopes of a peaceful settlement of the Middle East crisis.

In early January 1991, these hopes for peace were dashed and oil prices again bounded higher.

On the evening of January 16, 1991, United States and allied forces attacked Iraq. Initial reports suggested that the international coalition's heavy air strikes were a resounding success. Hopes for a quick and complete allied victory in the Persian Gulf war triggered a plunge in oil prices to the lowest level since July 1990, a sharp decline in U.S. Treasury bond yields, and a global rally in stock prices. After a remarkably successful four-day ground war, President Bush declared a cease-fire effective midnight February 27, 1991.

In the 1980s, Federal Reserve policy was notable for its successes. The Volcker Fed scored a spectacular victory against rampant inflation in the early 1980s, setting the stage for a record peacetime economic expansion of nearly eight years. During the period from late 1987 through 1989, the Greenspan Fed successfully fine-tuned monetary policy, though the verdict on subsequent Greenspan efforts is less favorable.

The Greenspan Fed's goal is sustainable, noninflationary economic growth. From March 1988 through February 1989, the Greenspan Fed sought to counter accelerating real economic activity and mounting inflationary pressures at a time of high productive resource utilization by tightening reserve pressures in small but frequent moves and by pushing interest rates higher. In contrast, from June 1989 through December 1989, Fed policymakers sought to ease reserve pressures in small steps, to push interest rates lower in light of weakening tendencies in real economic activity and indications that inflationary pressures would soon begin moderating. After maintaining an unchanged policy stance in the first half of 1990, the Fed eased further in the second half of the year, at first tentatively, then stepping up the pace in December 1990 with rapid-fire use of all three major Fed policy "guns"—including the already noted reserve requirement cut, two further easing steps through open market operations and a discount rate decline. Further easing actions were taken by the monetary authorities in the early months of 1990.

The Greenspan Fed has until recently de-emphasized the monetary and credit aggregates as intermediate policy targets, in contrast with the heavy monetary orientation of the Volcker Fed. The Greenspan Fed favors instead the approach of "casting the net wide"[1] by monitoring many intermediate policy variables used to help diagnose undesired fluctuations in economic activity or price pressures. These many intermediate Fed policy signals include, in addition to the monetary and credit aggregates, quarterly real GNP growth, monthly industrial production, resource utilization rates, employment, the corporate purchasing managers' index, the balance of inventory stocks in relation to sales, and unfilled orders. The Greenspan Fed also scrutinizes wage pressures, commodity prices, the dollar, bond yields, equity prices, and the spread between short- and long-term interest rates.

During the 1980s, monetary authorities grew increasingly uncertain about monetary and economic relationships because of deregulation, financial innovation, and globalization. To avoid making cumulative policy errors in this new and uncertain environment, the wary Greenspan Fed formulated the technique of making small and usually frequent adjustments in its policy stance that could be promptly reversed if necessary.

Looking ahead, the 1990s will bring new challenges, and perhaps the harshest test yet of the Fed's modern money management techniques, on both the domestic and foreign fronts. Fed policy makers will face the daunting tasks of subduing inflationary pressures and correcting the financial excesses of the 1980s without triggering destabilizing corporate bankruptcies or bank failures that might severely depress the economy for an extended time. An emerging flaw in the Fed's modern policy approach is that it is currently trying to consider so many conflicting intermediate policy variables that the monetary authorities may be frozen into inaction, as appeared to be the case at times during 1990. Also complicating the Fed's efforts are, on the fiscal policy front, Washington's growing domestic fiscal activism, in the form of the government's cuts in entitlement programs and defense spending and increases in tax revenues. On the international front, there are increasingly important foreign financial influences on U.S. longer-term interest rates, especially the prospects for high interest rates and soaring credit demands in a united Germany and capitalist Eastern Europe.

Part One

Policy Process and Indicators

Monetary policy is the government's most flexible and reliable weapon for keeping the domestic economy on a sustainable, noninflationary growth course. Ideally, fiscal policy (changes in government taxation and spending) should also assist in this job; but Washington politicians tend to get bogged down in partisan squabbles and hamstrung by pressures from special interests, thereby seemingly rendering fiscal policy incapable of influencing economic activity in a timely fashion. Indeed, the agonizingly slow and unseemly process by which the Republican Bush Administration and Democrat-controlled Congress finally passed the October 1990 Deficit Reduction Bill that cut the deficit by an estimated $492 billion over five years through higher taxes and spending cuts could *not* have come at a worse time for the slumping economy.

In its usually more timely and effective money management process, the Federal Reserve seeks to adjust bank reserve pressures in a manner that influences the cost and availability of money and credit in order to affect economic activity and inflation. Fed policymakers seek to diagnose the state of the economy by examining continuous economic and financial data. When economic conditions threaten to become unhealthy, the monetary authorities typically will react promptly.

The Greenspan Fed (1987–91) has focused primarily on the dual policy objectives of reining in inflationary pressures (progress toward price stability) and maintaining sustainable economic growth (avoiding recession). To accomplish these objectives, the Greenspan Fed pursued a novel "soft landing" policy approach in the 1988–89 period in which it fine-tuned reserve pressures in a manner that sought to ease real GNP growth down to a pace somewhat but not too far below the economy's longer-term growth potential. It was expected that this experimental policy approach, if pursued for a sufficiently long time, would eventually relieve pressures on nearly fully employed productive resources thereby eventually operating to moderate inflationary pressures.

By 1990, however, the Greenspan Fed's soft landing policy approach seemed to be in danger of failing. The underlying rate of inflation was accelerating early in that year, despite an extended period of sluggishness in economic activity. To make matters worse, an unusual bank-induced credit squeeze started to become evident in the spring of 1990. Then, as if matters were not difficult enough, the August Persian Gulf war threat and oil price shock created additional uncertainties. Also complicating Fed policy was Washington's prolonged budget negotiations. At times during 1990, Fed policymakers seemed to lapse into a condition of near policy paralysis. At other times, the Fed's policy responses seemed to be conditioned primarily by unusual forces (such as in July when the Fed eased in response to the bank-induced credit squeeze) or by forces outside the Fed's control (such as in October when the Fed eased in response to Washington's deficit-cutting bill). Finally, in December 1990, in light of alarming signs of an economic downturn, an intensifying bank-induced credit crunch, and slumping monetary growth, the Fed dramatically stepped up the pace of its easing actions, and more such actions came in the early months of 1991.

CHAPTER 1

The Fed's Policy-Making Process

To understand the Fed's policy-making process and to try to anticipate how the monetary authorities might respond to policy challenges, it is a good idea to try to put yourself in its place. Fed policy meetings are gatherings of informed and highly trained individuals. Given their different regional perspectives, however, Fed officials participating in these meetings are more likely to express the common sense of the person on main street than the high-powered formulas of a laboratory scientist. This is not to say that Fed policy meetings don't take on an academic or technical monetary tone at times. (How could it be otherwise, given the fact that so many Fed policymakers are trained economists?) But the fact is that the Fed's choice of policy objectives, the means to achieve them, and the guidelines used along the way are all mainly the product of common sense give and take.

COMPOSITION OF THE FOMC

The key Fed policy-making body is the Federal Open Market Committee (FOMC).[1] It is in charge of the Fed's primary policy instrument, open market operations. The FOMC is composed of 12 voting members—including the 7 members of the Board of Governors and 5 voting Federal Reserve Bank Presidents. The Chairman of the Board of Governors also serves as Chairman of the FOMC. The New York Fed President serves as Vice Chairman of the FOMC and has a permanent vote on this body. The remaining 4 voting positions on the FOMC are filled by the remaining 11 Reserve Bank Presidents on a rotating basis.[2] (It should be noted that all 12 Reserve Bank Presidents, both voting and nonvoting, participate at each FOMC meeting, as can be seen in Exhibit 1.1.) The FOMC (which meets in Washington, D.C. approximately eight times a year on a regularly scheduled basis and more frequently in special telephone conferences if conditions dictate) influences reserve pressures and the cost and availability of money and credit in order to try to achieve the economic objective of sustainable, noninflationary growth.

The FOMC operates directly through purchases (or sales) of government securities in order to ease (or tighten) reserve pressures. These actions are taken with a view to reducing (increasing) the cost and increasing (decreasing) the availability of money and credit in order to influence the course of spending and output and ultimately inflationary pressures. The object at each FOMC meeting is to diagnose the state of the economy and to take into account special factors such as financial tensions and international considerations in shaping, through majority vote, a policy directive that guides Fed open market operations during the five to six week interval between FOMC meetings.

MOMENTOUS MEETING

The "room" is anything but intimate. It has a lofty, two-story high ceiling from which is suspended a huge, heavy, menacing, metal chandelier adorned by vigilant eagles perched on its upper edge. The towering, solemn walls are covered by a richly textured but drab material. In the

Exhibit 1.1. Seating Arrangement For October 2, 1990, FOMC Meeting

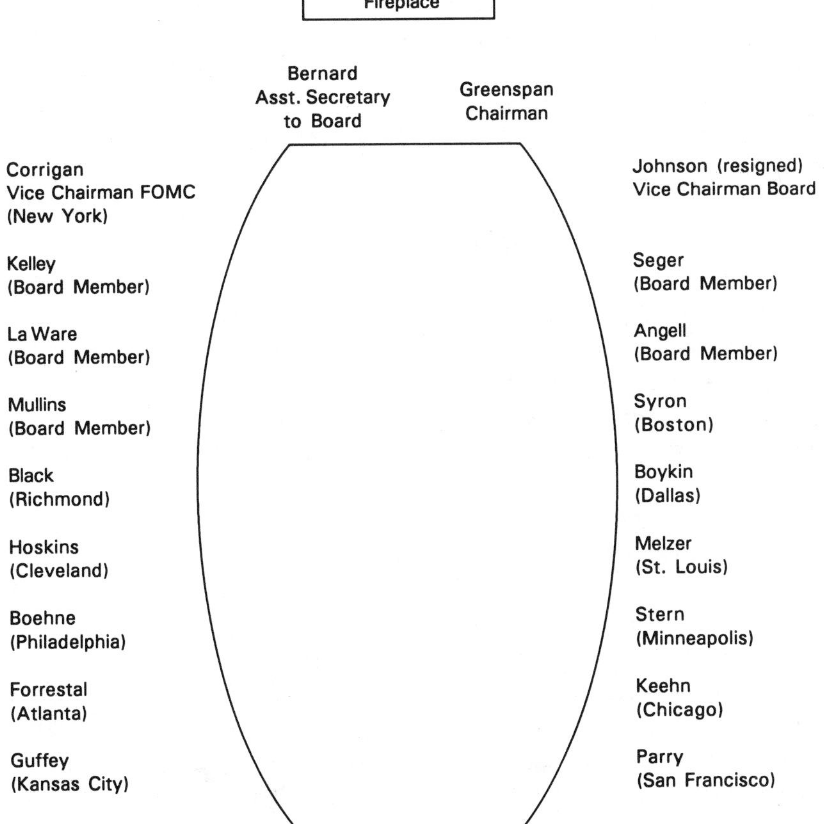

Source: Federal Reserve and Aubrey G. Lanston & Co. Inc.

center of the room is a gigantic mahogany conference table surrounded by straight-back chairs in which stern-faced monetary policymakers are about to sit. At one end of the room there is a large, rarely used and uninviting fireplace encased in cold and imposing marble—the same material which encases the oversized main door and other entrances to the room, including one from the Chairman's office. Looming above the fireplace is an over-sized scowling likeness of the national eagle symbol with arrows in one claw and an olive branch in the other, similar to, but not exactly like, the official seal that appears on U.S. currency.

The room is steeped in tradition. It had been used in 1942–43 as a "war" room by the combined U.S. and British military chiefs of staff to plot the strategies ultimately leading to victory in Europe. Now the room was about to be used for the "monetary wars." The icy formality of the room, with its musty, institutional smell of aged furniture wax and floor cleaner, foretold the serious business that was about to transpire in this special place.

The month of October seems to have historical significance in Fed policy deliberations, as evidenced by the October 6, 1979, "Saturday Massacre" (also called the "Saturday Night Special") and the October 19, 1987, "Black Monday" stock market crash. There was also the less severe but still unnerving October 13, 1989, stock market collapse.

The October 2, 1990, FOMC meeting about to start in this Federal Reserve Board room (where both the Federal Reserve Board and the FOMC meet) was no exception. It was a watershed meeting that posed more challenges than perhaps any other single policy meeting in the Greenspan era. Fed policymakers faced mounting financial tensions: intensifying banking, thrift, and insurance industry problems; a severe credit squeeze; a weakening economy; a stunning oil price shock; and a declining dollar; among other problems.

CAST OF CHARACTERS

The cast of characters at this crucial October 2, 1990, FOMC meeting was impressively long on academic degrees but somewhat shorter on senior level monetary policy experience. The FOMC was also short one member, Vice Chairman Manuel Johnson who resigned effective August 3, 1990, and had not yet been replaced.

Most senior among the members of the Board of Governors at the October 2, 1990, FOMC meeting was Martha Seger who was sworn in only slightly more than five years earlier on July 2, 1984. (Board members are seated at each meeting according to seniority.) She received her Ph.D. degree in finance and business economics from the University of Michigan. Prior to joining the Board, she had been Professor of Finance at Central Michigan University, and before that, Commissioner of Financial Institutions for the State of Michigan. Seger, born in Adrian, Michigan, was without question the most outspoken "dove" on the FOMC, consistently urging an easier Fed policy stance. She dissented at the October 2 meeting, favoring an immediate easing step, rather than a future easing move conditioned on a budget agreement. (Governor Seger announced her resignation from the Board of Governors on January 23, 1991.)

Next in seniority among the members of the Board of Governors was Wayne Angell who was sworn in February 7, 1986. He received his Ph.D. in economics from the University of Kansas. Previously, he had been Professor of Economics at Ottawa University and member of the Investment Committee of now defunct Franklin Savings Association. Angell, born in Liberal, Kansas, and who owed his Fed appointment to his friendship with Senator Robert Dole (Republican-Kansas), was an important swing vote on the Board, along with former Vice Chairman Johnson. Angell tended to favor the use of commodity prices and other auction market indicators as important intermediate indicators for policy. He cast a dissenting vote against any easing following the October 2 meeting.

Next in line came Edward (Mike) Kelley who was sworn in as a Board member only slightly more than three years earlier on May 26, 1987. He received his MBA from Harvard University. Prior to being named to the Board, he had been Chairman of Investment Advisors Incorporated in Houston, Texas, and, not insignificantly, was a friend of then-Treasury Secretary James Baker. Kelley was born in Eugene, Oregon.

Following in order of seniority was Board Chairman Alan Greenspan (seated at the head of the Board table) who was sworn in August 11, 1987. The always cautious, considerate, and serious-minded Fed Chairman, well-regarded by his fellow policymakers, received his Ph.D. from New York University. Prior to being named Fed Chairman, he had been chairman of a private economic consulting firm and also served as a corporate director for an impressive cross-section of corporate America: Aluminum Company of America (Alcoa); Automatic Data Processing Inc.; Capital Cities/ABC; Mobil Corporation; Morgan Guaranty; and the Pittston Company. Greenspan was born in New York City. As a widely respected economic analyst, he had an eye for real sector imbalances; his numbers-crunching ability was legendary. Greenspan thrived on the wealth of data made available to him as a Fed policymaker; he often short-circuited the chain of command at the Board research staff to obtain information directly from junior specialists.

Next in order of seniority came John LaWare who was sworn in on August 15, 1988. He holds an MA in political science from the University of Pennsylvania. Previous to being named to the Board, he had been Chairman of Shawmut Bank and before that he had served as a lending officer at Chemical Bank and as Chairman of the Association of Bank Holding Companies. LaWare was born in Columbus, Wisconsin.

The most junior Board member, but already a rising star, was David Mullins who had been recently sworn in on

May 21, 1990. He received his Ph.D. in finance and economics from MIT and had been Assistant Secretary of the Treasury for Domestic Finance, and before that a professor at Harvard Business School. He was born in Memphis, Tennessee. Governor Mullins apparently saw very sluggish growth at the time, but no recession on the horizon. He felt that all the Fed could do was to try to keep money and credit growing at a pretty restrained pace and let the economy take care of itself.[3]

Nevertheless, Mullins voted with the Greenspan-led majority at the October meeting (against an unusually large four-person dissent). The majority voted in favor of an initially unchanged policy stance followed by a Fed easing move if a Federal budget-cutting agreement was reached. Moreover, the majority agreed to permit further easing if incoming data warranted it—though this step was never taken. Joining Governor Mullins in the Greenspan-led majority were Governors Kelley and LaWare, along with Reserve Bank Presidents Corrigan, Boehne, and Stern. (On January 14, 1991, Mullins was nominated by President Bush to become Vice Chairman of the Federal Reserve Board to replace Manuel Johnson.)

Most senior in service among the five voting Reserve Bank Presidents at the October 2 meeting was Robert Boykin, President of the Dallas Reserve Bank, who took office January 1, 1981. He was a lawyer by profession with a JD degree from the University of Texas. Prior to being named Dallas Fed President he had served in the Dallas Reserve Bank's legal department. Boykin was born in Eugene, Oregon. In the policy deliberations on October 2, Boykin dissented, arguing against any easing. He was unwilling to concede that the economy was in a recession (although evidence subsequently suggested that it was); rather, he took the view that it was entering a phase of declining economic activity and rising inflation.[4] Another senior voting Reserve Bank President was Edward Boehne, President of the Philadelphia Reserve Bank who took office February 1, 1981. He received his Ph.D. degree in economics from Indiana University and had previously served in the research department at the Philadelphia Reserve Bank. Boehne was born in Evansville, Indiana.

Next in seniority among the voting Reserve Bank Presidents was E. Gerald Corrigan, Vice Chairman of the FOMC and President of the New York Reserve Bank, who took office January 1, 1985. He received his Ph.D. in economics from Fordham University and had previously been President of the Minneapolis Reserve Bank. Prior to that he had worked up through the research ranks to become Senior Vice President at the New York Reserve Bank and had been special advisor to former Fed Chairman Volcker. Corrigan, who tends to be hawkish on monetary policy questions, was born in Waterbury, Connecticut. Also voting at the October 2 FOMC meeting was Gary Stern, President of the Minneapolis Reserve Bank who took office March 16, 1985. He received his Ph.D. degree in economics from Rice University and had previously served in both the Minneapolis Reserve Bank and New York Reserve Bank research departments. Stern was born in San Luis Obispo, California.

Most junior among the voting Reserve Bank Presidents, but most persuasive as leader of the monetary policy hawks was W. Lee Hoskins, President of the Cleveland Reserve Bank, who took office October 8, 1987. Hoskins argued that the Fed should maintain a strong anti-inflation stance, and not give in to pressures to ease monetary policy to promote economic growth. He dissented, warning against any easing following the October 2 meeting. He received his Ph.D. degree in economics from UCLA and had previously headed the economic research departments at Pittsburgh National Bank and prior to that at the Philadelphia Reserve Bank. Hoskins was born in Los Angeles, California.

Chairman Greenspan opened the meeting by seeking approval of the minutes of the previous August 21 FOMC meeting (see Exhibit 1.2).[5] Next he asked for reports by the managers for foreign operations and for domestic open market operations. After questions and discussion, the

Exhibit 1.2. FOMC Sample Agenda

Sample Agenda

I. Approval of minutes of actions taken at the last meeting of the Federal Open Market Committee.

II.* Foreign currency operations.
- A. Report on operations since the last meeting.
- B. Action to ratify transactions since that meeting.

III.* Domestic open market operations.
- A. Report on operations since the last meeting.
- B. Action to ratify transactions since that meeting.

IV. Economic situation.
- A. Staff report on economic situation.
- B. Committee discussion.

V. Longer run ranges for monetary policy (February and July meetings).
- A. Staff comments.
- B. Committee discussion and actions on longer run ranges.
  1. Review of ranges for year in progress.
  2. Establishment of tentative ranges for following year (July meeting).

VI. Current monetary policy and domestic policy directive.
- A. Staff comments.
- B. Committee discussions.
- C. Action to adopt directive.

VII. Confirmation of date for next meeting.

*At the February and July meetings, reports on operation in foreign currencies and the domestic securities market and their discussion are sometimes deferred until after the longer run ranges are developed.

Source: Federal Reserve

FOMC ratified the foreign and domestic open market operations conducted over the interval since the previous FOMC meeting. The next item on the agenda was Board staff review of current and prospective economic and financial developments, summarizing the material on the major economic and financial trends in the *green* book. This is one of three basic briefing books (each identified by its color) that are presented to FOMC members in advance of each meeting.

The Committee members (including the nonvoting Reserve Bank Presidents who all attend each FOMC meeting) then presented their own views on the economic situation and outlook. Sometimes the Committee members' views on the economic situation and outlook will differ from those of the Board staff. However, there seemed to be general agreement (erroneous as it turned out) at the October 2, 1990, meeting that the "available data did not point to cumulating weakness and the onset of a recession." Additional material on the regional economic situation in each of the 12 Federal Reserve Bank districts is presented in the *beige* book, made public two weeks before each FOMC meeting.

The FOMC members typically employ a wide range of analytical approaches at each meeting; some use traditional Keynesian aggregate demand analysis, some focus more on key industries with certain cyclical characteristics or special regional developments, and some rely on "auction market" indicators such as the spread between the Federal funds rate and the 30-year Treasury bond rate, the dollar, or commodity prices. Other members prefer instead to emphasize the relationship between monetary or credit aggregates and economic activity.

Next came the staff presentation (by the Monetary Affairs Division Director) of alternate short-run growth paths for the monetary aggregates, along with associated amounts of discount window borrowings and ranges for the Federal funds rate. This presentation draws on and amplifies material presented to FOMC members in the highly secret *blue* book. Typically, three short-term policy options are offered: option A specifies higher money growth and a lower-than-prevailing borrowings target and Federal funds rate level; option B specifies monetary growth rates that are consistent with unchanged borrowings and Federal funds rate levels; and option C specifies lower monetary growth and a tightening in reserve pressures reflected in higher borrowings and

Federal funds rate levels, relative to those specified in option B. The *blue* book also incorporates these policy options into sample wordings of alternative FOMC directives.

This staff presentation of short-term policy targets was then discussed by the FOMC members themselves who offered their own modifications. At this critical point in the policy deliberations at the typical FOMC meeting, the Fed Chairman can exert perhaps his greatest influence in shaping the monetary policy outcome. He may open the discussion and thus set the terms of the debate regarding short-term policy targets. Alternatively, the Chairman may sum up and mold a "consensus" to his liking. By this point in the policy deliberations the Chairman can, with knowledge of the on-going discussion and debate, usually present ranges for the monetary and credit aggregates that will command the support of the majority of the FOMC members. At the October 2 meeting, Greenspan favored Fed easing actions. However, he recognized that in order to prod along the difficult federal budget negotiations at that time, any Fed easing steps should be conditioned on the achievement of a creditable deficit-cutting agreement. Finally, a Greenspan-led compromise between the hawks and doves was reached and the wording of the FOMC policy directive guiding Fed open market operations until the next FOMC meeting was decided on.

FORMULATION OF DIRECTIVE

Fed policymakers can specify in their FOMC directive several alternative means of adjusting reserve pressures through open market operations during the intermeeting period. For example, the monetary authorities may provide for a symmetrical directive (as in the July 5–6, 1989 meeting) in which "somewhat greater reserve restraint or somewhat lesser reserve restraint would be acceptable" (see Exhibit 1.3). Alternatively, Fed officials might decide on an asymmetrical directive but with the potential size of the

Exhibit 1.3. FOMC Directive

Operating Paragraphs from Selected FOMC Policy Directives
Meeting Held July 5-6, 1989

In the implementation of policy for the immediate future, the Committee seeks to decrease slightly the existing degree of pressure on reserve positions. Taking account of indications of inflationary pressures, the strength of the business expansion, the behavior of the monetary aggregates, and developments in foreign exchange and domestic financial markets, somewhat greater reserve restraint or somewhat lesser reserve restraint would be acceptable in the intermeeting period. The contemplated reserve conditions are expected to be consistent with growth of M2 and M3 over the period from June through September at annual rates of about 7 percent. The Chairman may call for Committee consultation if it appears to the Manager for Domestic Operations that reserve conditions during the period before the next meeting are likely to be associated with a federal funds rate persistently outside a range of 7 to 11 percent.

Meeting Held August 22, 1989

In the implementation of policy for the immediate future, the Committee seeks to maintain the existing degree of pressure on reserve positions. Taking account of progress toward price stability, the strength of the business expansion, the behavior of the monetary aggregates, and developments in foreign exchange and domestic financial markets, slightly greater reserve restraint might or slightly lesser reserve restraint would be acceptable in the intermeeting period. The contemplated reserve conditions are expected to be consistent with growth of M2 and M3 over the period from June through September at annual rates of about 9 and 7 percent, respectively. The Chairman may call for Committee consultation if it appears to the Manager for Domestic Operations that reserve conditions during the period before the next meeting are likely to be associated with a federal funds rate persistently outside a range of 7 to 11 percent.

Meeting Held October 2, 1990

In the implementation of policy for the immediate future, the Committee seeks to maintain the existing degree of pressure on reserve positions. Taking account of progress toward price stability, the strength of the business expansion, the behavior of the monetary aggregates, and developments in foreign exchange and domestic financial markets, slightly greater reserve restraint might or somewhat lesser reserve restraint would be acceptable in the intermeeting period. The contemplated reserve conditions are expected to be consistent with growth M2 and M3 over the period from September through December at annual rates of about 4 and 2 percent, respectively. The Chairman may call for Committee consultation if it appears to the Manager for Domestic Operations that reserve conditions during the period before the next meeting are likely to be associated with a federal funds rate persistently outside a range of 6 to 10 percent.

Source: Federal Reserve

policy shift equal in either direction (as in August 22, 1989) in which slightly greater reserve restraint might or slightly lesser reserve restraint would be acceptable." Still another directive wording indicates on asymmetrical policy bias both in terms of magnitude and direction (as in the October 2, 1990 meeting) in which "slightly greater reserve restraint might or somewhat lesser reserve restraint would be acceptable."

Apart from the precise wording of the Fed policy directive covering the intermeeting period the Committee members may reach agreement on conditional adjustments in reserve pressures. For example, at the December 15, 1988, meeting, the FOMC agreed that an initial tightening in reserve pressures during the intermeeting period should be followed by a further tightening move (as actually occurred on January 5, 1990), "unless incoming evidence on the behavior of prices, the performance of the economy, or conditions in financial markets differed greatly from current expectations." Of course, at the October 2, 1990, FOMC meeting, the conditional step was in the opposite easing direction, and it was hinged on a budget agreement.

POLICY ISSUES

Fed policymakers faced a classic policy dilemma at their October 2, 1990, meeting. Too much easing too soon could mean accelerating wage and price pressures on the heels of the oil price shock triggered by Iraq's August invasion and occupation of Kuwait; but too little easing too late could threaten to intensify a threatened economic downturn (actually the recession appears to have begun two months before in August 1990), especially given the fragile condition of the financial sector.

According to the official record of policy actions, the majority of FOMC members favored, at the October 2 meeting, unchanged reserve pressures for a short period, followed by an easing move if a budget agreement could be achieved. In addition, Fed officials left room for a further easing in reserve pressures "if warranted by incoming data on economic and financial conditions in the context of an already sluggish economy." However, this additional easing step was never taken.

At the October 2 meeting, Fed policymakers devoted "considerable attention" to the unusual bank-induced credit squeeze. A number of Committee members said that the risk of recession didn't stem from traditional forces "but from the possible aggravation of the strains in financial markets, further retrenchment in lending by banks and others, and the increased difficulty of many heavily indebted businesses and individuals to meet and service their debt obligations in a sluggish economy." Many Committee members "stressed that a considerable divergence appeared to have developed between available economic indicators, which suggested continued if only sluggish growth, and deteriorating business confidence."

Striking a cautionary note with regard to the extent of any future Fed easing steps, Committee members generally felt that on the inflation front "under foreseeable circumstances and assuming no sharp movements in oil prices, whose course remained highly uncertain, over all prices were likely to remain under upward pressure for some time." Although Committee members "still anticipated eventual progress in reducing inflation as continued sluggish demand was reflected in diminished pressures on productive resources," a major concern in the interim was that "the rise in oil prices would become more firmly entrenched in the cost structure of the economy, thereby making more difficult and delaying progress toward price stability."

On balance, Fed policymakers, facing a myriad of forces at the meeting, decided to proceed timidly. Indeed, they tied the next easing step to budget negotiations, something beyond their control. Subsequently, at the November 13 FOMC meeting, the Fed responded belatedly to the more seriously slumping economy (the recession had already been underway for 3½ months). But, like earlier easing actions, the Greenspan Fed's mid-November easing in reserve pressures was modest and carefully defined.

Finally, in December 1990, the Fed picked up the pace of its easing actions.[6] On December 4, the Fed announced a cut in reserve requirements to counter the intensifying bank-induced credit crunch. On December 7, following a dismal November employment report released on that day, the Fed moved to ease reserve pressures through open market operations pushing the Federal funds rate down to 7¼% from 7½%. Then, on December 18, the Fed employed its third and final major policy tool in announcing a discount rate cut to 6½% from 7%. In addition, the Fed decided on this same day to nudge the funds rate down to 7% from 7¼% through open market operations. The Fed's stepped-up pace of easing actions continued into early 1991. On January 8, 1991, the Fed moved, in response to sluggish monetary growth, to ease the funds rate to 6¾% from 7% through open market operations. Then, on February 1, 1991, the Fed acted, following extremely weak employment and corporate purchasing managers reports, to cut the discount rate to 6% from 6½%, paralleled by a decline in the funds rate to 6¼% from 6¾%. On March 8, 1991 the Fed eased yet again, pushing the Federal Funds rate down to 6% from 6¼%, following February's disturbingly weak employment report.

CONTEMPORARY PRIORITIES

Generally, the Greenspan Fed has focused on four primary categories of intermediate policy variables to help decide when to change reserve pressures. For most of Chairman Greenspan's tenure, the intermediate policy indicators have been grouped, in order of importance, as inflation indicators, the indicators of business expansion, money and credit aggregates, and conditions in the foreign exchange market and domestic financial markets. The first two Fed priorities—price stability and sustainable expansion—are the *ultimate objectives* of monetary policy. The third Fed priority—moderate growth in the monetary aggregate—is really an *intermediate* Fed indicator (target). The fourth Fed priority, summed up in the catch-all phrase "conditions in the foreign exchange and domestic financial markets," is actually intended to capture Fed policymaker concerns about market instability.

As a first priority, from the August 1988 FOMC meeting through the February 1991 FOMC meeting, Fed policymakers focused on intermediate inflation indicators as the primary factor to consider in making intermeeting modifications in reserve pressures (see Table 1.1). Such inflation indicators include measures of pressures on productive resources such as the unemployment rate and the rate of industrial capacity utilization, along with the employment cost index, producer prices, and other auction market indicators of inflationary expectations.

As a general policy approach, the Greenspan Fed was, during most of the period from late 1987 through early 1990, "leaning against the wind" to curtail excess demand at a time of near full employment that might cause higher wage and price pressures. Without question, the Greenspan Fed's highest priority was to first stabilize and then reduce the rate of price increase. Ideally, the Fed wanted, over the coming five years, to reduce the rate of price increase to zero, or at least to a point where it no longer exerted a significant influence on consumer or business spending decisions. This premier role for intermediate inflation indicators in Fed policy deliberations has prevailed during virtually the entire Greenspan tenure, with the exception of the period immediately following the 1987 stock market crash when the Fed's desire to stabilize domestic financial market conditions (especially the stock market) temporarily reigned supreme. In March 1987, the preceding Volcker Fed had moved the dollar into first place among intermediate indicators to consider in making modifications in reserve pressures.

The Greenspan Fed's second policy priority was to try to sustain the business expansion (or to avoid recession). The fear was that the "critical mass" of the huge thrift industry crisis—real estate deflation, bank debt downgradings, and excessive debt burdens, especially in the corporate sector—

could turn a recession into a depression. In connection with this second priority, the Fed focused on real sector intermediate indicators such as monthly statistics on industrial production, nonfarm payroll job growth, the corporate purchasing managers' index, inventory/sales ratios, and unfilled orders. In trying to make a short-term reconciliation of the first and second priorities, the Greenspan Fed experimented with an untried "soft-landing" approach. In this soft-landing experiment, the Greenspan Fed sought to gradually slow previously strong real GNP growth and then to maintain it for a prolonged period at a pace slightly, but not too far below the economy's potential (currently estimated, based on trends in labor force and productivity growth, at about 2½% per year). In 1990, the Fed's projected (and presumably desired) central tendency pace for real GNP growth was 1½ to 2%.

The basic premise was that if the monetary authorities maintained this soft-landing pace of real GNP growth long enough (perhaps several years), pressures on labor and capital resources would lessen, thereby easing inflationary pressures. This would, in turn, make it possible for the Fed to reduce the core rate of inflation below its undesirably high 4 to 5% pace (see Exhibit 1.4) without enduring the customary recession.

In the 1987–90 period, the bulk of the increasing wage and price pressures (as can be seen in Exhibit 1.5) were concentrated in the service sector (which accounts for about 75% of total nonfarm payroll employment). In contrast, wage and price pressures were more moderate in the goods producing sector (accounting for 25% of total employment) owing largely to a prolonged period of sluggish demand growth in this sector, though, much to the dismay of Fed officials, employment costs in even the goods producing sector began to accelerate in late 1989 and early 1990. Because of prolonged demand weakness in the goods producing sector, there was temporarily some moderation by mid-1990 in the rate of increase in producer prices of fin-

Table 1.1. Fed Policy Priorities

Order in which Policy Variables Conditioning Reserve Pressure Appeared in the FOMC Directive

Meetings	First	Second	Third	Fourth	Fifth
3/85 to 7/85	Monetary aggregate	Strength of expansion	Inflation	Credit market conditions	Exchange rates
8/85 to 4/86	Monetary aggregate	Strength of expansion	Exchange rates	Inflation	Credit market conditions
5/86	Monetary aggregate	Strength of expansion	Financial market conditions	Exchange rates	
7/86 to 2/87	Monetary aggregate	Strength of expansion	Exchange rates	Inflation	Credit market conditions
3/87	Exchange rates	Monetary aggregate	Strength of expansion	Inflation	Credit market conditions
5/87	Inflation	Exchange rates	Monetary aggregate	Strength of expansion	

7/87	Inflation	Monetary aggregate	Strength of expansion		
8/87 to 9/87	Inflation	Strength of expansion	Exchange rates	Monetary aggregate	
11/87 to 5/88	Financial market conditions	Strength of expansion	Inflation	Exchange rates	Monetary aggregate
6/88	Inflation	Strength of expansion	Foreign exchange and domestic financial markets	Monetary aggregate	
8/88 to 2/91	Inflation	Strength of expansion	Monetary aggregate	Foreign exchange and domestic financial markets	

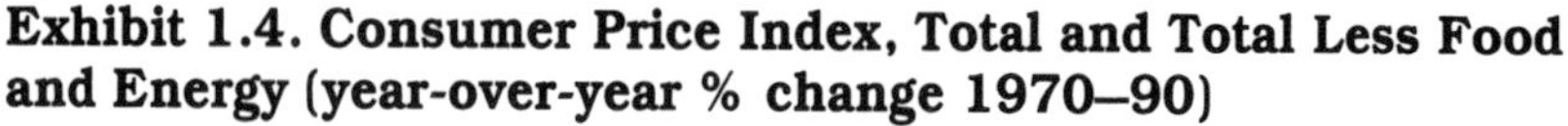

Exhibit 1.4. Consumer Price Index, Total and Total Less Food and Energy (year-over-year % change 1970–90)

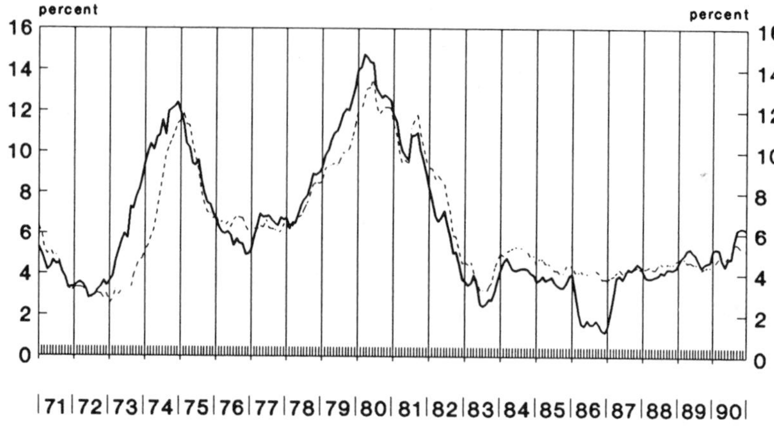

Source: Bureau of Labor Statistics

ished goods and in prices of partially processed or intermediate goods (see Exhibit 1.6). However, this favorable inflationary trend was promptly reversed in August 1990 by the oil price shock.

Needless to say, the Fed faced a delicate balancing act. It was not easy to keep its policy stance just tight enough to ensure that economic activity hovered in the twilight zone between expansion and recession, especially when economic activity was also influenced by fiscal actions and by foreign trade imbalances, among other things. The Fed had little cushion on the downside. The Greenspan Fed closely followed real sector indicators, such as the Inventory-Sales ratio (see Exhibit 1.7), to determine if any imbalances were emerging. When real GNP growth threatened to turn negative, the Fed had to be alert to a possible need to ease reserve pressures and to push interest rates lower. Of course, classic

Exhibit 1.5. Employment Cost Index: Goods Producing Sector vs. Services (year-over-year % change 1982–90)

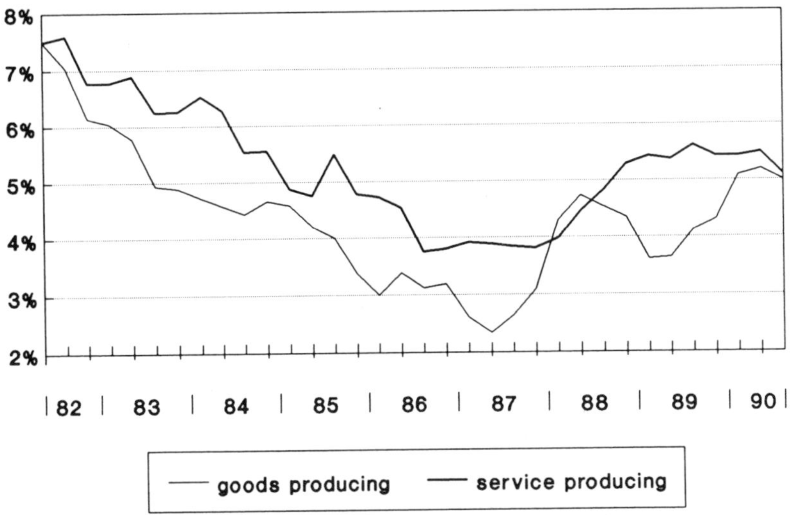

Source: Bureau of Labor Statistics

supply-side shocks and related financial instability such as caused by the August 1990 Middle East hostilities and the possible disruption of oil supply presented Fed policymakers with an even greater challenge.

A less emphasized third Fed policy priority is to maintain moderate monetary growth. This priority actually serves as an intermediate indicator or target. If M-2 growth, for example, exceeds the Fed's target, the monetary authorities will act to tighten reserve pressures and to push the Federal funds rate and other money market rates to higher and more attractive levels. This widening of the spread by which the funds rate and other money market rates exceeds the more sticky rates on many M-2 components reduces the public's appetite for M-2 balances. Conversely, if M-2 growth falls below the Fed's target, Fed policymakers will react by easing reserves and pushing the funds rate and other money market rates to lower and less attractive levels, relative to the less

Exhibit 1.6. Producer Price Index: Monthly, Finished, and Intermediate goods (year-over-year % change 1980–90)

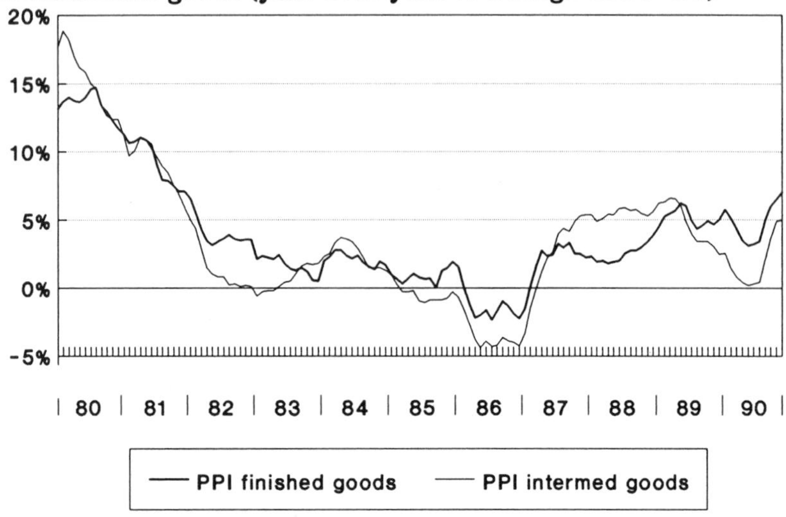

Source: Bureau of Labor Statistics

frequently adjusted rates on many M-2 components, thereby increasing the public's demand for M-2 balances.

During much of the 1980s, however, the relationship between monetary growth and nominal GNP (velocity) became both unstable and unpredictable, largely because of deregulation and financial innovation. This undermined the role of the monetary aggregates as an intermediate policy target, particularly for the month-to-month and quarter-to-quarter periods in which Fed policy decisions are made. Nevertheless, the Greenspan Fed at least looked favorably enough on the monetary aggregates to act in August 1988 to move them up to third priority among the groupings of intermediate policy variables to be considered in modifying reserve availability.

In January 1991, the Greenspan Fed placed renewed emphasis on undesirably sluggish M-2 growth. This was the main factor triggering a further Fed easing step on January 8, 1991.

Exhibit 1.7. Inventory/Sales Ratios and Order Backlogs

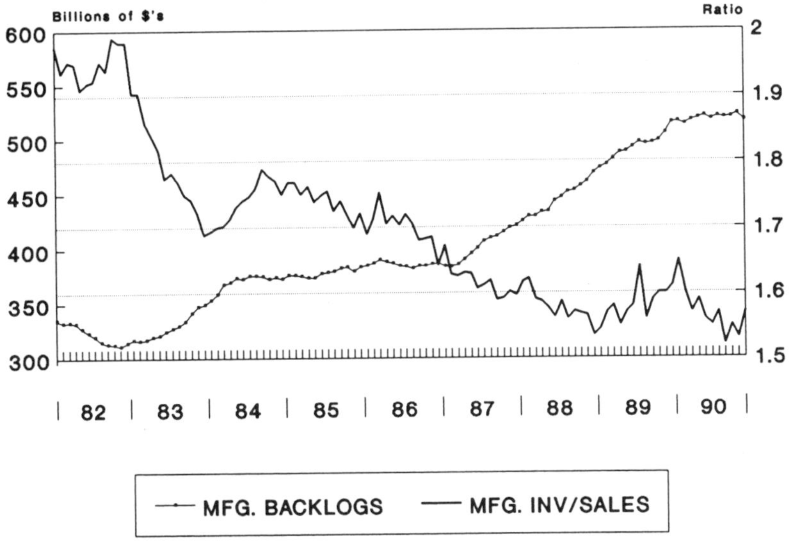

Source: Bureau of Labor Statistics

It is important to note, however, that the Greenspan Fed's renewed emphasis on monetary aggregate growth arose not because of some sort of sudden conversion to monetarism. Rather, the Greenspan Fed viewed the sluggishness of monetary growth as partly a symptom of an intensifying bank credit squeeze or crunch. In essence, the monetary authorities were seeking to avoid a repeat of the 1930s situation in which bank financial troubles and insolvencies, bad loan problems, related declining deposit (monetary) growth, and contracting economic activity all interacted in a downward "death" spiral. Of particular importance in the Great Depression was the fact that the huge 35% contraction in the money supply reflected a large number of bank failures. (From 1929 until the national bank holiday was declared in March 1933, there were a whopping 7,000 bank failures.) This banking collapse resulted in the rupture of countless credit "lifelines" between bank lenders and individual borrowers. To avoid a similar danger posed by the current unusual bank credit squeeze or crunch, the Greenspan Fed has sought to ease reserve pressures with a view to restimulating sluggish monetary growth.

The Fed's targets for money and credit growth and its projections of selected economic measures for 1990 and 1991 are revealed in Table 1.2. The Greenspan Fed is still somewhat uncertain about the short-term relationship between nominal GNP growth and fluctuations in M-2 growth. Furthermore, Exhibit 1.8 shows that the 1980s brought increased volatility in the rate of increase in the velocity of M-2, owing mainly to deregulation and financial innovation. Money velocity (or the income velocity of money) is defined as nominal GNP divided by M-2 (GNP/M-2), or the number of times M-2 balances must turn over to support a given level of economic activity in any given quarter.

In their routine policy deliberations, Fed policymakers currently tend to focus primarily on the M-2 monetary aggregate (M-1 plus savings accounts and small-denomination time deposits plus money market demand accounts and household money market mutual funds plus overnight repurchase agreements (RPs) and overnight Eurodollars). Over the longer term, the monetary authorities are seeking to maintain growth in the M-2 aggregate at a pace that is commensurate with the economy's sustainable growth. In the shorter term, this objective translates into a Fed effort to set the annual target for M-2 growth low enough to allow for some moderation in still excessive price pressures, but high enough to accommodate the economy's current underlying growth momentum so as not to starve the economy for money, thereby pushing it over the edge into recession.

In recent years, there has been a marked and prolonged divergence between the rate of growth in the M-2 aggregate and growth in the broader credit (domestic nonfinancial debt) aggregate (see Exhibit 1.9). From 1984 through 1989, in particular, M-2 growth lagged far behind that of the broader credit (domestic nonfinancial debt) aggregate. (Do-

Table 1.2. Federal Reserve Monetary Targets and Economic Projections (Humphrey-Hawkins Act Testimony) July 18, 1991

Ranges for Growth of Monetary and Credit Aggregates

Percent change, fourth quarter to fourth quarter	1989	1990 Adopted in February 1990	1991
M2	3 to 7	3 to 7	2½ to 6½
M3	3½ to 7½	1 to 5	1 to 5
Debt	6½ to 10½	5 to 9	4½ to 8½

Economic Projections for 1991

Measure	Memo: 1990 Actual	FOMC Members and Other FRB Presidents: Range	FOMC Members and Other FRB Presidents: Central Tendency	Administration
1991				
Percent change, fourth quarter to fourth quarter*				
Nominal GNP	4.3	3½ to 5½	3¾ to 5¼	5.3
Real GNP	.3	−½ to 1½	¾ to 1½	.9
Consumer price index†	6.3	3 to 4½	3½ to 4	4.3
Average level in the fourth quarter, percent**				
Unemployment rate	5.9	6¼ to 7½	6½ to 7	6.6

*Average for the fourth quarter of the preceding year to the average for the fourth quarter of the year indicated.

†Actual and FOMC forecasts are for all urban consumers; Administration forecast is for urban wage earners and clerical workers.

**Percentage of the labor force. Actual and FOMC forecasts are for the civilian labor force; Administration forecast is for the total labor force, including armed forces residing in the United States.

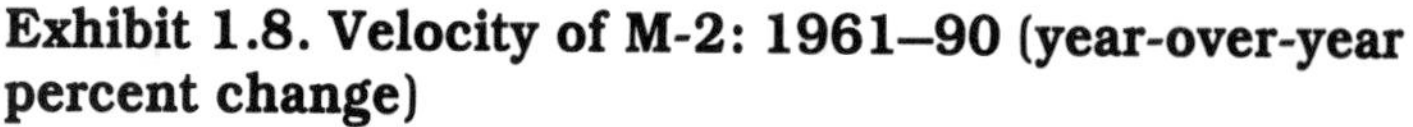

Exhibit 1.8. Velocity of M-2: 1961–90 (year-over-year percent change)

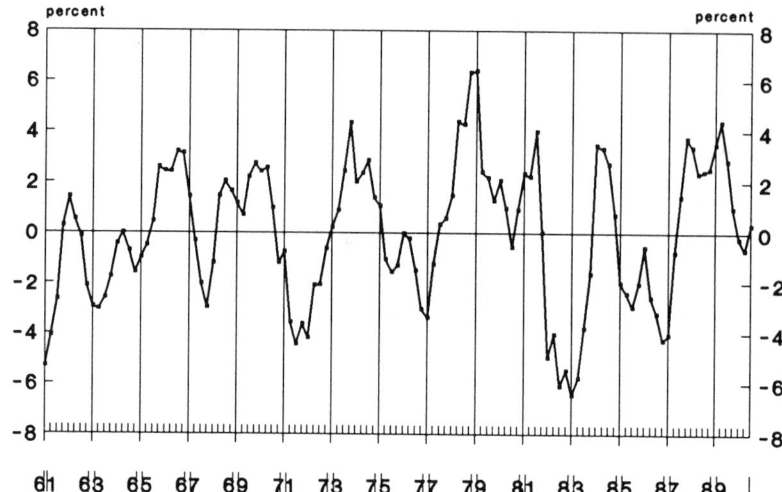

Source: Federal Reserve, U.S. Dept. of Commerce, Aubrey G. Lanston & Co. Inc.

mestic nonfinancial debt includes the outstanding credit market debt of the federal, state, and local governments, and private nonfinancial sectors. Private debt consists of corporate bonds, mortgages, consumer credit, other bank loans, commercial paper, banker's acceptances, and other debt instruments.) Taking a closer look at the relationship between M-2 and credit (nonfinancial debt) in Table 1.3, it is noteworthy that, measured on a fourth quarter by fourth quarter basis, M-2 growth was far outstripped by credit (nonfinancial debt) growth in each of the years 1987, 1988, and 1989, though by the end of this period the differential was narrowing somewhat.

This development is largely explained by the fact that the broader credit aggregate includes *both* bank and nonbank sources of funds. As a result, the broader credit aggregate has captured the effects of an increasingly important and popular financial innovation called "securitization."

Exhibit 1.9. M-2, Credit (domestic nonfinancial debt) GNP (constant $), GNP (current $) 1960–90 (quarterly year-over-year % change)

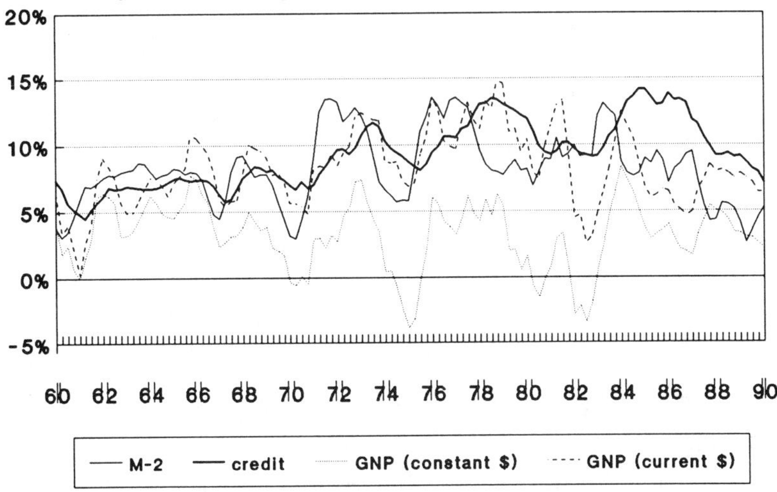

Source: Federal Reserve, U.S. Dept. of Commerce, Aubrey G. Lanston Co. Inc.

Securitization can be defined as the process which takes place when a commercial bank's or other lending institution's assets are removed in one way or another from the balance sheet of that lending institution and are funded instead by investors who purchase a negotiable financial instrument evidencing this indebtedness, without recourse (or in some cases with limited recourse) to the original lender. The securitization of home mortgages is now a fact of life; specifically, bank-originated home mortgages are bundled together and used as backing for marketable debt sold by issuing agencies to such institutional investors as pension funds. These investors benefit directly from the stream of revenues generated by the interest and principal payments made by borrowers on the underlying individual loans. This mortgage-backed securities market soared to approximately $1 trillion in outstanding issues in 1989, with the major participants on the supply (issuing) side

Table 1.3. Money and Debt Aggregates (Dollar amounts in billions, % change at an annual rate)

	M1			M2			M3			L			Nonfinancial Debt		
Date	Total	Monthly % chg	Qtrly % chg	Total	Monthly % chg	Qtrly % chg	Total	Monthly % chg	Qtrly % chg	Total	Monthly % chg	Qtrly % chg	Total	Monthly % chg	Qtrly % chg
1987															
Jan	730.3	9.3		2833.3	8.1		3519.1	8.4		4164.3	8.4		7654.1	10.4	
Feb	731.7	2.3		2835.2	0.8		3526.9	2.7		4177.9	3.9		7696.4	6.6	
Mar	734.1	3.9	13.0	2838.3	1.3	6.2	3532.7	2.0	6.5	4175.5	−0.7	6.3	7746.1	7.7	10.6
Apr	744.4	16.8		2850.4	5.1		3550.5	6.0		4186.4	3.1		7811.4	10.1	
May	747.8	5.5		2854.1	1.6		3568.4	6.0		4215.3	8.3		7882.7	11.0	
Jun	743.0	−7.7	7.1	2857.2	1.3	2.6	3584.8	5.5	4.7	4236.1	5.9	3.8	7946.0	9.6	9.4
Jul	743.5	0.8		2863.9	2.8		3593.1	2.8		4238.4	0.7		7992.3	7.0	
Aug	746.7	5.2		2878.6	6.2		3615.9	7.6		4265.0	7.5		8047.2	8.2	
Sep	749.0	3.7	0.7	2894.7	6.7	3.5	3637.9	7.3	5.4	4297.2	9.1	5.2	8109.8	9.3	8.6
Oct	757.3	13.3		2909.5	6.1		3659.6	7.2		4327.4	8.4		8177.3	10.0	
Nov	754.2	−4.9		2911.1	0.7		3675.2	5.1		4341.2	3.8		8254.1	11.3	
Dec	750.4	−6.0	4.1	2913.2	0.9	4.5	3678.7	1.1	6.1	4338.7	−0.7	6.5	8307.5	7.8	9.8
4th Q/4th Q		6.3			4.3			5.8			5.5			9.9	
1988															
Jan	757.5	11.4		2936.3	9.5		3705.2	8.6		4376.7	10.5		8349.9	6.1	
Feb	759.4	3.0		2959.4	9.4		3737.0	10.3		4410.3	9.2		8405.7	8.0	
Mar	763.0	5.7	3.2	2978.2	7.6	6.4	3760.3	7.5	6.9	4437.6	7.4	6.7	8471.7	9.4	7.9
Apr	770.1	11.2		2999.7	8.7		3785.4	8.0		4476.4	10.5		8538.3	9.4	
May	773.1	4.7		3013.3	5.4		3805.0	6.2		4506.3	8.0		8607.8	9.8	
Jun	778.9	9.0	7.4	3026.4	5.2	7.5	3827.3	7.0	7.7	4528.7	6.0	8.7	8677.3	9.7	9.5
Jul	783.4	6.9		3033.2	2.7		3847.1	6.2		4567.8	10.4		8741.2	8.8	
Aug	784.4	1.5		3037.7	1.8		3858.1	3.4		4584.8	4.5		8805.9	8.9	
Sep	784.8	0.6	5.3	3041.1	1.3	3.2	3867.2	2.8	5.4	4592.9	2.1	6.9	8922.7	15.9	10.0
Oct	785.1	0.5		3048.8	3.0		3883.8	5.2		4613.8	5.5		8981.1	7.9	
Nov	786.0	1.4		3064.1	6.0		3903.5	6.1		4644.2	7.9		9048.6	9.0	
Dec	787.5	2.3	1.0	3072.4	3.3	3.2	3918.3	4.5	4.6	4676.1	8.2	5.5	9107.6	7.8	10.1
4th Q/4th Q		4.3			5.2			6.3			7.1			9.7	

1989															
Jan	785.8	−2.6		3073.4	0.4		3925.9	2.3		4683.3	1.8		9150.3	5.6	
Feb	786.7	1.4		3078.0	1.8		3936.7	3.3		4702.0	4.8		9209.8	7.8	
Mar	785.5	−1.8	−0.1	3086.9	3.5	2.3	3956.5	6.0	3.9	4735.9	8.7	5.4	9279.9	9.1	7.4
Apr	782.1	−5.2		3089.4	1.0		3965.0	2.6		4762.0	6.6		9342.9	8.1	
May	776.2	−9.1		3085.3	1.6		3965.6	0.2		4761.9	0.0		9403.6	7.8	
Jun	773.7	−3.9	−4.4	3101.6	6.3	1.6	3984.9	5.8	3.3	4784.4	5.7	5.3	9457.9	6.9	8.2
Jul	779.1	8.4		3127.0	9.8		4007.6	6.8		4810.5	6.5		9506.9	6.2	
Aug	780.4	2.0		3146.9	7.6		4013.0	1.6		4825.2	3.7		9570.7	8.1	
Sep	782.9	3.8	1.8	3163.6	6.4	7.0	4013.5	0.1	4.0	4831.8	1.6	4.5	9629.1	7.3	7.1
Oct	788.1	8.0		3181.9	6.9		4018.1	1.4		4841.7	2.5		9689.0	7.5	
Nov	789.4	2.0		3201.2	7.3		4031.0	3.9		4858.1	4.1		9751.7	7.8	
Dec	794.8	8.2	5.1	3221.6	7.6	7.1	4044.3	4.0	2.0	4881.2	5.7	3.1	9790.4	4.8	7.3
4th Q/4th Q		0.6			4.6			3.3			4.6			7.7	
1990															
Jan	794.8	0.0		3231.0	3.5		4048.5	1.2		4882.5	0.3		9831.3	5.0	
Feb	801.4	10.0		3255.7	9.2		4064.3	4.7		4890.4	1.9		9889.9	7.2	
Mar	804.8	5.1	4.8	3271.0	5.6	6.4	4069.0	1.4	2.3	4906.6	4.0	2.7	9959.1	8.4	6.1
Apr	807.3	3.7		3279.1	3.0		4074.7	1.7		4917.9	2.8		10015.9	6.8	
May	805.4	−2.8		3274.4	−1.7		4068.4	−1.9		4889.8	−6.9		10059.9	5.3	
Jun	809.4	6.0	3.5	3282.6	3.0	3.2	4073.1	1.4	1.1	4909.0	4.7	1.0	10117.8	6.9	6.9
Jul	809.0	0.6		3287.8	1.9		4077.6	1.3		4918.4	2.3		10183.5	7.8	
Aug	815.8	10.1		3305.3	6.4		4093.4	4.6		4929.4	2.7		10256.6	8.6	
Sep	822.1	9.3	4.1	3319.8	5.3	3.1	4096.0	0.8	1.7	4954.3	6.1	2.3	10313.6	6.7	7.4
Oct	820.0	3.1		3320.3	0.2		4091.6	1.3		4947.4	−1.7		10354.7	4.8	
Nov	822.6	3.8		3316.6	1.3		4085.8	1.7		4954.4	1.7		10412.4	6.7	
Dec	825.2	3.8	0.9	3320.3	1.3	0.4	4085.9	0.0	0.1	NA	NA	NA	NA	NA	NA
4th Q/4th Q		4.0			3.7			1.2			NA			NA	

Notes: M-1: The sum of nonbank public holdings of currency, traveler's checks, demand deposits, and other checkable deposits, including interest-bearing NOW accounts.

M-2: M-1 plus overnight RPs, overnight Eurodollars, household money market mutual fund (MMMF) balances (general and broker/dealer), money market demand accounts (MMDAs), savings, and small-denomination time deposits.

M-3: M-2 plus large-denomination time deposits, term RPs, term Eurodollars, and institution MMMF balances.

Liquidity (L): M-3 plus nonbank public holdings of U.S. savings bonds, short-term Treasury securities, commercial paper, and banker's acceptances, net of money market mutual fund holdings of these securities.

Debt (domestic nonfinancial debt): Outstanding credit market debt of the U.S. government, state and local governments, and private nonfinancial sectors. Private debt consists of corporate bonds, mortgages, consumer credit, other bank loans, commercial paper, banker's acceptances, and other debt instruments.

Source: Federal Reserve and Aubrey G. Lanston & Co. Inc.

being the Government National Mortgage Association (GNMA) and the Federal National Mortgage Association (FNMA), which together account for about half of the total offerings of these securities.

In addition, bank loans for such things as mobile homes, cars, boats, and credit cards are also each bundled together and used as backing for marketable debt instruments that are, in turn, sold directly in the financial markets. These are called asset-backed securities. In effect, this securitization process shifts credit from bank to nonbank sources. Banks can earn the fees from originating and processing these loans while at the same time either reducing, or at least limiting the growth in their asset and liability footings so as to strengthen their capital ratios.

The short-lived but spectacular explosion of high yield, junk bond debt to a peak total of $200 billion from 1984 to 1989 also served to shift business credit from bank to nonbank sources. In a typical takeover, the raiding group of investors usually relied heavily on longer-term funds borrowed in the junk bond market. Moreover, the junk bond market became an attractive nonbank source of funds for many companies of low credit that previously could find a welcome only at banks.

This process of shifting a significant portion of business credit from bank to nonbank sources actually began in the 1960s with the development of the commercial paper market (unsecured short-term IOUs) which corporations typically issue to each other or to institutional investors such as mutual funds. In particular, large corporations with the highest credit rating found they could borrow less expensively in the commercial paper market than at banks. In 1990, the downgrading of both short- and long-term debt of many bad-loan plagued money center banks caused many of their corporate customers to find an even greater cost advantage in borrowing directly in the commercial paper or longer-term debt markets, as compared to borrowing at banks.

ROLE OF THE DOLLAR

The Greenspan Fed's lowest priority is really a dual aim of seeking a steady U.S. dollar in the foreign exchange markets and stable conditions in the domestic financial markets, the latter being a catch-all grouping of financial indicators. However, it is important to note that the Greenspan Fed places considerably less emphasis on the dollar as an influence on its policy actions than did the preceding Volcker Fed. Indeed, the dollar at times carried top billing among the Volcker Fed's policy priorities. This was the case in March 1987, for example, when trade sanctions against the Japanese threatened an all-out trade war (and thus no end to the chronic U.S. trade deficit). In these circumstances, the Fed sought to counter a possible freefall in the U.S. dollar as private foreign investors sought to sell their dollar investments, forcing official institutions to mount massive dollar-support operations.

In contrast, the Greenspan Fed believes that it is more important, as a rule, to focus on the domestic objective of achieving sustainable, noninflationary economic growth, thereby leaving the determination of the value of the U.S. dollar to foreign exchange market forces. Among recent Fed leaders, perhaps former Fed Vice Chairman Manuel Johnson was the most outspoken on the desirability of leaving the determination of the U.S. dollar's level to market forces. He signaled his concerns on this issue in unusually forthright terms at a special September 25, 1989, FOMC meeting by voting against a routine increase in the limit in the overall open position in all foreign currencies held in the System Open Market Account, proposed to facilitate increased direct Fed intervention against the dollar. Two days earlier, on September 23, 1989, the U.S. Treasury, which has responsibility for international financial affairs and works jointly with the Fed when official intervention to influence the foreign exchange value of the dollar is necessary, along with the other G-7 countries (Germany, France, Japan, United Kingdom, Italy, and Canada) had decided on coordinated official intervention to push the dollar lower, especially in terms of the D-Mark and the Japanese yen. These officially coordinated efforts to push the dollar lower were taken to restimulate U.S. exports and reduce the threat of inflation in Japan and Germany posed by earlier weakness in both the yen and D-mark.

However, as revealed in the records of policy actions at the October 1989 and March 1990 FOMC meetings, Fed policymakers took issue with these official Treasury-commanded dollar-depressing actions by forthrightly arguing that Fed open market policy changes solely for purposes of pushing the dollar lower would be counterproductive. The Fed argues that its moves to ease reserve pressures and to push interest rates lower as part of coordinated official efforts to push the dollar lower would also push import prices higher and cause an acceleration in U.S. price pressures, thus posing a potential conflict with the Fed's highest policy priority.

Finally, additional intermediate policy variables are grouped under the catch-all category of "conditions in the domestic financial markets." To be sure, since equity prices are included in this category, Fed policymakers may bring this grouping of intermediate policy variables to the fore at times of financial tension, as actually was done in the post-October 19, 1987 stock market crash period.

OTHER INSTITUTIONAL AND TECHNICAL FEATURES

The Federal Reserve System is composed of a Board of Governors located in Washington, D.C. and of 12 district Federal Reserve Banks (Boston, New York, Philadelphia, Cleveland, Richmond, Atlanta, Chicago, St. Louis, Minneapolis, Kansas City, Dallas, and San Francisco).[7] The 7 members of the Board of Governors are each appointed to 14-year terms by the President, with the advice and consent of the Senate. The Chairman and Vice Chairman of the Board of Governors are each appointed by the President to hold these titles for four-year terms, renewable at the President's pleasure, with the advice and consent of the Senate.

The Presidents of each of the 12 district Federal Reserve Banks are chosen by their respective Board of Directors with the approval of the Board of Governors in Washington. Each Reserve Bank has its own Board of Directors consisting of nine members. Each Reserve Bank Board is made up of three Class A directors, representing member banks; three Class B directors, who are engaged in pursuits other than banking, elected by the member banks in each Federal Reserve district; and three Class C directors appointed by the Board of Governors, one of whom it designates as Chairman and another as Deputy Chairman.

The Fed's two primary policy tools are the discount rate (the rate that the Fed charges depository institutions for the privilege of borrowing funds at its discount window) and open market operations. Discount rate changes are initiated by the Board of Directors of one or more Reserve Banks; but only the Board of Governors in Washington may approve, by majority vote, an actual change in the Federal Reserve discount rate.

The Federal Reserve Board has also infrequently used authority to adjust reserve requirements that banks must legally hold against all transactions accounts (currently roughly 12%) and on certain certificates of deposit with maturities of less than 18 months (previously 3%).[8] After imposing new reserve requirements to limit bank credit growth on October 6, 1979, the Fed Board avoided making any additional reserve requirement adjustments for policy purposes during the entire decade of the 1980s. However, the Fed had under consideration a cut in reserve requirements, beginning in summer of 1990. For a given level of total reserves, such a cut in required reserves would increase the amount of earning assets that banks may hold. It was hoped that this, in turn, would improve bank profitability and help counter a widening bank-induced credit squeeze. On December 4, 1990, the Federal Reserve Board announced that it was eliminating the 3% reserve requirement on nonpersonal time deposits with maturities of less than 18 months which are mostly corporate certificates of deposit.

The Fed's primary policy tool is open market operations. The Fed injects (drains) bank reserves through purchases (sales) of U.S. government securities, on either a temporary basis by means of System RPs (reserve RPs) or on a permanent basis by means of outright purchases (sales). The FOMC is in charge of open market operations. System RPs call for the Fed to purchase government securities for a specified period (usually one day) and then sell this Fed-determined amount back to primary dealers at an agreed upon interest rate (see Chapter 5). The FOMC (consisting of the seven members of the Board of Governors plus five voting Reserve Bank Presidents) acts to adjust bank reserve pressures through open market operations by using any of three alternative policy levers (operating procedures), discount window borrowings, the Federal funds rate, or nonborrowed reserves (see Exhibit 1.10).

Since 1983, the Fed has been following a discretionary reserve control approach. Currently, in its open market operating procedures, the Fed uses joint discount window borrowings and Federal funds rate guidelines. The Fed adjusts these borrowed reserves and funds rate guidelines from time to time, depending on certain intermediate policy indicators (or targets). Alternatively, during 1979–82, the Fed adopted an automatic reserve control approach in which it targeted a path for nonborrowed reserve growth that would be consistent with moderate increases in demand for money and reserves. Under this reserve control approach, imposed at a time of double-digit inflation, stronger-than-desired increases in demand for money and reserves—perhaps sparked by speculative consumer and business spending motivated by rampant inflation psychology—would result

Exhibit 1.10. Fed Policy Objectives, Intermediate Indicators and Alternative Open Market Operating Procedures

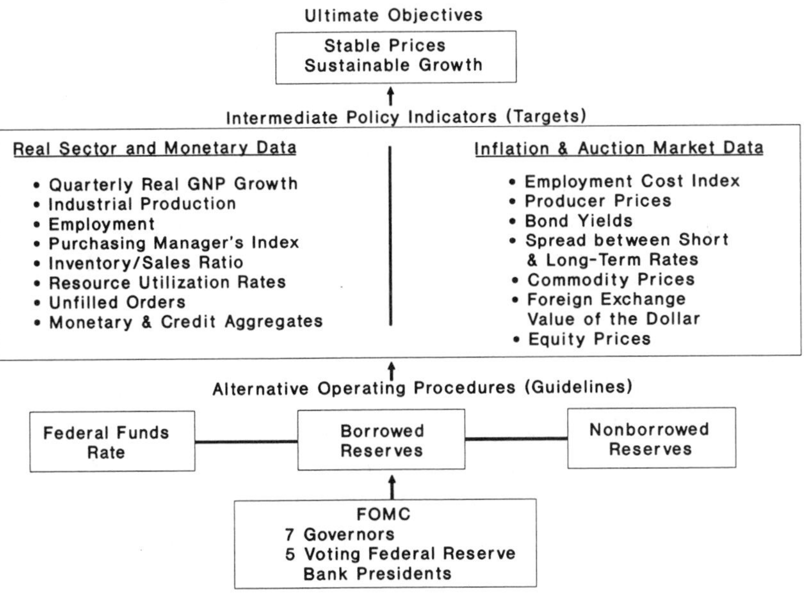

Source: Aubrey G. Lanston & Co. Inc.

more or less automatically in a tightening pressure on bank reserve positions as reflected in sharp increases in borrowed reserves and the Federal funds rate (the rate on reserve balances at the Fed loaned and borrowed among banks, usually overnight). Prior to 1979 the Fed targeted the Federal funds rate as its primary open market operating procedure.[9]

Recently, the Greenspan Fed has developed a sort of *hybrid* approach as a means of influencing reserve pressures through open market operations. This open market operating procedure involves a system of joint discount window borrowings and Federal funds rate guidelines. This modified Fed open market approach lies somewhere between the discretionary discount window borrowings targeting procedure that prevailed during the period from 1983 to 1987 and the rigid Federal funds rate targeting approach that was employed prior to 1979.

Because of an increasingly unstable relationship between money and economic activity, the Greenspan Fed has deemphasized, though not completely ignored, money as an intermediate policy target. An intermediate policy target must meet two major criteria: it must be subject to some Fed control and it must show a meaningful relationship to economic activity and inflation. The Fed focused instead on several intermediate policy variables bearing more directly on economic activity and inflation including quarterly real GNP growth, monthly industrial production, employment, the corporate purchasing managers' index, the balance in inventory stocks relative to sales, unfilled orders, and resource utilization rates. The Fed also considers as intermediate policy indicators wage pressures, bond yields, commodity prices, the dollar, stock prices, and the spread between the Federal funds rate and the 30-year Treasury bond yield. Fed policymakers use this large array of policy variables, along with growth in the broader money and credit aggregates, to assess excess demands on productive resources and related price pressures as well as, most importantly, to gauge changes in the public's inflationary expectations.

These intermediate policy indicators are thus used to identify abnormal economic or price conditions in order to determine when Fed adjustments in reserve pressures should be made. In modern money management, some Fed policymakers feel that the old-fashioned intermediate targeting procedure, which involved focusing only on the M-1, M-2, or M-3 monetary aggregates may be inherently inefficient in determining when the Fed should tighten or ease reserve pressures because it ignores information from other variables.

CHAPTER 2

Fed Culture, Leadership, and Indicators of Policy Shifts

To help analyze and anticipate Fed policy shifts, it is useful to closely track Fed day-to-day operations as well as to identify the most helpful indicators of Fed policy shifts. Also, the Fed's institutional structure came to play an increasingly important role during Chairman Greenspan's leadership as the dovish Board of Governors in Washington, D.C. was pitted against the more hawkish and increasingly persuasive district Federal Reserve Presidents.

THE FED'S "CORPORATE CULTURE"

Traditionally, the corporate culture inside the Fed has been Fed Chairman-centered but collegial. It has been a culture of easy familiarity and reasoned debate. Basically,

Fed internal policy meetings can be described as a cross between those of a university economics faculty and a bank Board of Directors.

Modern Fed Chairmen are chosen, in effect, by the financial markets. The political process is secondary. Typically, the White House leaks to the press a list of potential nominees for the top job at the U.S. central bank and leaves the choice largely to the collective judgment of the financial markets.

Fortunately, this process, which might be called "market Darwinism," has usually produced the brightest and the best contemporary Fed Chairmen. In order to be viewed favorably by market opinion such a Fed leader should be intellectually overpowering both within and outside Fed policy circles, analytically keen, consistent within his own policy framework, a credible communicator, and have good policy instincts. Without the financial markets' strong approval, for example, former Fed Chairman Paul Volcker might have been neither initially appointed by President Carter in August 1979 nor reappointed by President Reagan in August 1983.[1]

The Fed Chairman gains special power within the Fed's policy hierarchy by setting the tone and shaping the outcome of both the meetings of the Board of Governors and the FOMC. The Chairman, by carefully timing his remarks during the policy discussion, can play a key role in shaping the policy directive. The Chairman may open the discussion of policy targets by expressing his own preferences or he may summarize the sense of these meetings once deliberation and debate has been concluded. The Fed Chairman also enhances his power by representing the Federal Reserve System in all its major dealings with Congress and the Administration, as well as in key foreign policy coordinating bodies such as the Group of Seven (G-7). (The G-7 major industrial nations consist of the United States, Germany, Japan, United Kingdom, France, Italy, and Canada.) In addition, all major editing decisions concerning key Fed documents and reports, together with all significant internal personnel decisions pass through the Chairman's office.[2]

The backbone of the Fed is its powerful and effective 200 member Board research staff (arguably the best in Washington, D.C.). The Board staff is rigidly structured almost to the point of being aristocratic in nature; its senior officers might be considered akin to the famed knights of King Arthur's roundtable, though, admittedly, they spend more overtime hours defending the King (Chairman) at their desks than riding prancing steeds and proclaiming the merits of monetary policy throughout the kingdom. The senior Board staff officers play a key role in presentations at all major internal Fed meetings, especially the FOMC. A Fed Chairman (or other Board members) who earns the respect of the highly competent Board staff will benefit from this powerful ally in policy debates both inside and outside the Fed. Each of the 12 Reserve Banks also have their own research staffs but they are more modest-sized and less powerful. The Federal Reserve System's well-earned reputation for economic professionalism is in no small measure attributable to the outstanding quality of its research staff.

Today, the Fed Chairman's nearly absolute power in all internal administrative matters and Fed policy formulation has been weakened somewhat by mass media scrutiny and the growing practice of the Washington policy "leak." Being well-versed in the modern ways of Washington politics, some ambitious, new-breed Fed policymakers have, in competition with the Fed Chairman, begun to effectively use the mass media and public relations to sell themselves or their own ideas (perhaps in seeking recognition for future Administration appointments to the Fed Chairman's job itself or other key government positions). Through background press interviews and the infamous Washington policy "leak," they can advance their own policy positions. This modern monetary policy manifestation of Washington politics may be a primary factor behind the rising tide of policy leaks from anonymous Fed sources (see Chapter 5).

FINE-TUNING POLICY METHODS

The Greenspan Fed's technique in implementing policy shifts is, for the most part, to adjust reserve pressures in small and frequent steps that could be easily reversed if necessary. In contrast, the preceding Volcker Fed, operating in a different economic environment, had a flair for more dramatic policy measures, as in the case of the infamous October 6, 1979, "Saturday Massacre." Actually, Chairman Greenspan's initial success in achieving an economic soft-landing helped put the much maligned concept of Fed policy fine-tuning in a better light, at least temporarily. In 1988, for example, in light of evidence indicating that real economic activity was expanding at a vigorous pace and that inflation might intensify at a time of high labor and capital resource utilization, the Greenspan Fed responded with five small but frequent steps to tighten reserve pressures effected through open market operations (during the March–June period) followed by a discount rate increase to 6½% from 6% in August of that year (see Table 2.1). Then, at the December 1988 FOMC meeting, the Greenspan Fed decided on a further two-part reserve tightening move by means of open market operations, implemented in mid-December and early January 1989. Subsequently, in a bolder move, in response to a sharp early-1989 flare up in inflationary pressures, the Greenspan Fed moved in mid-February to tighten reserve pressures through open market operations, promptly followed by a discount rate hike to 7% from 6½%. (Actually, Fed policymakers moved on February 23, the day before the discount rate hike, to further tighten reserve pressures through open market operations, but this move was reversed the following day when the discount rate increase was agreed on.)

Table 2.1. Actual and Estimated Fed Policy Shifts 1987–91

	Type of Fed Shift in Reserve Pressures*	Fed Borrowings Guideline* (millions $)	Associated Fed Funds Rate (Percent)	Discount Rate (Percent)
1987				
February 10–11	No change	300	6	
March 31	No change	300	6	
April 30	Modest tightening	400	6¼	
May 19	No change	400	6¼	
May 21	Modest tightening	500	6½	
July 7–8	No change	500	6½	
August 18	No change	500	6½	
September 3	Modest tightening	600	7¼	6 (9/4/87)
September 22	No change	600	7¼	
October 23	Modest easing	500	7	
October 28	Slight easing	450	6⅞	
November 3	No change**	450	6⅞	
November 4	Slight easing	400	6¾–6⅞	
December 4	Modest easing	300	6½–6⅝	
December 15–16	No change	300	6½–6⅝	
1988				
January 28	Slight easing	250	6⅜–6½	
February 11	Slight easing	200	6¼–6⅜	
March 30	Modest tightening	300	6½–6⅝	
May 9	Modest tightening	400	6¾–6⅞	
May 25	Modest tightening	500	7–7⅛	
June 22	Slight tightening	550	7¼–7⅜	
July 1	Slight tightening	600	7½–7⅝	
August 16	No change	600	8–8⅛	6½ (8/9/88)
September 20	No change	600	8–8⅛	
November 1	No change	600	8¼–8⅜	
November 22	No change	400††	8⅜–8½	

Table 2.1. Continued

	Type of Fed Shift in Reserve Pressures*	Fed Borrowings Guideline* (millions $)	Associated Fed Funds Rate (Percent)	Discount Rate (Percent)
December 15	Modest tightening	500	$8\frac{3}{4}$–$8\frac{7}{8}$	
1989				
January 5	Modest tightening	600	9–$9\frac{1}{8}$	
February 14	Modest tightening	700	$9\frac{1}{4}$–$9\frac{3}{8}$	
February 23	Modest tightening	800***	$9\frac{1}{2}$–$9\frac{5}{8}$	
February 24	Modest easing	700	$9\frac{3}{4}$–$9\frac{7}{8}$	7 (2/24/89)
March 9	No change	500†††	$9\frac{3}{4}$–$9\frac{7}{8}$	
May 17	No change	600****	$9\frac{3}{4}$–$9\frac{7}{8}$	
June 6	Modest easing	500	$9\frac{1}{2}$	
July 7	Modest easing	600****	$9\frac{1}{4}$	
July 27	Modest easing	550	9	
August 22	No change	550	9	
October 5	No change	500††††	9	
October 19	Modest easing	400††††	$8\frac{3}{4}$	
November 2	No change	350††††	$8\frac{3}{4}$	
November 6	Modest easing	300	$8\frac{1}{2}$	
November 9	No change	250††††	$8\frac{1}{2}$	
November 15	No change	200††††	$8\frac{1}{2}$	
December 11	No change	150††††	$8\frac{1}{2}$	
December 20	Modest easing	125	$8\frac{1}{4}$	
1990-e				
February 6-7	No change	150*****	$8\frac{1}{4}$	
March 27	No change	150	$8\frac{1}{4}$	
April 13	No change	175*****	$8\frac{1}{4}$	
May 15	No change	325*****	$8\frac{1}{4}$	
July 2-3	No change	550*****	$8\frac{1}{4}$	
July 13	Modest easing	450	8	
October 29	Modest easing	325††††	$7\frac{3}{4}$	
November 16	Modest easing	225	$7\frac{1}{2}$	
December 7	Modest easing	125	$7\frac{1}{4}$	$6\frac{1}{2}$ (12/18/90)
December 19	Modest easing	100	7	
1991-e				
January 8	Modest easing	50	$6\frac{3}{4}$	
February 1	No change	100*****	$6\frac{1}{4}$	6 (2/1/91)

e estimated
*Through Fed open market operations.

Table 2.1. Continued

†Bank adjustment plus seasonal borrowings at the discount window.

**The published record of the November 3, 1987, FOMC meeting indicated that in the post-stock market crash period the monetary authorities gave greater weight than usual in their day-to-day open market operations to maintaining a stable Federal funds rate (presumably in the vicinity of 6¾%) in order "to facilitate the return to a more normal functioning of financial markets and to minimize the chances that the Committee's intentions would be misinterpreted." This special Fed emphasis on the funds rate in its day-to-day operations continued through the March 29, 1988 FOMC meeting.

††In a special Committee consultation on November 22, 1988, the FOMC decided that, "in light of recent information suggesting that the economic expansion retained considerable strength," it would be appropriate for the federal funds rate to continue to trade in the slightly higher range that had prevailed recently. At the same time, the Fed in an unusual move lowered its discount window borrowings target to take into account an unusual development in which "depository institutions had reduced their demands on the discount window."

*** On February 23, 1989 the Fed borrowings target was increased to $800 million, but it was returned to $700 million on the next day when the discount rate was raised.

†††In light of the accumulating indications of additional weakness in depository institutions' discount window borrowings demands relative to earlier patterns, the borrowing assumption was adjusted downward in the maintenance period beginning March 9, 1989.

**** Technical upward revision in Fed target for adjustment plus seasonal discount window borrowings, reflecting unusual strength of seasonal borrowings.

†††† Technical downward adjustments in Fed target for adjustment plus seasonal discount window borrowings, reflecting a decline in seasonal borrowings.

***** Technical upward adjustment in the Fed's target for adjustment plus seasonal borrowings to allow for a "likely turnup" in seasonal borrowing from its "January lows."

Source: Federal Reserve, Aubrey G. Lanston & Co. Inc.

More fine-tuning came in the second half of 1989, when the Greenspan Fed reversed course, in response to weakening tendencies in real economic activity and some indications suggesting a gradual reduction of inflation, and eased reserve pressures in six small steps (see Exhibit 2.1).

Exhibit 2.1. Federal Funds Rate (effective guideline) and Discount Rate

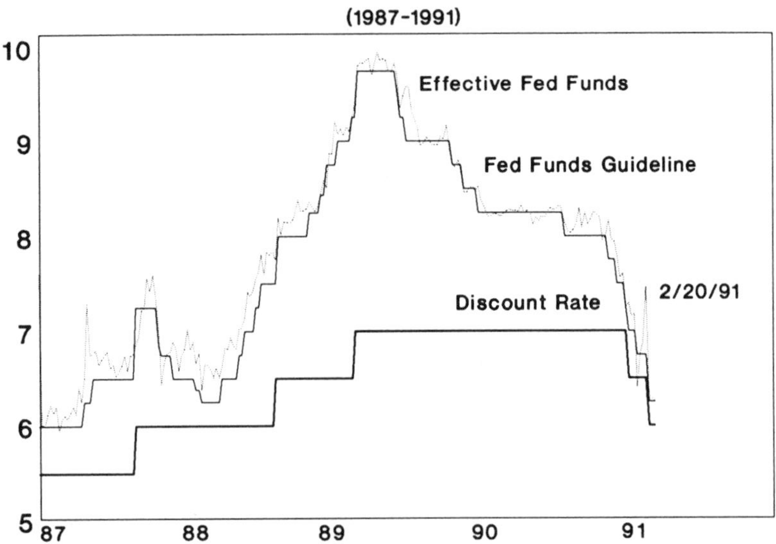

However, in early 1990, wage and price pressures flared up again. This raised questions both inside and outside the Fed as to whether the Greenspan Fed's experimental soft landing approach—aimed at keeping the nearly-fully employed economy balanced in the twilight zone between expansion and contraction—could actually do the job of first stabilizing and then reducing core inflationary pressures.

To complicate matters, there was, beginning in the spring of 1990, an unusual bank-induced credit squeeze (see Chapter 7). To some extent, greater bank selectivity in lending reflected a healthy unwinding of the financial excesses and bad-loan experience of the 1980s. But the bank credit stringency went far beyond the fine line that separates normal cyclical behavior from an all-out credit contraction and financial asset deflation. The threat of a widespread credit contraction arose as many banks sought to reduce their asset and liability footings in order to improve their capital ratios. The Fed initially responded to this problem with a modest easing step through open market operations in July. At the same time, the monetary authorities also began to consider a possible cut in bank reserve requirements in order to increase potential bank profitability and to counter the increasingly dangerous bank-induced credit squeeze. The Federal Reserve Board finally announced such a reserve requirement cut on December 4, 1990 (see Chapter 1).

Also adding to the Fed's problems was the oil price shock stemming from Iraq's sudden (August 2, 1990) invasion and occupation of Kuwait. This caused analysts (both inside and outside the Fed) to focus, as in the 1973 and 1979 oil price shocks, on the cost and availability of oil and on slumping consumer confidence (see Exhibit 2.2). This latest oil price shock posed a major dilemma for Fed policymakers; they faced a cost-induced spurt in inflationary pressures, the threat of a Middle East war, and a record drop in consumer confidence that threatened to push the economy over the brink into recession. Initially, at least, the Fed's main concern was that a premature easing move to fight recession, at a time of rising inflation fears and a declining dollar, could further destabilize the financial markets possibly resulting in rising rather than declining bond rates.

DISTINGUISHING TECHNICAL MOVES FROM POLICY SHIFTS

As regards Fed daily open market operations, there are some hints that help distinguish between Fed technical operations and operations signaling intended policy shifts. For example, when the Fed engages in daily open market

Exhibit 2.2. Consumer Confidence

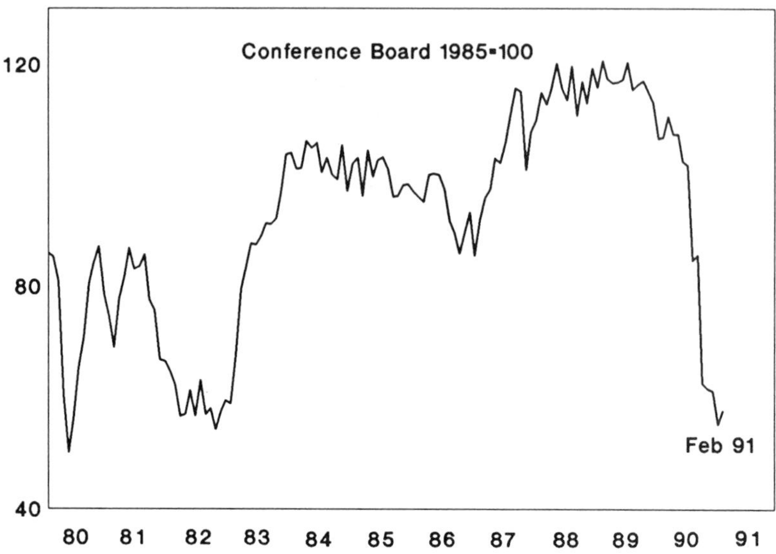

Source: Conference Board

reserve supplying operations merely for technical purposes of offsetting the drain from market factors (e.g., float, currency in circulation, Treasury deposits at the Fed, etc.)[3] the type of Fed action (System RPs, customer RPs, or outright purchases of U.S. government securities) will depend *solely* on the projected size and duration of the reserve adding need in any given two-week bank reserve maintenance period. If, for example, the reserve-adding need is $3 billion or less and is either uncertain or projected to last for only a day or two, the Fed will typically do customer RPs. (Customer RPs reduce the drain on bank reserves that would otherwise have occurred if the customer funds were instead invested internally at the Fed in the form of reverse RPs.) Alternatively, if the reserve adding need is more than $3 billion, or lasting for several days, the Fed will supply reserves through System RPs. Or, lastly, if the reserve-adding (draining) job is more than $3 billion, lasting for three consecutive weeks or more, the Fed will supply (absorb) reserves permanently through outright purchases (sales) of U.S. government securities.

In contrast, the strongest signal of intended Fed easing actions would be for the Fed to supply reserves through one-day System RPs with the Federal funds rate trading below the prevailing level. Conversely, Fed tightening actions would be most strongly signaled by a Fed move to drain reserves through one-day reverse RPs with the Federal funds rate trading above the prevailing level. A somewhat more ambiguous signal of Fed easing intentions would be for the Fed to do customer RPs with funds trading below the prevailing level. Infrequently, Fed easing intentions may also be signaled by permanent reserve-adding operations through outright purchases of U.S. government securities in a bank reserve maintenance period in which little or no adding needs are indicated.

INDICATORS OF FED POLICY SHIFTS

In analyzing the Fed's primary operating procedures, it is important to remember that the monetary policy process is a continuous one; it is partly a reactive process and partly one of trying to anticipate future trends in real economic activity and inflationary pressures. Under the Fed's current operating arrangement, the FOMC will decide on the directive for open market operations prevailing during intermeeting intervals, and this policy directive will then be communicated to and implemented by the Manager for Domestic Operations, System Open Market Account, located at the New York Reserve Bank. In essence, the best indicators of Fed policy shifts are those policy operating signals used in conveying an FOMC policy decision to the New York Fed Manager for Domestic Operations, and those policy guidelines in particular for which the New York manager is held accountable.

SPECIAL NATURE OF DISCOUNT WINDOW BORROWINGS

When the FOMC communicates desired changes in reserve pressures with the Manager for Domestic Operations, System Open Market Account, it places more emphasis in its primary operating procedures on the borrowed and nonborrowed reserve components of total reserves than on the reserve total itself. (Total reserves equal borrowed reserves plus nonborrowed reserves.) This is because reserves borrowed at the Fed discount window (excluding extended credit) are special. These borrowed reserves are temporary because of the Fed's surveillance of the discount window (as to the purpose, frequency and amount of these borrowings) and because of the bank tradition against such borrowings (since repeated use of the discount window can be viewed as a sign of an institution's weakness). For these reasons, a rising share of borrowed reserves in relation to total reserves represents a tightening in reserve pressures for the banking system as a whole. (At the end of 1990, the Fed's guideline for discount window borrowings was estimated at about $100 million, while the level of total reserves was a much higher $60 billion.)

The special nature of borrowed reserves serves as the basis for a positive correlation between these borrowings and the Federal funds rate. Thus, when the Fed tightens reserve availability through open market sales of U.S. government securities, banks will find themselves hard-pressed for funds and will fall back temporarily on extra discount window borrowings. But, because limitations are placed on access to the discount window, banks must seek to promptly extricate themselves from the discount window; in this effort to cut their reliance on the discount window, banks will bid up rates on Federal funds and on other substitute sources of lendable funds such as Eurodollars, RPs, and certificates of deposit. Thus, for any given level of the discount rate and set of rules of access to the discount window, a rising borrowings total will be associated with a rising Federal funds rate, and conversely, a declining borrowings total, during periods when the Fed is easing reserve pressures, will be associated with a falling funds rate.

RELATIONSHIP BETWEEN BORROWINGS AND FEDERAL FUNDS RATE

Presently, a relatively loose but positive relationship exists between discount window borrowings and the Federal funds rate. An FOMC decision to slightly tighten reserve pressures through open market operations would cause the Fed to increase its guideline for discount window borrowings (measured from one bank two-week reserve maintenance period to the next). This minimal Fed tightening move would, for any given level of the discount rate, be associated with an increase in the Federal funds rate. The typical modest Fed tightening step might involve roughly a $100 million increase in the Fed's guideline for discount window borrowings, and this would be associated with approximately a one-quarter percentage point increase in the Federal funds rate. This is the normal size of the Greenspan Fed's tightening step; the Greenspan Fed favors small but frequent policy steps in hopes of avoiding major cumulative policy errors.

AUCTION MARKET INDICATORS

Some Fed policymakers are currently using auction market policy variables to provide more information than under the Fed's old intermediate money targeting procedure. ("Auction" markets are those commodities and financial markets in which prices are determined by the relatively free interaction between large numbers of buyers and sellers.) Former Vice Chairman Manuel Johnson and Governor

Wayne Angell took the lead in exploring this relatively new policy frontier. Former Vice Chairman Johnson focused primarily on three auction market indicators: the spread between the Federal funds rate and the 30-year bond yield (see Exhibit 2.3),[4] the foreign exchange value of the dollar (see Exhibit 2.4), and commodity prices (see Exhibit 2.5). When, as in early 1989, Fed tightening moves push the Federal funds rate up more sharply than longer-term bond yields, the yield curve will flatten or, as in the case in early 1989, early 1982, most of 1981, and early 1980 even become inverted (short-term rates in excess of long-term rates). This development, according to Johnson's line of reasoning, suggests that bond investors are impressed by the Fed's anti-inflation resolve. Other signs suggesting that collective financial market inflationary expectations may be moderating would be a strengthening dollar and declining commodity prices.

Exhibit 2.3. Selected Interest Rates: Federal funds and 30-year Treasury Bonds

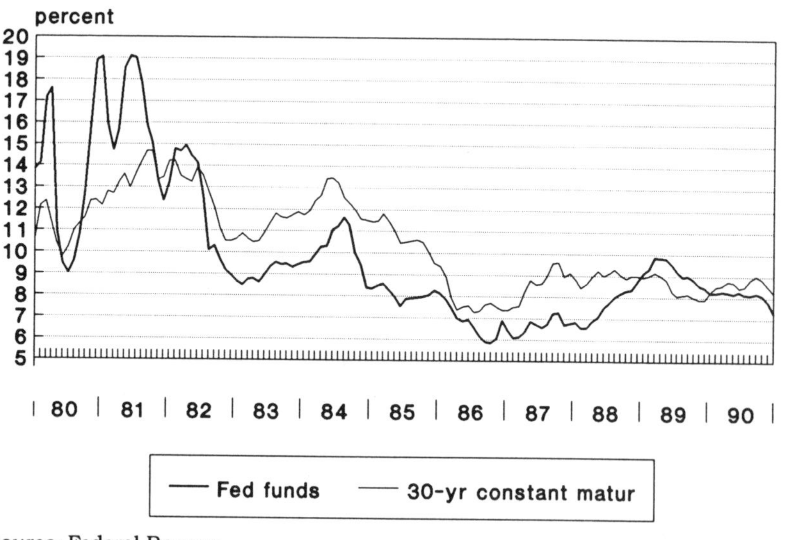

Source: Federal Reserve

Exhibit 2.4. Yen and D-Mark Foreign Exchange Rates (monthly 1985–90)

Source: Federal Reserve

Collective participant perceptions and expectations are at the core of the auction market indicators. Thus, as a rule, a central bank bent on convincing bond investors that it is ever vigilant in its fight to curtail inflationary pressures and expectations should follow a monetary policy of tightening *twice* as much as collective market expectations and, conversely, easing only *half* as much as market expectations.

Conversely, a steepening yield spread (long-term rates in excess of short-term rates), especially when combined with a declining dollar and rising commodity prices, could be signaling that a series of Fed easing steps might be going too far, thereby reawakening collective financial market inflationary expectations. This appears to have been the case in December 1989 when the Fed took the last of a series of six easing steps. On the heels of the Fed's December 1989 easing step, the Federal funds rate declined to 8¼% from 8½%, the

Exhibit 2.5. Commodity Prices (year-over-year % change, 1980–90)

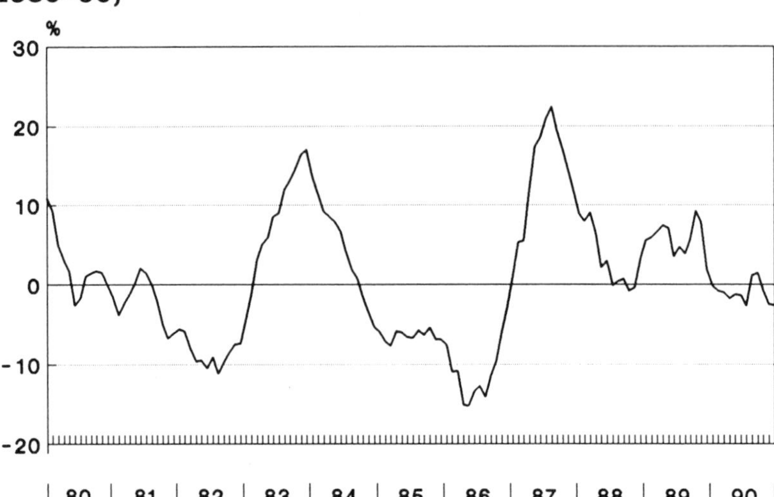

Sources: Journal of Commerce and Aubrey G. Lanston & Co. Inc.

bond yield rose, and the dollar declined. Fed Governor Wayne Angell, who voted against the December 1989 easing move, has stated that these auction market signals were telling Fed policymakers that they should not have taken this extra easing step. The yield curve also steepened following the Fed's July 13, 1990 easing step, largely because this sudden action was perceived as being partly political and thus potentially inflationary.

The main problem with auction market indicators is that they can be misleading. For example, yield curve shifts may be entirely attributable to changes in technical supply conditions or foreign financial influences rather than to public reactions to Fed policy shifts or related changes in market inflationary expectations. In early 1990, for example, the Treasury announced that it might need to issue an additional $40 to $50 billion in mostly short-term securities to meet Resolution Trust Corporation (RTC) working capital needs in connection with government thrift takeovers in the second quarter of that year; there was also growing concern that additional longer-term funds might be needed because the magnitude of the thrift problem had initially been underestimated. This prospective mountain of new supply exerted considerable upward pressure on rates in various maturity sectors of the yield curve, independently of any Fed policy considerations. Also, in the early months of 1990, U.S. bond rates moved higher in sympathy with sharp increases in foreign longer-term interest rates, especially in Germany. These foreign longer-term rate increases exerted upward pressure on U.S. longer-term rates as the competition for a limited amount of global capital intensified, quite independently of market perceptions of Fed policy shifts. Finally, yield curve shifts may be particularly difficult to interpret when it is unclear as to whether the shifts reflect market perceptions of *past* Fed policy shifts and related changes in market inflationary expectations or whether they reflect expectations of *future* Fed policy shifts.

HOW TO DO IT LIST

Perhaps aiding in the establishment of a practical framework for analyzing Fed policy indicators and anticipating Fed policy shifts would be a "How To Do It List."

1. Find the weekly average level for adjustment and seasonal discount window borrowings in the Friday edition of the *Wall Street Journal.* Compute two-week averages for discount window borrowings for each bank reserve maintenance period. (Take note of and make adjustments—as the Fed does—for the fact that, within each year, seasonal borrowings tend to rise from a low in January to a peak in August.)
2. Look up the daily Federal funds rate in the *Wall Street Journal.* Compute two-week averages for the

Federal funds rate covering each bank reserve maintenance period. The Federal funds rate is also available on a weekly average basis in the Federal Reserve's weekly release on "Selected Interest Rates" (H.15).

3. Keep a daily calendar on Fed open market operations (see Exhibit 2.6). Note the time of the day when the Fed acts and what type of action was taken (i.e., system RPs, reverse RPs, customer RPs, etc.). Take note of the Federal funds rate level prevailing at the time of the Fed's action (or lack of action). Keep a record of the daily consensus of Fed watchers, as reported on the Dow-Jones capital markets news

Exhibit 2.6. Fed Daily Open Market Operations: September 1990

MONDAY	TUESDAY	WEDNESDAY	THURSDAY	FRIDAY
HOLIDAY	4 Fed funds 8% 11:33 AM $1.5B customer RP Consensus: $1.5B -$2.5B customer RP Lanston: possible modest add need	5 Fed funds 8 3/8% 11:33 AM Overnight System RP Consensus: $2.5B customer RP;chance of System RP Lanston: likely System RP	6 Fed funds 8 1/8% 11:33 AM 4-day RPs not fixed; 7-day RPs fixed Consensus: 4 day System RPs; chance of $2.5B $2.5B Customer RP Lanston: 4 day System RPs	7 Fed funds 8 1/16% 11:33 AM $2.0B customer RP Consensus: Split between large customer RP & 6-day System RP Lanston: likely large customer RP but System RP possible
10 Fed funds 8 1/16% 11:33 AM 3-day System RPs Consensus: $1.5-$2.5B customer RP Lanston: 3-day System RP likely	11 Fed funds 8 1/16% 11:32 AM 2-day System RPs Consensus: Split between $1.5-$2.5B customer RP & no action Lanston: Customer RPs possible	12 Fed funds 7 15/16% No action Consensus: No action; possible customer or 5-day System RP Lanston: No intervention likely	13 Fed funds 7 15/16% 11:35 AM 4-day and 7-day fixed RPs Consensus: Split between customer, multi-day System RPs Lanston: Potential for 4- and 7-day RPs	14 Fed funds 7 15/16% No action Consensus: Split between no action & $1.5-2.0B customer RPs Lanston: No action likely
17 Fed funds 7 15/16% 11:33 AM 3-day fixed RP Consensus: 3-day System RP Lanston: 3-day System RPs anticipated	18 Fed funds 7 15/16% No action Consensus: Split between 2-day System RP & $2-2.5B customer RP Lanston: 2-day System RP expected	19 Fed funds 7 7/8% No action Consensus: No action Lanston: No action expected	20 Fed funds 8 1/16% No action Consensus: Split between no action & multi-day RPs Lanston: Customer RPs likely	21 Fed funds 8 1/8% 11:33 AM $1B customer RP Consensus: $1.5-$2.5B customer RP Lanston: Customer RPs expected
24 Fed funds 8 1/4% 11:31 AM 1-day System RP Consensus: Term System or customer RP Lanston: Likely customer RP RP but chance of System RPs	25 Fed funds 8 5/16% 11:33 AM 1-day System RP Consensus: Overnight System RP Lanston: System RPs are likely	26 Fed funds 8 1/4% 11:33 AM 1-day System RP Consensus: overnight System RP RP Lanston: overnight system RP expected	27 Fed funds 8 1/8% 11:33 AM 1-day System RP Consensus: 4-day or overnight System RP Lanston: Customer RP likely but chance of System RP	28 Fed funds 8% No action Consensus: No action Lanston: No action expected

Source: Aubrey G. Lanston & Co. Inc.

wire, to determine whether the Fed has an indicated reserve adding job in the current bank maintenance period. Of course, you might make your own estimate of the Fed's indicated reserve adding job as well. Double check, after the Federal Reserve figures are released each Thursday afternoon, to see if this consensus on (or your own estimate of) the Fed's indicated daily reserve job is confirmed by the actual reserve data. This information is available in the Federal Reserves' weekly release on "Factors Affecting Reserves of Depository Institutions" (H.4.1).

4. In order to analyze auction market indicators, it would be a good idea to maintain daily figures on the spread between the Federal funds rate and the 30-year Treasury bond yield (also available in the *Wall Street Journal*). Also note the foreign exchange value of the dollar in terms of major currencies such as the D-mark and the Japanese yen (likewise available in the *Wall Street Journal*). In addition, take note of the daily JOC commodity index (available in the *Journal of Commerce*, a daily business newspaper published by Knight-Ridder). This important index covers prices for 18 key industrial materials.
5. In setting the stage for anticipating impending Fed shifts in its policy stance, investors and Fed watchers should do two essential things. First, watch for signs of financial tensions or credit market instability to which the Fed might respond, such as the October 1987 stock market crash or the mid-1990 bank-induced tightening in loan terms. The Fed is likely to respond to major financial shocks if they threaten to spill over to negatively affect real economic activity. Second, investors or Fed watchers seeking to anticipate Fed policy shifts should scan recent Fed leaders' speeches, statements, and Congressional testimony, as well as the record of policy actions for recent FOMC meetings, to determine if

either real economic activity or indicators of price pressures are deviating from the expectations of Fed policymakers.

A good case study in helping to anticipate Fed policy shifts during periods of financial tension was the October 19, 1987, stock market crash. The Fed promptly announced officially, on the day following the "Black Monday" plunge of 500 points in the Dow-Jones industrial average, that it was prepared to meet any liquidity needs. This Fed announcement at that time of considerable financial upheaval foreshadowed subsequent Fed easing steps on October 23, 1987, and October 28, 1987. These Fed easing steps, along with fears of a crash-related economic downturn (later proven unfounded), triggered substantial declines in both short- and long-term interest rates. Further Fed post-Crash easing steps were taken in November and December 1987 and January and February 1988.

In another case, in June 1989, Fed policymakers took the first of a series of six modest easing steps that were spread over the second half of the year. At that time, economic activity was weakening more than the Fed expected, and there was some hope that inflationary pressures would moderate further. The weakness was especially evident in the goods producing sector, notably in the case of autos and other durable goods. Among the most obvious signals of sluggish economic growth at that time were a pronounced decline in the National Association of Purchasing Management's composite index (see Exhibit 2.7) and a slowing in nonfarm payroll employment growth (see Table 2.2), especially in the goods producing sector. In July 1990, the Fed eased to counter indications of unusually severe bank loan stringency.

For investors and Fed watchers seeking to be the first to identify such Fed easing steps, the following

Exhibit 2.7. National Association of Purchasing Management Composite Index

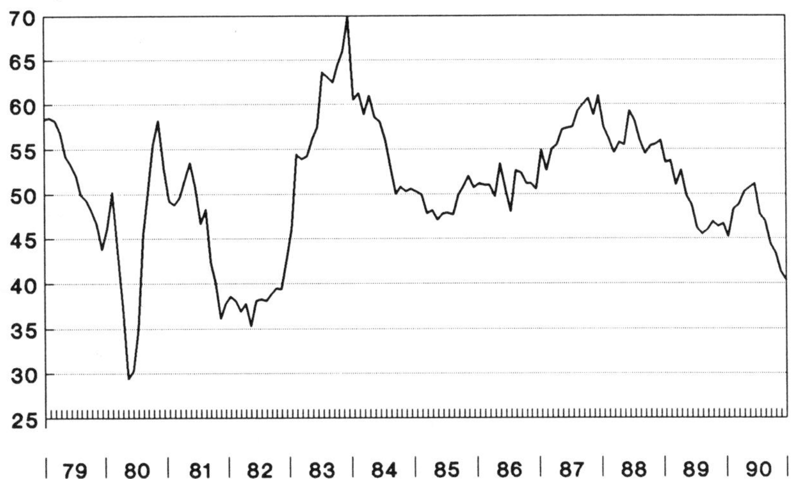

Source: National Association of Purchasing Management

helpful hints are offered. Usually, Fed easing steps will be signaled by Fed reserve supplying action through one-day System RPs at a time when the Federal funds rate level is at or below the prevailing level. Alternatively, a Fed move to do customer RPs at a Federal funds level distinctly below the prevailing level can also signal Fed intentions to ease reserve pressures. For example, the Fed's move to ease reserve pressures on December 7, 1990, in response to the shockingly weak November employment report released on that day, was signaled by $1.5 billion in customer RPs done with funds trading at 7¼%, distinctly below the prevailing level of 7½%.

Other hints of Fed easing steps might be a Fed move to buy government securities outright when only a modest adding job (or none at all) may be indicated. Also hinting at a Fed easing step might be a Fed move to "front load" an indicated reserve add-

Table 2.2. Nonagricultural Payroll Employment: (average monthly change per quarter in thousands of workers)

	1=2+11	2=3+5+6	3	4	5	6=7+10	7	8	9	10	11=12+13+14+15+16+19	12	13	14	15	16	17	18	19
	Total nonag-ricul. payrolls	Total goods pro-ducing payrolls	Mining	Oil & gas	Con-struc-tion	Total manu-fac-turing	Durable goods mfg.	Transp. equip.	Motor vehi-cles	Non-durable goods mfg.	Total ser-vice produc-ing pay-rolls	Trans-porta-tion & util.'s	Whole-sale trade	Retail trade	Fin-ance insur-ance real es-tate	Ser-vices	Busi-ness ser-vices	Health ser-vices	Govt.
1980:1	125	(52)	6	7	(27)	(32)	(13)	(22)	(24)	(19)	177	(4)	16	15	20	84	13	28	47
1980:2	(346)	(324)	10	12	(56)	(277)	(231)	(46)	(40)	(46)	(22)	(19)	(17)	(62)	9	34	(1)	21	33
1980:3	42	(14)	0	8	0	(14)	(10)	8	7	(4)	56	(2)	8	7	12	72	18	25	(42)
1980:4	253	104	16	9	8	80	72	14	11	8	149	6	13	26	17	80	16	27	7
1981:1	89	5	13	12	(6)	(2)	(0)	1	0	(1)	84	7	10	29	12	49	8	23	(22)
1981:2	81	18	9	15	(32)	41	32	8	8	10	63	3	9	26	9	54	23	22	(37)
1981:3	9	(20)	19	12	(19)	(20)	(22)	(14)	(13)	2	28	6	3	8	8	57	9	24	(53)
1981:4	(201)	(202)	5	7	(26)	(181)	(141)	(28)	(19)	(40)	0	(12)	(5)	(44)	(0)	48	6	22	13
1982:1	(162)	(162)	0	4	(29)	(133)	(90)	(8)	0	(43)	0	(8)	(10)	3	3	26	(4)	19	(14)
1982:2	(165)	(196)	(25)	(12)	(16)	(155)	(117)	(12)	(5)	(38)	31	(9)	(12)	28	5	13	(5)	22	7
1982:3	(216)	(168)	(24)	(16)	(20)	(124)	(110)	(11)	(2)	(14)	(48)	(17)	(15)	2	2	19	(1)	17	(39)
1982:4	(159)	(183)	(20)	(10)	(11)	(151)	(125)	(17)	(12)	(27)	24	(12)	(15)	(6)	3	33	5	14	20
1983:1	92	(22)	(18)	(14)	(16)	12	10	8	12	2	114	(12)	(3)	47	12	62	37	11	9
1983:2	350	130	(6)	(6)	42	95	70	13	13	25	220	7	20	66	17	101	47	18	9
1983:3	415	150	2	2	45	103	79	15	14	24	265	17	21	89	25	103	44	13	9
1983:4	306	135	5	2	29	102	83	16	13	19	170	(4)	24	75	17	72	46	9	(14)
1984:1	408	148	2	1	46	100	79	19	9	21	260	28	32	82	18	93	42	11	7
1984:2	359	102	4	3	42	57	50	5	0	6	257	15	20	67	16	103	37	9	35
1984:3	316	82	3	3	31	47	50	13	12	(3)	235	13	22	73	19	67	33	(9)	40
1984:4	316	(1)	(7)	(1)	23	(18)	(2)	(1)	(4)	(16)	317	3	18	126	22	121	26	28	28

1985:1	188	(1)	(3)	(3)	16	(14)	(5)	10	2	(10)	189	10	11	32	21	101	34	17	15
1985:2	266	(3)	(1)	(2)	40	(42)	(26)	6	1	(17)	269	4	11	85	25	107	38	17	37
1985:3	197	(30)	(9)	(6)	22	(43)	(39)	2	(2)	(4)	227	3	6	31	27	110	37	16	50
1985:4	204	3	(6)	(6)	14	(4)	(6)	10	3	1	200	4	5	43	32	100	32	21	16
1986:1	115	(27)	(16)	(14)	11	(22)	(18)	1	(3)	(4)	142	(1)	(6)	42	25	64	17	21	18
1986:2	61	(68)	(26)	(25)	(4)	(37)	(34)	2	(2)	(3)	128	(35)	(3)	49	30	79	28	21	9
1986:3	261	(20)	(14)	(11)	9	(15)	(16)	3	(1)	1	281	39	12	71	27	86	28	23	46
1986:4	213	13	(4)	(4)	20	(3)	(13)	3	0	10	201	10	3	33	25	96	30	20	33
1987:1	211	20	(1)	(0)	14	7	3	5	2	5	191	10	10	36	19	104	34	23	11
1987:2	246	27	2	3	14	11	2	(3)	(4)	9	219	8	10	51	20	107	27	22	24
1987:3	253	64	4	3	3	56	33	5	(1)	23	189	18	14	37	13	105	22	25	3
1987:4	364	74	1	1	29	44	29	(1)	(2)	15	290	15	16	69	9	110	27	26	71
1988:1	274	16	(2)	(1)	8	10	3	(5)	(4)	7	258	14	14	60	9	127	37	25	33
1988:2	288	46	(1)	(1)	19	28	24	7	3	5	242	11	25	43	2	138	34	30	23
1988:3	230	(1)	(5)	(4)	2	2	9	0	2	(7)	230	8	15	39	1	132	38	31	35
1988:4	298	39	(4)	(5)	4	39	28	9	5	11	259	12	18	50	9	141	29	35	29
1989:1	247	1	(0)	(1)	(6)	8	(0)	2	(0)	8	245	5	24	63	3	121	12	35	29
1989:2	184	1	0	1	18	(17)	(14)	(4)	(4)	(2)	183	17	12	12	10	94	17	40	37
1989:3	168	(10)	6	2	12	(28)	(25)	(6)	(6)	(3)	178	0	12	26	13	87	14	40	40
1989:4	172	(29)	3	2	(3)	(29)	(24)	(6)	(5)	(4)	200	40	14	25	11	96	2	47	15
1990:1	246	14	4	2	32	(22)	(12)	(1)	(1)	(11)	233	11	6	18	12	109	12	49	77
1990:2	236	(32)	5	3	(14)	(23)	(20)	(0)	0	(3)	268	13	7	19	8	92	13	53	129
1990:3	(72)	(77)	(3)	(1)	(31)	(43)	(44)	(13)	(7)	1	5	8	(4)	7	2	72	4	47	(80)
1990:4	(203)	(172)	1	1	(64)	(109)	(79)	(26)	(15)	(30)	(31)	4	(13)	(58)	7	44	(18)	53	(1)
1991:1	(229)	(173)	(2)	0	(65)	(106)	(83)	(21)	(11)	(23)	(56)	(13)	(26)	(50)	(3)	17	(16)	38	18

Note: Parentheses indicate declines.
Source: Bureau of Labor Statistics, Aubrey G. Lanston & Co. Inc.

ing need. In a front-loading action, the Fed supplies reserves early in a given two-week bank reserve maintenance period in which an adding job is indicated, or, if a draining job is indicated, it drains reserves late in a given reserve maintenance period. Conversely, the Fed might signal tightening intentions by "backloading" actions in which the Fed supplies reserve late in a given two-week maintenance period in which a reserve adding need is indicated, or by draining reserves early in a maintenance period in which a draining job is projected.

NEW CHANNELS OF MONETARY POLICY INFLUENCE

Viewing the monetary policy process in a cyclical perspective, there are two current policy channels of special note. The first channel of policy influence on the business cycle is the spread between short-term interest rates (most directly influenced by Fed policy shifts) and long-term rates. When Fed policymakers tighten aggressively enough to convince bond investors that inflationary pressures will be curtailed, for example, the Federal funds rate and other short-term interest rates will rise more sharply than long-term rates, and the yield curve will flatten or even become inverted (short-term rates in excess of long-term rates). For financial intermediaries that borrow "short" and lend "long," this tight money condition squeezes profits and creates a disincentive to lend, resulting in a slowing in loan and deposit (money) growth. Consumer and business borrowers facing the resulting reduced availability and increased cost of credit and money will, in turn, curtail spending, thus causing a slowing in economic activity. Certainly, this was the case when an inverted yield curve in portions of 1980, most of 1981, and early 1982 helped bring on the brief recession in 1980 and the much deeper and longer recession of 1981–82. (Of course, the 1980 recession was also greatly influenced by credit controls which prevailed from March to July of that year.) In 1989, the yield curve inverted again, though to a lesser extent than in 1981–1982, producing a slowing in economic activity. Conversely, when the Fed eases aggressively, and pushes short-term rates sharply lower, the yield curve will usually steepen, setting the stage for an acceleration in economic activity.

A second channel of policy influence is the spread between interest rates on six-month corporate debt and six-month Treasury bills.[5] This spread measures the default risk on private debt. Usually, as the Fed continues to tighten monetary conditions just before a recession, this spread tends to widen as lenders begin to question the ability of firms borrowing from them to repay their loans. A widening of the spread of the six-month corporate debt rate over six-month Treasury bill rate could be a signal that bank lenders tend to prefer liquidity over extending risky new credits.

The National Bureau of Economic Research (NBER), which officially dates U.S. business cycles, has included these two channels of monetary policy influence (the spread between short- and long-term rates and the spread between the six-month Treasury bill rate and the six-month commercial paper rate) in an "experimental recession index." The other components of this experimental index include new housing permits, unfilled orders of durable goods manufacturers, the trade-weighted dollar, part-time work in nonfarm industries and the change in ten-year Treasury bond yield.

More basically, the traditional economic channels of monetary policy have changed as a result of the earlier deregulation of interest rates and foreign exchange rates as well as the greater integration of world financial markets.[6] For example, the elimination of deposit interest rate ceilings and the emergence of secondary mortgage markets in the 1980s may have weakened the strong effect of monetary policy on housing activity. In effect, this combination of deregulation and financial innovation meant that the Fed no longer could make policy restraint take hold abruptly through disintermediation. Second, the rising indebtedness of U.S. corporations in the 1980s may have made them more sensitive to changes in interest rates. Third, the increased openness of the U.S. economy has clearly made exchange rates a more important channel of monetary policy influence. Note in Table 2.3 the sharply increased share of exports and imports in relation to total economic activity from 1960 to 1990. Exports (as a share of GNP) rose dramatically from 5.7% in 1960 to 14.5% in 1990, while over the

Table 2.3. Major Components of GNP (amounts in billions of 1982 dollars)

	I-1960		I-1990	
	Level	% of GNP	Level	% of GNP
GNP	1,671.7	100.0	4,195.9	100.0
Consumption expenditures	997.1	59.6	2,710.1	64.6
Durables	96.9	5.8	437.1	10.4
Motor vehicles and parts	47.7	2.9	182.2	4.3
Other durables	49.2	2.9	254.9	6.1
Nondurables	460.7	27.6	912.2	21.7
Services	439.6	26.3	1,360.7	32.4
Business fixed investment	288.7	17.3	710.9	16.9
Nonresidential	161.1	9.6	520.2	12.4
Residential	100.9	6.0	188.1	4.5
Inventory (change)	26.7	1.6	2.6	0.1
Net exports	−9.3	−.6	−41.2	−1.0
Exports	95.0	5.7	608.0	14.5
Imports	104.3	6.2	649.2	15.5
Government	395.2	23.6	816.1	19.4

Source: U.S. Dept. of Commerce

same period, the share of imports rose from 6.2% to 15.5%. A strong dollar loomed large as a cyclical influence when it helped produce a large trade deficit (by making exports more expensive and imports less expensive) that nearly brought the U.S. economy to its knees in 1986 (see Exhibit 2.8).

Exhibit 2.8. Quarterly Real GNP Growth 1980–90 (year-over-year change at an annual rate)

Source: U.S. Dept. of Commerce

Part Two

Fed Leaders, Power, Politics

Strong leaders have played an important role in shaping monetary policy objectives and the means to achieve them. Great Fed chairmen have been the product of situations in which a strong leader faced a major challenge. Insight into how Fed Chairmen formulate policy objectives, develop operating techniques to achieve them, exercise power, interact with fellow policymakers, and deal with outside political pressures can be found in the analysis in this section. Chapter 3 is a comparative grading of post-World War II Fed chairmen. Great Fed chairmen must possess vision, insight, courage, commitment, and an instinctive sense of good policy timing. Also in this Part, to help gain insight into the importance of personalities in shaping policy aims and implementing them through specific policy measures, are chapters on the routine Fed Board meeting that almost triggered an international incident (Chapter 4) and on the Fed's more recent Thanksgiving fiasco (Chapter 5). Finally, there is an examination of the continuing political assault on the Fed's independence by various Congressional and Administration sources (Chapter 6).

CHAPTER 3

An Evaluation of Contemporary Federal Reserve Chairmen[1]

Monetary policy is more art than science. Like painting colors on a canvas, Fed leaders must shape monetary policy in harmony with fiscal policy and international policy considerations, while blending in harsh political pressures, periodic oil price shocks, and other prominent items on the landscape to try to achieve the objective of a pleasing economic picture.

On a practical level, monetary policy is a continuous process of observation and adjustment, of modifying unfinished brush strokes to make the painting a better one. Specifically, Fed policymakers must digest a continuous stream of incoming economic and financial data to determine when to make adjustments in bank reserve pressures. Basically, the policy process is partly reaction to unforeseen events and partly Fed efforts to anticipate future trends.

In monetary policy, as in most other pursuits, timing is everything. Too much Fed tightening too soon can, for example, prematurely snuff out a budding economic expansion; conversely, too little Fed easing too late might help cause an already sluggishly growing economy to come to a complete halt or even to turn down.

Complicating matters for Fed policymakers is the primitive state of economic forecasting.[2] Moreover, there is no settled body of monetary theory; the theoretical framework for monetary policy is still evolving and monetary linkages to economic activity are at times highly uncertain. Accordingly, each Fed policymaker typically has his or her own framework for monetary analysis; the best hope in these uncertain conditions is that they each react consistently within their own framework. For this reason, investors and Fed watchers seeking to anticipate Fed policy shifts and related interest rate movements must learn as much as possible about each Fed leader's own monetary policy framework and personal traits.

The Chairman of the Federal Reserve Board of Governors is, under certain circumstances, the second most powerful person in our government. These special conditions, it is true, usually prevail only if a strong Fed leader happens to be in office when a major economic or financial challenge arises. Such was the case, for instance, when Chairman Marriner Eccles faced the challenge of the Great Depression and, more recently, when Chairman Paul Volcker met the challenge of rapidly accelerating and psychologically embedded inflationary pressures.

On a less lofty level, some Fed chairmen have from time to time been accused of covering up political motives for taking easing actions or avoiding tightening. Critics have gone so far as to portray these Fed chairmen as being like flim-flam men, because they are seemingly so adept at disguising the real motives behind some policy shifts.[3]

The necessary qualities of a great Fed chairman (grade: A) are that such a person must have, in addition to at least some technical knowledge of the job, an instinctive feel for the appropriate timing of monetary policy shifts, a trait that is perhaps more inbred than acquired. A great Fed Chairman must also have penetrating insight into the major economic or financial problems at hand. Moreover, this person must have the courage to stand up to critics and must make a lasting commitment to implementing the appropriate monetary policy actions to solve the prevailing problems. In addition, a great Fed Chairman must have a lofty vision of the longer-term adaptive role of monetary policy (in combination with fiscal policy) necessary to maintain a prolonged condition of sustainable, noninflationary economic growth. In this connection, the Fed chairman (and other policymakers as well) must remain independent of unreasonable political pressures. Most important, a great Fed Chairman must be consistent and credible; this person must be clearly understood by and believable to economic and financial decision makers (both domestic and foreign).

The quickest way for a Fed chairman to lose this prized credibility is to be perceived as caving in to political pressures. Such an unwanted event will be promptly signaled in the auction markets; the yield curve will steepen (longer-term rates in excess of short-term rates) as bond investors become skeptical of the Fed's anti-inflation resolve, commodity prices will rise, and the dollar will fall.

The following analysis focuses first on the current Fed Chairman Alan Greenspan and then on a comparative grading of contemporary Fed leaders. In his young adulthood, Greenspan was an accomplished musician and a member of the close-knit band of followers of philsopher Ayn Rand,[4] the fervant advocate of "rugged individualism" and "titanic self-assertion." One of the foremost proponents of capitalism, Rand envisioned a society in which each person could realize his or her potential in any chosen field without significant government interference or regulation. Perhaps partly because of this early influence, Greenspan has favored virtually all forms of bank deregulation, including the elimination of the 1930s Glass-Stegal barriers between commercial banking and investment banking.

In his business career, Greenspan ran a highly successful private economic consulting firm specializing in industrial sector analysis. Subsequently, the politically well-connected[5] Greenspan interrupted this private economic consulting business to serve as Chairman of President Ford's Council of Economic Advisers (1974–77) and later to serve in the Reagan Administration as Chairman of the bipartisan National Commission on Social Security Reform (1982–83).

ALAN GREENSPAN

Alan Greenspan is the ultimate, high level "numbers cruncher." He collects as many economic facts and figures as he can get his hands on in order to thoroughly diagnose the state of the economy, much as a doctor would diagnose a patient. Greenspan, who constantly scans computer screens near his desk, prides himself in being among the first to identify real sector imbalances; he even goes so far as to figure the precise odds of a recession (which, by his calculation, in early 1990, dropped to 20% from 30% in the spring of 1989 before rising again in late 1990).

To illustrate his attachment to computers and to the quantitative and market information that they provide, Greenspan reminisced in his Humphrey-Hawkins congressional testimony on February 20, 1991 about where he was the night that the United States and allied forces attacked Iraq (January 16, 1991). While most Americans were tied to their television sets, Greenspan was glued to his computer. He recounted, "I recall vividly sitting by my computer screen on the night of the air attacks on Iraq." He continued, "It became fairly clear at that point that the war would not evolve into a pattern which would create a major destruction of oil resources in the Middle East." Seemingly in awe of global financial market interrelationships, Greenspan added, "And when that became apparent as the night evolved, you could basically see not only the price of oil coming down very sharply across the world, but you could see the effects minute by minute in the exchange markets, in the interest rate markets, in the gold markets, all arbitraged across and around the world."

Personally, Greenspan is courteous, judicious, fair-minded, low-key, and highly respected by his fellow policymakers. At times self-conscious almost to the point of shyness, he leads by persuasion rather than by attempts to dominate others. Greenspan is intellectually brilliant, perhaps to the point of being too academic at times in his policy approach and is sometimes deadly dull in his personal testimony before Congress. But, commendably, he seldom, if ever, talks down to people.

Greenspan is intense in his work and meticulous in defining his policy shifts. He is most considerate of the opinions of others; by all accounts Greenspan is a very good listener, so much so that Greenspan-led FOMC meetings have acquired the reputation of being anything but brief. Indeed, Greenspan's seemingly limitless patience and democratic leadership approach (giving other Fed policymakers their full say) has contrasted sharply with his predecessor Volcker's more secretive and personally dominating approach.

However, the Greenspan Fed's "watch everything" approach raised the threat that the monetary authorities might end up watching so many conflicting signals that they would become indecisive, as appeared to be the case in the first half of 1990. In this connection, while it officially recognized as early as the July 2–3, 1990, FOMC meeting the emergence of the unusual bank-induced "credit crunch," the Greenspan Fed, perhaps because it was trying to watch so many other indicators at the same time and because it favored quantitative information over anecdotal evidence, failed to give early and adequate weight to this factor as a primary economic depressant.

To be sure, Greenspan's personal policy priority clearly remains that of curtailing inflationary pressures. Nevertheless, the negative side of Greenspan's democratic leadership approach is that it has resulted in too much Fed infighting and too many press leaks. At time, Fed deliberations seemed to lapse into periods of near policy paralysis. The fundamental conflict was between the Fed "hawks" and "doves." The hawks (mostly Volcker-selected Reserve Bank Presidents) would risk recession if necessary to rein in inflationary pressures; the doves, in contrast, wanted to avoid recession at all costs.

Perhaps Greenspan's greatest leadership success in a crisis situation was the Fed's appropriate response to the stock market Crash of October 19, 1987. Fed policymakers, under Greenspan's able leadership, moved promptly to inject liquidity into the financial system and to push interest rates lower in order to protect the real sector of the economy from the unsettling stock market plunge. In successfully meeting this early test of his leadership, Greenspan greatly increased his personal credibility on Capitol Hill.

In contrast, the collapse in stock prices on October 13, 1989, left some uncertainty about who within the Fed was calling the shots. Specifically, Vice Chairman Johnson, who acted without Greenspan's approval and against his better judgment, leaked to the *New York Times* and the *Washington Post* during the weekend following this stock price plunge the fact that the Fed was again (as in October 1987) ready to meet the financial sector's liquidity needs. Greenspan's contrasting view was that this particular stock price plunge reflected the appropriate correction of excesses in the corporate takeover area and thus was not deserving of the special provision of additional Fed liquidity.

In late 1989, the New York Fed's domestic trading desk came under market criticism for the "Thanksgiving Fiasco" (*see* Chapter 5). This problem arose most innocently on the day before Thanksgiving—November 22, 1989—when the Fed faced an adding job to meet seasonal needs arising from a jump in currency in circulation. Market participants misinterpreted the Fed's open market reserve supplying operations (five-day System RPs) on that day, wrongly concluding that it was a Fed easing step. Two major factors contributed to this costly mistake. First, market participants, most of whom held heavy positions in U.S. government securities on the heels of a huge 1989 bond market rally, allowed wishful thinking about a possible stepped-up pace of Fed easing to get in the way of their better judgment. Second, the Greenspan Fed had unfortunately become increasingly ambiguous in its day-to-day open market operations.

Specifically, the New York Reserve Bank's domestic trading desk, in contrast with greater precision under Volcker, had failed to distinguish clearly between open market operations for the purpose of signaling policy shifts and those for the technical purposes of merely offsetting the impact of market factors on bank reserve positions. For example, each of the two Fed easing steps on November 6 and October 16 had in fact been signaled by a relatively subtle Fed move to do customer RPs with funds trading below the prevailing level. Perhaps for this reason as well as to avoid putting off the adding job until late in the reserve maintenance period, Fed officials opted instead, on November 22, to do the five-day System RPs. (An alternative Fed reserve-adding move to meet the moderate-sized seasonal reserve need at the time might have been for it to do one-day customer RPs on November 22 and then, following the Thanksgiving holiday, on November 24, to do System weekend RPs, though the latter might have been hampered by skeleton post-holiday staffs.) Fed officials must have been shocked when market participants misinterpreted their technical move on November 22 as a Fed easing step.

Ideally, the Fed trading desk should be more precise in signaling policy shifts. The Fed should signal easing actions through open market operations by adding reserves through the relatively stronger action of one-day System RPs with the funds rate trading below the prevailing level. (To be fair, it should be emphasized that Fed policymakers have appropriately signaled their policy shifts much more clearly since the

Thanksgiving fiasco.) Conversely, to signal tightening intentions, the Fed should drain reserves through one-day System reverse RPs with funds trading above the prevailing level.

More recently, although the Fed has more clearly signaled its policy shifts, the circumstances of the July 13, 1990, easing step were perhaps the most unusual of any Fed easing move in the post-World War II era. The official explanation of this easing step was that the monetary authorities were easing in order to try to offset the credit-tightening effects of greater bank loan stringency. The problem was that only a few weeks earlier Greenspan had testified before Congress that he saw little, if any, evidence of a bank-induced credit squeeze. Moreover, Treasury Secretary Brady had, at the beginning of the same week (on July 9), urged that the Fed ease further. This led market observers to conclude that this Fed easing move was at least partly political.[6]

The Bush Administration had been putting increasing pressure on Greenspan to ease in order to restimulate lagging economic growth and to lessen the destructive effects of the savings and loan (S&L) crisis and declining real estate prices. The Bush Administration also wanted Greenspan to ease to counter the potentially depressing economic impact of a prospective budget deficit-cutting agreement that would raise taxes and cut spending. The implicit threat in these Bush Administration pressures on Greenspan to ease was that he would not be reappointed Fed Chairman if he didn't respond.

In contrast with the Fed's usual secrecy, the Fed Chairman telegraphed this July 13, 1990, easing step on the preceding day in Congressional testimony before the Senate Banking Committee on the unrelated subject of deposit insurance. In answer to an apparently eagerly anticipated question, Greenspan read from already prepared notes that he favored an easing move in response to evidence that banks were increasing interest rates on new business loans, relative to their cost of funds, and requiring more collateral as backing for these loans.

Just prior to Greenspan's testimony on July 12, 1990, the monetary authorities unearthed additional unpublished evidence (from the quarterly bank lending practices survey) of the mounting bank-induced credit squeeze. Also, the Board staff may have developed around that time (for internal use only) more precise quantitative measures of the degree of tightening in bank lending rates and other credit terms, relative to their cost of funds.

In any case, Chairman Greenspan regained at least some of his lost market credibility when the record of the July 2–3, 1990, FOMC meeting was released in late August. This policy record disclosed that the FOMC discussed the bank-induced loan stringency ten days before the July 13 Fed easing step and that the FOMC intended that the Fed Chairman would ease after a short wait unless data on the economy and the monetary aggregates indicated greater economic strength.

The historical contributions of other post-World War II Fed leaders range from exceptional (Eccles and Volcker) to deplorable (Miller). A comparative grading of contemporary Fed Chairmen is offered in Table 3.1. A common theme running through the records of these contemporary Fed Chairmen is that great Fed leaders are distinguished more by their policy instincts, timing, effective and credible communications, and performance under pressure than by their

Table 3.1. Comparative Grading of Contemporary Fed Chairmen

Chairman		Grade
Eccles	(1934–48)	95
McCabe	(1948–51)	65
Martin	(1951–70)	90
Burns	(1970–78)	75
Miller	(1978–79)	60
Volcker	(1979–87)	93
Greenspan	(1987–)	85

SCALE (90's - A, 80's - B, 70's - C, 60's - D)

technical monetary policy competence and numbers crunching ability, though the latter should not be minimized.

MARRINER ECCLES

Eccles, whose term as Fed Chairman spanned the immediate pre- and post-World War II period, set the standards by which contemporary Fed leaders should be judged. This man seemed an unlikely candidate for greatness. Eccles had no formal college education; indeed, his father came penniless to the United States from Scotland. But Eccles' greatness came at a time when it was needed most, during the Great Depression. He correctly saw that monetary policy did not operate in a vacuum. Eccles played a major role in convincing the Roosevelt Administration that fiscal stimulus—spending in excess of tax receipts—was required, in addition to aggressive monetary accommodation, to help pull the economy out of the clutches of the Great Depression.[7]

Among his other contributions, Eccles also had a major influence on the Banking Act of 1935 which helped restore confidence in the U.S. banking system and strengthened the Fed Board of Governors' hand in formulating and implementing monetary policy. Eccles, who tended to be somewhat long-winded, nevertheless had a dominating personal presence in policy meetings. Perhaps most important of all, Eccles led the fight for Fed independence from undue Treasury influence. Indeed, largely through Eccles' influence, the Banking Act of 1935 created the important FOMC policymaking body and excluded the Secretary of the Treasury and the Comptroller of the Currency from the Board of Governors. Eccles also fought toe-to-toe with Treasury Secretary Snyder with respect to the Treasury's demand that the Fed continue to peg Treasury securities rates. This Fed rate pegging approach had helped facilitate Treasury financing in support of the war effort; but, in the postwar period, it threatened to make the Fed, in Eccles' words, "an engine of inflation." Eccles was a major force behind the 1951 Treasury-Federal Reserve Accord which appropriately freed the Fed from pegging Treasury securities rates.[8]

THOMAS McCABE

Thomas McCabe, appointed by President Truman as Eccles' successor, was a pleasant and likable person with a good understanding of the business sector. (Prior to his appointment McCabe was Chairman of Scott Paper Corporation and Chairman of the Philadelphia Reserve Bank Board of Directors.) But McCabe was a disappointingly weak Fed Chairman, particularly on the issue of Fed independence from Treasury pressures. He deserves no better than a barely passing grade. McCabe was overpowered by then-Treasury Secretary Snyder who wanted to continue to force the Fed to peg interest rates, as had been done to facilitate Treasury borrowing to finance World War II. McCabe's effectiveness as Fed Chairman was also undermined by the fact that the powerful Eccles stayed on as a Board member, despite not being reappointed as Chairman.

WILLIAM McCHESNEY MARTIN, JR.

In contrast with his predecessor, Martin, who reigned as Fed Chairman for a record 19 years, was a master of the art of central banking. He had a deep understanding of financial markets and an instinctive feel for making the right monetary policy move at the right time. Within Fed policy-making circles, Martin was the consummate politician, always soliciting opinions from other Fed policymakers in order to shape a consensus, a consensus that, curiously, often bore less resemblance to the collective judgment of his fellow Fed policymakers than to Martin's own view of the Fed's most appropriate policy course.

The Fed's main objective, according to Martin, should be to "lean against the wind" by tightening bank credit when economic growth is excessive and inflationary pressures are accelerating or, alternatively, to ease bank credit when the economy falters. Martin sought to encourage postwar growth and prosperity while guarding against accelerating price pressurers. As an inflation fighter, he saw himself as the person who takes away the punch bowl before the party gets too wild. Under Martin's leadership, there were recurring periods of Fed restraint in the second half of the 1950s, which helped set the stage for a "golden age" of sustained economic growth with low inflation in the first half of the 1960s.

Subsequently, Martin's anti-inflation move to increase the discount rate in late 1965 infuriated then-President Johnson. Reportedly, in order to try to intimidate Martin into backing down on the discount rate hike, Johnson invited Martin down to the President's Texas ranch and drove him around on dirt roads in a big Lincoln convertible at excessive speeds; but, despite the dust and danger, Martin didn't budge.

However, Martin's "magic" touch disappeared in the second half of the 1960s when the Fed eased prematurely. The Martin-led Fed acted on the mistaken assumption that the belated 1968 tax increase (required to help finance the Vietnam War) would promptly depress U.S. economic activity.

ARTHUR BURNS

Arthur Burns was the most political of contemporary Fed Chairmen.[9] Burns, who seemed to thrive on Washington political intrigue, was quick to offer advice on fiscal policies and was deeply involved in President Nixon's 1971 imposition of price controls.

Burns presided over a brief but severe credit crunch in 1973–74. The resulting sharp spike in interest rates put the Fed, for the first time, on the front page of the newspapers and sent housing activity into a tailspin.

No one questioned Burns' intellectual and academic credentials. A former long-time economics professor at Columbia University, an early guiding light in the prestigious National Bureau of Economic Research (NBER), and Chairman of the President's Council of Economic Advisors in the Eisenhower Administration, he was a respected pioneer in U.S. business cycle research. As Fed Chairman, Burns was intellectually overpowering both inside and outside Fed policy circles. But, Burns' blunt and condescending manner and his autocratic management style clashed with the collegial atmosphere created inside the Fed by his predecessor.

Moreover, when it really counted, Burns was remarkably ineffective. In particular, perhaps because of lingering excessive political sensitivities, Burns consistently underreacted during the period from 1975 through early 1978, as inflationary psychology and speculative excesses built up in an environment of negative real interest rates.

G. WILLIAM MILLER

The booby prize for the most ineffective Fed Chairman of the post-World War II era goes to G. William Miller. He failed not so much from a lack of intelligence as from a lack of interest. Miller seemed almost more preoccupied with proclaiming no-smoking edicts in Board meetings[10] than with making forceful Fed policy moves. Miller's business sense was good; he was formerly chairman of Textron Inc. However, Miller seemed out of his element in dealing with macroeconomic issues and policy questions.

Fortunately, Miller's term was short; but his reluctance to aggressively tighten monetary policy to fight rapidly mounting price pressures could not have come at a worse time. Miller, like his predecessor, also appeared to cave in to political pressures at times. Miller has the dubious distinction of being the only Fed Chairman ever outvoted by the Board of Governors on a discount increase (1978), and this incident severely undercut Miller's effectiveness as Fed Chairman.

PAUL VOLCKER

It has been said that Paul Volcker was born to be Fed Chairman.[11] Certainly, in terms of training and temperment, it would be hard to conceive of anyone better prepared for the job. His monetary policy expertise ranged from the technical intricacies of day-to-day Fed open market operations up to the highest levels of monetary policy strategy and conceptualization. And Volcker had cultivated, primarily through his stints at both the U.S. Treasury and the New York Fed, close personal friendships with many foreign central bankers and the major world financial figures, friendships that would come in handy in future efforts at international monetary policy coordination. During the five years from 1979 through 1984, Volcker's instinctive sense of policy timing and purpose in successfully curtailing soaring inflationary pressures is unprecedented in the annals of central banking.

Volcker's boldest policy stroke came at a special Saturday FOMC meeting on October 6, 1979 (dubbed the "Saturday Massacre" or the "Saturday Night Special").[12] His keen sense of anti-inflation policy tactics and timing suggested the need for a dramatically announced change in operating procedures aimed at disciplining monetary growth more effectively. These new operating procedures involved a largely "automatic" reserve control approach that targeted moderate growth in the supply of nonborrowed reserves. Volcker also raised the discount rate to a record (at that time) 12% from 11% and imposed new reserve requirements to limit the growth of bank credit.

This surprise Fed move produced a surge in the Federal funds rate and in other market rates to unimagined heights. The higher cost of loanable bank funds was soon reflected in sharp increases in the prime rate and other rates charged business and consumer borrowers. (The prime rate soared to a peak of 21.5% in late 1980.) Spending declined sharply and the economy was eventually dragged into the deep inflation-killing recession of 1981–82. This bold monetary policy stroke should, nevertheless, be given much of the credit for helping to set the stage for the longest peacetime expansion on record (December 1982 to July 1990).

However, during the 1985–87 period, Volcker's effectiveness as Fed Chairman waned somewhat. His basic problem was too much secrecy and personal dominance in the formulation of monetary policy. Volcker's domination of the policy process increasingly conflicted with the wishes of the Reagan-appointed Board members.

By early 1986, Reagan-appointed Board members represented a majority of the seven-member Board of Governors. In a widely publicized incident in late February of that year, Volcker was initially outvoted by the Reagan-appointed Board majority favoring an immediate discount rate cut to 7% from 7½% (*see* Chapter 4). However, before the discount rate cut was officially announced, an angry Volcker, who reportedly threatened to resign, was able to hammer out a compromise. In this compromise, the discount rate was delayed until early March when it could be coordinated with discount rate cuts by both Germany and Japan so as to minimize the negative impact on the U.S. dollar. The fallout from this unpleasant experience served to weaken Volcker's firm grip on the monetary policy process.

CHAPTER 4

The Routine Board Meeting That Almost Triggered An International Financial Crisis

The nearly disastrous day for monetary policy (February 24, 1986) started routinely and calmly at the marble-encased Federal Reserve Board of Governors building on Constitution Avenue in Washington, D.C.[1] The seven-member Board (consisting of Chairman Paul Volcker, Vice Chairman Preston Martin, and Governors Wayne Angell, Manuel Johnson, Martha Seger, Emmet Rice, and Henry Wallich) met in a regular morning session to consider requests by eight district Federal Reserve Banks for a discount rate cut to 7% from 7½%. Chairman Volcker started the meeting by mumbling through lips tightly clenching a cigar that his recommendation was that any Board action on the discount rate cut requests should be delayed until a Fed discount rate cut could be coordinated with similar actions by Japan and Germany. Such a coordinated move was needed, Volcker explained, to minimize the negative effect of a Fed discount rate cut on the dollar. However, Volcker cautioned that Germany remained reluctant to reduce its discount rate and, although Japan was more willing to cooperate, it wanted to delay the move.

Expecting prompt approval, the Fed Chairman asked whether there was any discussion of his recommendation for a delay in the discount rate cut. Ever the dissenter who coveted Volcker's job, Vice Chairman Martin immediately challenged the Chairman. "I think we should discuss this issue," Martin asserted. The Fed Chairman bristled with uncharacteristic contempt. There ensued an extended discussion of whether the discount rate should be cut immediately or delayed, as favored by the Chairman.

It was never easy to challenge Volcker on a major policy decision because he seemed to operate with special insight and intuition on a more lofty policy level than his fellow policymakers. Although he was quite familiar with and often intimately involved in the Fed's day-to-day policy routine, Volcker seemed, at times like this, to reach above this mundane policy level almost as if to tap received wisdom from some higher source. To be sure, Volcker's aloofness and secrecy in arriving at the key policy decisions was sometimes resented by his fellow policymakers. But to go along with his hallowed policy perspective, Volcker also seemed to be just plain lucky in making the right policy calls at the right time.

VOLCKER OUTVOTED

On this fateful day it soon became evident that Chairman Volcker (supported by Governors Wallich and Rice) would be outvoted by the Reagan-appointed Fed majority (Martin, Seger, Angell, and Johnson). Only once before had a Fed Chairman been outvoted in such an important policy matter; Volcker's predecessor G. William Miller had been outvoted on a discount rate increase in 1978. Fed policymakers recognized that this might be a bombshell leading to Volcker's resignation. With a final admonition that he, as their Chairman, urged a delay, Volcker called for the formal vote. The jarring results were as expected; four Board members in favor of an immediate discount rate cut, three (including Volcker) against.

The room fell silent. Senior Fed staff members that were present—including Steve Roberts (assistant to Volcker), Joe Coyne (public affairs), and Michael Bradfield (legal)—were stunned. Following the usual routine after a Board decision to change the discount rate, Roberts, Coyne, and Bradfield began a preliminary drafting of the official discount rate cut announcement. Volcker angrily stalked out of the meeting. Soon thereafter, on the same day, the Fed Chairman attended a previously scheduled lunch with Treasury Secretary Baker and threatened to resign.

SEEDS OF DOOM

The seeds of doom had been sown by two intervening events. First, there had been growing antagonism between the Fed Chairman and Vice Chairman Martin, who could not hide his ambition to become Fed Chairman. As a long-time associate of President Reagan, Martin had a direct, inside political track to the White House. Much to Volcker's consternation, Martin used this important White House channel frequently, going even so far as to interview the Administration's prospective candidates for the Fed Board of Governors behind Volcker's back. Nor was there any love lost between Volcker and Governor Seger, who intensely disliked Volcker for his secrecy (bordering on arrogance, she thought) in arriving at policy decisions. She felt left out of the policy loop. Earlier, Seger had been traveling in Europe, but she arrived back just in time for the February 24 meeting.

A second event that helped set the stage for the fateful February meeting was the early February 1986 swearing in of two new Reagan appointees, Governors Johnson and Angell. These appointments were highly politicized. Manuel Johnson was the fair-haired boy from the supply-side camp at the Reagan Administration's Treasury Department. The market speculation was that he would be pro-growth, at least most of the time. There was a similar political ring to Wayne Angell's appointment to the Fed Board which arose out of Angell's friendship and political backing of Senator Robert Dole (Republican-Kansas), Senate minority leader. The prevailing political wisdom was that these appointments now represented a Reagan-majority Board which would cut the imperious Volcker down to size.

To clear the air, soon after joining the Board, Governor Johnson asked for a private meeting with Volcker. Johnson told Volcker that he would support the Fed Chairman 90% of the time. However, on the subject of a possible near-term discount rate cut, Johnson said he wanted to go on record as favoring one. Volcker pointedly asked Johnson if he had other reasons for favoring such action. Johnson took this to be a backhanded way of asking if he was excessively beholden to the Reagan Administration for appointing him. The implication was that Johnson was urging a discount rate cut for the political purposes of pleasing the Reagan Administration in return for appointing him. Johnson replied that he could see how Volcker might conclude this, but that actually Johnson was following his own economic judgment that the economy was weakening and his personal conscience as to the right policy response. Johnson quietly but emphatically stated that he was not succumbing to political pressures in recommending this action.

FINAL COMPROMISE

The afternoon of February 24, 1986, turned out to be at least as eventful as the morning. Volcker, after cooling off from his unusual display of anger at the contentious morning meeting, had returned to his office after what must have been a tense lunch with Treasury Secretary Baker.

Fortunately, Governor Angell saw the opening for a workable compromise. He asked Steve Roberts, assistant to Volcker, to set up an appointment with the Chairman after lunch. Vice Chairman Preston Martin, who happened to be walking by the Chairman's office at the same time that Angell was arriving, joined in the meeting with the Chairman. A compromise on a delayed discount rate cut was discussed. As Vice Chairman Martin was leaving the meeting he called over to Joe Coyne, who happened to be standing in the hall near the Chairman's office, that Coyne should hold up on drafting the discount rate cut announcement. Martin told Coyne that a second Board meeting on the proposed discount rate cut would be held later that afternoon.

This incident forshadowed an idealogical split in Fed policymaker ranks that was destined to deepen under Chairman Volcker's successor, Alan Greenspan. At one extreme, there were the hawkish Reserve Bank Presidents (mostly Volcker proteges) who wanted to doggedly fight inflation even to the point of risking a recession. At the other extreme, there was the loosely constituted majority of dovish Governors consisting of some pro-growth supply siders and some more traditional doves who emphasized the need to avoid a recession at all costs, especially at a time when unusually large debt burdens weighed heavily on both the private and public sectors of the economy. Historically, because of the politically sensitive nature of their appointments, members of the Board of Governors have been found in their dissents to favor Fed easing initiatives, while, in contrast, the presumably more independent and conservative Reserve Bank Presidents tend in their dissents to favor anti-inflationary Fed tightening moves.[2]

Just 45 minutes before the impending afternoon announcement on February 24, the Board, in its unusual second meeting, switched its vote to favor a delay in the discount rate cut. Thus, a potential international financial crisis triggered by Volcker's almost certain resignation was narrowly averted. A surprise resignation by the highly respected U.S. central bank head (which was a strong possibility had the Board's initial vote overruling him been allowed to stand) would almost certainly have triggered a free-fall in the U.S. dollar in the foreign exchange markets. Such a dollar crisis would most likely have been accompanied by fears of renewed inflation and a loss of confidence in the Reagan Administration. This, in turn, would almost certainly have triggered a pullback of private foreign investors desperately needed to help finance excessive U.S. budget deficits, resulting in upward pressures on U.S. longer-term interest rates.

On May 7, just 12 days later, the Fed, in a coordinated move with Japan and Germany, lowered the discount rate to 7% from 7½%. In all likelihood, this highpoint in international monetary coordination was motivated not so much out of international policy altruism as by the desire to do a personal favor. Perhaps, in the final analysis, an international financial crisis was averted because Volcker's trusted German and Japanese central banking friends acted primarily out of a common human motivation, to get a good friend out of an embarrassing jam.

CHAPTER 5

The Thanksgiving Fiasco

For Federal Reserve officials, the day before Thanksgiving—November 22, 1989—seemed to be starting as just another routine day. The monetary authorities faced the very ordinary task of supplying reserves through open market operations to offset a predictable seasonal reserve drain stemming from a Christmas spending-related increase in currency in circulation. There was not the slightest hint on this day that such routine Fed reserve-supplying operations were about to escalate into a Fed watchers nightmare of misinterpretation, uncertainty, confusion, and recrimination.

DAILY OPEN MARKET ROUTINE

Normally, the focal point of the Fed's daily open market routine[1] is the "morning call" which usually begins at 11:15

A.M. eastern standard time and ends about 11:35 A.M. The participants in this daily morning call include senior officers of the New York Fed domestic trading desk, senior Board staff members in Washington, D.C., and one of the Reserve Bank Presidents who is currently a voting member of the FOMC (other than the permanently voting New York Fed President). Occasionally, a member of the Board of Governors will sit in on the morning call at the Board. The Fed Chairman does not typically attend the morning call but he is kept fully informed of daily open market operations that may be agreed on. Among the topics normally discussed at the morning call is the projected bank reserve need in the current two-week bank maintenance period. Also considered are the Treasury's daily Tax and Loan calls and any special seasonal reserve influences. At the morning call, Fed officials might also take note of any unusual financial market developments, including excessive volatility in either the U.S. dollar or in stock prices. Immediately following the morning call, the New York Fed's trading desk will execute, subject to close Fed-watcher scrutiny, any necessary daily open market operations that might have been agreed on.

The Fed's discussion at the November 22, 1989, morning call almost certainly focused on the need to provide reserves through open market operations to offset the seasonal drain stemming from the increase in currency in circulation. One Fed reserve-supplying option, given the moderate indicated reserve need at the time, would have been for the monetary authorities to act on Wednesday (November 22) to supply reserves through customer RPs. (Customer RPs, the mildest Fed action to lessen reserve pressures through open market operations, actually reduce the drain on reserves that would otherwise have occurred had the customer funds instead been invested internally at the Fed in the form of a Fed reverse RP.) Then, on Friday (November 24), following the Thursday Thanksgiving holiday, Fed officials could have met the remainder of the indicated reserve need by doing weekend System RPs.

Fed RPs represent repurchase agreements calling for the monetary authorities to purchase government securities from any of 40 or so primary dealers in government securities for a specified period (usually one day) and then to sell this Fed-determined amount of government securities back to these primary dealers at an agreed upon interest rate. These Fed RPs are the most common means through which the monetary authorities temporarily add reserves to the banking system, say, to offset the reserves drained through market factors. Most commonly such a reserve drain through the operation of market factors might reflect an increase in currency in circulation (as in the current case of the Thanksgiving fiasco), or an increase in Treasury deposits, or perhaps a decline in float. (Float represents Federal Reserve credit extended to banks for checks not collected within the time period prescribed by an automatic schedule.)

The problem for many market observers is that the Fed may do RPs (or reverse RPs) not only for technical purposes of offsetting the reserve impact of market factors but also for purposes of signaling Fed intentions to shift its policy stance. For example, the Fed may signal a tightening move to doing one-day reverse RPs at a Federal funds level distinctly higher than the prevailing level. Conversely the Fed may signal an easing move by doing one-day RPs with funds at a level distinctly below the prevailing level. This distinction between technical open market operations and Fed intentions to signal policy shifts (see Chapter 2) can be an endless source of confusion for Fed watchers.

PROBLEMS FACED

However, there were at least two difficulties with the November 22, 1989 open market strategy. Most immediately, the Federal funds rate was 8⅜% at the time of the November 22 morning call, below the prevailing level of

8½%. The danger was that if the Fed did customer RPs at a funds rate below the prevailing level, market participants might misinterpret this Fed move as a policy shift toward ease rather than as a routine technical operation. This must have been a source of concern for Fed policymakers, who are quite sensitive to how the market perceives their actions.

The problem was that the Fed's two preceding easing steps on November 6 and October 19 had been signaled by precisely such a Fed operation, namely a Fed move to do customer RPs at a funds rate lower than that which had been prevailing. To make matters worse, there was pre-Thanksgiving speculation by some market participants that the Fed might be about to step up the pace of its easing steps from approximately one a month to two a month.

There was a second reason for rejecting the open market strategy to meet the seasonal reserve need by starting with customer RPs, subsequently followed, after the Thanksgiving holiday, by weekend System RPs. This was that Fed open market operations following the Thanksgiving holiday would most likely be hampered by reduced postholiday staffing (both at the Fed and at government securities dealers) and by the announced early market closing time on Friday, November 24. Fed trading desk officials reasoned that since many market participants might be on vacation on this day following Thanksgiving, it would make for relatively inactive securities trading and financing activity.[2]

To overcome these difficulties and especially to avoid delay in addressing the estimated reserve shortage which would leave the Fed with a very large reserve adding job toward the end of the reserve maintenance period, Fed policymakers chose instead to do five-day System RPs on Wednesday, November 22. The monetary authorities must have assumed that the market could not possibly misinterpret such a straightforward operation. Customarily, such term RPs have been viewed as devoid of policy significance because they are funds rate insensitive and because they routinely are executed only to meet predictable or recurring reserve needs such as the seasonal type that the Fed faced at that time.

Undoubtedly, Fed policymakers were shocked when market participants wrongly jumped to the conclusion that the Fed's five-day System RPs on November 22 were an easing signal. The resulting outburst of market easing psychology temporarily drove the funds rate lower, making the easing psychology a self-fulfilling prophecy. Even the usually reliable *Wall Street Journal,* in an article on November 24, offered the mistaken view that the Fed had eased further. Apparently, the *Wall Street Journal* reporter failed to check with Fed officials before publishing this article. This press account played an important role in misleading the markets on the Fed's policy intentions.

DESPERATE POLICY SIGNALS

In an effort to convince market participants that they were not easing, the monetary authorities reversed course, despite continued seasonal reserve adding requirements, and drained reserves through System reverse RPs on both Friday, November 24, and again on Monday, November 27. However, it was not until the Fed's Monday reverses, done a full hour earlier than usual with funds at 8⁵⁄₁₆%, that market participants finally became convinced that no Fed easing move had been intended on the previous Wednesday. (And even then, some misguided market observers clung to the patently incorrect alternative view that the Fed must have eased briefly on November 22 and then, upon seeing the dollar fall and the gold price rise, turned around and tightened on November 27.)

The Fed's post-Thanksgiving signal that no easing had occurred was unusually explicit and dramatic. With few exceptions, the Greenspan Fed has avoided such dramatic policy measures. The Greenspan trademark of moving in modest, carefully defined, and orderly steps, was evident both when the Fed was moving in a tightening direction, as seen in most of the firming steps during the period from March 1988 through February 1989, and when it was moving in an easing direction, as in the six small, carefully defined easing steps taken from June 1989 through December 1989.

One notable exception to these cautious and discrete policy steps came in February 1989, when the monetary authorities tightened aggressively in response to a surge in inflationary pressures. In February 1989, the Fed acted boldly both through a tightening in reserve pressures by means of open market operations, and a February 24 discount rate hike. Subsequently, in light of a deepening recession, intensifying bank loan stringency, and sluggish monetary growth, the Fed moved in the opposite direction to ease with uncharacteristic aggressiveness in December 1990 and again in early 1991.

TROUBLING DEVELOPMENTS

Actually, the necessity for the Fed to provide its eye-catching, post-Thanksgiving message that it had not eased appears to be the culmination of some mildly disturbing tendencies from both within and outside the Greenspan Fed. For one thing, the Greenspan Fed increasingly had been beset from within by too many conflicting policy statements by monetary officials and by a mounting number of split votes on policy actions decided on in FOMC meetings. From the outside, the increasingly divided Greenspan Fed had been beset by growing pressure to ease by Budget Director Richard Darman and other Administration officials. In addition, there had been an array of press leaks about Fed policy from "government sources" (including Administration sources as well as those from inside the Fed). This troubling pattern of fragmented and conflicting Fed policy statements had earlier become evident on the weekend following the October 13, 1989, stock market collapse. At that time, Vice

Chairman Johnson, without Chairman Greenspan's permission and contrary to his better judgment, leaked to the press the fact that the Fed was prepared to supply the financial markets with adequate liquidity (*see* Chapter 3).

To make matters worse, actual Fed open market operations had recently become increasingly difficult for market participants to discern. There had been no clear Fed signals differentiating policy shifts on the one hand from routine technical actions to offset the impact of market factors on the other. As a result, Fed credibility suffered. Both domestic and foreign market observers alike became confused and annoyed by the Fed's lack of open market policy clarity.

The Fed's unusually explicit actions on November 24 and especially November 27 to demonstrate that it had not eased showed overeager market participants who was boss. The problem was that this unpleasant experience left market participants gun-shy and confused. The uncertainty almost certainly was reflected in higher average Treasury borrowing costs in the period immediately following the Thanksgiving fiasco than otherwise would have been the case.

Looking ahead, the most obvious solution to the Thanksgiving fiasco would be for the Fed to be more explicit in signaling policy shifts through open market operations (as it has in fact done). Of course, the Fed could always rely more heavily on the alternative, unmistakable policy signal of discount rate adjustments, but this is sometimes an overpowering policy tool, akin to killing a fly with a baseball bat.

ENCOURAGING SOLUTION

Fortunately, in the wake of the Thanksgiving fiasco, the Fed made a prompt step in the right direction by being appropriately explicit in implementing its December 20, 1989, easing step through open market operations. The Fed policymakers, after deliberations at their December 18–19 FOMC meeting, provided a refreshingly clear signal that they had decided to ease further in response to a pronounced weakening in economic activity. Specifically, the Fed provided reserves through one-day System RPs at a time when funds were trading at 8 7/16%, or slightly below the prevailing level. In contrast with the Thanksgiving fiasco, market participants immediately understood this intended easing message. In addition, to help curtail conflicting policy statements and leaks in the wake of the Thanksgiving fiasco, the Fed Chairman invoked a policy that discourages officials from talking to the media within one week of an FOMC meeting. This informal ban limits the ability of enterprising press reporters to poll a significant block of FOMC members just prior to any given FOMC meeting, thereby prejudging the outcome of that meeting.

In the future, it is hoped that similar unambiguous Fed signals of easing (or tightening) moves can be provided through open market operations. If, for example, the Fed wishes to indicate easing actions it can, in the future, supply reserves through one-day System RPs when funds are trading below the prevailing level. Alternatively, the Fed can signal tightening intentions by draining reserves through one-day reverse RPs with funds trading above the prevailing level.

To be sure, there remains a more straightforward means of indicating policy shifts—that of *immediate official Fed announcements* of each policy shift. But this method, most recently urged in proposed legislation by Representative Lee Hamilton (Democrat—Indiana), has two major drawbacks. First, formal announcements of each policy shift could reduce the Fed's flexibililty. The Fed might find it difficult to adjust its policy stance in a timely fashion without triggering undue financial market volatility. Second, immediate official announcements of Fed policy shifts, especially if such policy shifts are in a restrictive direction around election time, would almost certainly bring a flood of political criticism, if not outright political intimidation. This potential political firestorm could unduly limit Fed restraint, resulting in a pro-inflation policy bias.

CHAPTER 6

Unrelenting Political Pressures

The Federal Reserve is a political lightning rod.[1] One school of thought as to why so many politicians seem to get so much pleasure from criticizing Fed policymakers might be called the "whipping boy" or "scapegoat" school.[2] Politicians are eager to bad-mouth the Fed because they want to have someone other than themselves to blame if something goes wrong with the economy. For example, if the economy tilts into recession, thereby putting the jobs and financial well-being of their constituents in jeopardy, politicians can conveniently blame the Fed for being too slow to ease.

Another school of thought might be called the political "self-interest" school. These politicians have an ax to grind. For instance, as an unrepentant Fed critic, Budget Director Richard Darman, a key Bush Administration spokesman, has repeatedly tried to browbeat the monetary authorities into easing more aggressively, presumably in order to stimulate economic activity, thereby increasing badly needed budget revenues. The harsh reality was that for every one percentage point decline in real GNP growth engineered through the Fed's soft-landing, anti-inflation approach there is a loss of about $25 billion in budget revenues. Obviously, Budget Director Darman would rather have seen a "strong takeoff" in economic activity, with related increases in budget revenues, rather than the Fed-desired soft landing.

CONGRESSIONAL MEDDLING

Since the Fed is an independent agency answerable to Congress, it is not surprising that members of Congress have occasionally sought to modify the Fed's policy apparatus or at least to influence Fed thinking. For instance, Congressman Wright Patman (Democrat—Texas), the Texas populist who devoted nearly 50 years in Congress to assaulting the Federal Reserve System, struck fear into the hearts of countless Fed officials. Patman's congressional mentor, Sam Rayburn (Democrat—Texas) Speaker of the House of Representatives, advised Patman to use the Fed as a whipping boy. This Fed bashing could do nothing but help Patman's populist image in the eyes of his Texas constituents. Thus, Patman invariably argued that Fed policy was too restrictive and interest rates too high. As long-time Chairman of the House Banking Committee, Patman investigated everything from Fed expense accounts (he once criticized a district Fed Bank for its excessive spending on table-tennis balls) to the Fed's policy guidelines and reserves. Rumor has it that Patman burst in the front door of the New York Reserve Bank one day demanding that he be able to see and touch bank reserves on account at the Fed (which, of course, are merely untouchable bookkeeping entries). Patman also introduced unsuccessful legislation that would abolish the FOMC and turn its functions over to the Board of Governors. (Ironically, Patman's long Fed-bashing career came down to a crafty practice of threatening Fed independence in public but protecting it in private.)

Striking a more positive note, Congress appropriately has sought to increase the Fed's public accountability for its policy decisions. This has been done through the Joint Congressional Resolution of 1975 and the Full Employment and Balanced Growth (Humphrey-Hawkins) Act of 1978. The latter legislation calls for the Fed to report to Congress in February and July of each year on the Fed's analysis of the economic outlook and its monetary targets, and of how the Fed's economic projections and targets relate to the Administration's goals.

Actually, the current Congressional contacts of Fed officials are quite numerous. Under current arrangements, senior Fed policymakers actually testify before Congressional committees or subcommittees approximately 40 times per year.[3] The Fed Chairman alone testifies before Congress approximately 20 times a year. Of particular note is the fact that Chairman Greenspan is unusually forthright in these sessions about Fed policy intentions. In contrast, some of his predecessors (notably Burns and Martin) deliberately chose to reveal as little as possible about actual Fed motives in their Congressional testimony so as to leave maximum room to maneuver.

In 1986, however, Senator Melcher (Democrat—Montana), following the low road, sued the Fed in court to disallow Reserve Bank voting status on the FOMC, on the grounds that the Reserve Bank Presidents were not Presidential appointments. Melcher lost the case when a Federal court ruled that it is inappropriate for Congress to try to use the courts to change the Fed's structure when Congress itself has the direct remedy of legislating any changes it desires.

More recently, in 1989, Congressman Lee Hamilton (Democrat—Indiana) proposed legislation (the successful passage of which is doubtful) further increasing political interference with Fed activities.[4] This proposed legislation calls for the immediate official disclosure of Fed policy decisions rather than the current five to six week delay. In addition, the Hamilton legislation initially called for the Treasury Secretary and the Comptroller of the Currency to be put back on the Fed Board, as in the pre-Banking Act of 1935 days, though, after a private meeting with Greenspan, Hamilton subsequently modified this latter feature. Also, this legislation proposed that the four-year term of the Fed Chairman run concurrently with the four-year term of the President and that the Fed's operating budget be subject to greater Congressional scrutiny. Commenting on the Hamilton legislation, Chairman Greenspan warned it ran the risk of "compromising the Federal Reserve's effectiveness" because the Fed might feel heightened pressure from Congress "to exercise other than its best professional judgment on policy matters."[5]

Still another piece of legislation was introduced in September 1989 by Congressman Stephen Neal (Democrat—North Carolina). The Neal legislation was more favorably received by most, if not all, Fed policymakers (though it also had little chance of being signed into law). House Joint Resolution 409 directs the Federal Reserve to make price stability the primary goal of monetary policy. Specifically, it requires the monetary authorities to pursue policies aimed at gradually reducing the inflation rate to zero over five years. This legislation then requires Fed policymakers to pursue policies that would maintain price stability thereafter. Casting the Neal legislation in the best possible light, W. Lee Hoskins, President of the Reserve Bank of Cleveland, said that the clear mandate provided in this legislation would allay fears of inflation in the financial markets. In a similar vein, Richmond Fed President Robert Black has stated that probably all FOMC members supported the Neal legislation.[6]

U.S. TREASURY INFLUENCE ON THE FED

The U.S. Treasury Department has mounted perhaps the most dangerous threat to the Fed's independence. A seemingly endless bombardment of Treasury attempts to influence Fed policy decisions—with the Treasury's unsolicited advice nearly always tilted in the direction of easier money and lower Treasury borrowing costs—have been aimed at the Fed almost from its very beginning in 1913. In the Fed's earliest days, a Treasury contingent within the Board of Governors was led by the first Fed Chairman Charles Hamlin. (In fact, from 1913 to 1935, the Treasury Secretary, along with the Comptroller of the Currency, were ex officio members of the Board of Governors.) This meant that the Treasury's "low borrowing cost" viewpoint was ever-present on the inside at Fed meetings.

Following World War II, Treasury Secretary Synder sought to force the Fed to continue to peg interest rates, as had been done during the war to facilitate Treasury financing of the massive war budget deficit. The Treasury secretary was backed strongly by President Truman (who personally had suffered capital losses on his World War I Liberty bonds because of the Fed's 1920 tightening moves). This provoked, in early 1951, a Treasury—Fed donnybrook, pitting former Fed Chairman Eccles (who stayed on as a member of the Board of Governors despite President Truman's decision not to reappoint him as Fed Chairman in 1948) against Treasury Secretary Synder. Eccles asserted that the postwar Fed pegging of interest rates made the Fed an "engine of inflation." In addition, Eccles argued, much to the Truman Administration's dismay, that the Fed should assert its independence and fight inflation by disciplining money and credit growth thereby leaving the determination of interest rate levels to market forces. Subsequent Treasury—Fed discussions (in which William McChesney Martin, Jr., of all people, represented the Treasury) eventually led in March 1951 to the Treasury—Fed Accord in which the Fed was appropriately freed from pegging interest rates. Soon thereafter, in April 1951, President Truman named William McChesney Martin, Jr. as Fed Chairman.

More recently, during the Reagan Administration, Treasury Secretary (and later White House Chief of Staff) Donald Regan badgered Fed Chairman Volcker mercilessly. However, the barrage of criticism was primarily aimed at the Fed's seeming inconsistency in disciplining monetary growth. Rarely before had top Administration officials ever complained about the Fed's methodology or about how it implemented policy as opposed to the content and aim of its policy.[7] Indeed, the Fed's policy aim was not in dispute. The Reagan Administration explicitly encouraged the Volcker Fed to pursue tight money policies aimed at fighting inflation vigorously.

Still more recently, the Greenspan Fed has also been the object of a steady stream of unsolicited advice by Administration officials as to how the Fed should adjust its policy stance. The Treasury's assault was particularly intense at the beginning of 1988. For example, Fed Chairman Greenspan was infuriated when a senior Treasury Department economist (Michael Darby) distributed a letter (written on official Treasury Department stationery) to all FOMC members just prior to the February 1988 FOMC meeting warning that unless the Fed further eased its stance and restimulated lagging money growth, a recession could ensue.

Even more strikingly, Chairman Greenspan was, in one now infamous week in July 1990, subjected to an unusually heavy barrage of Bush Administration admonitions to ease the Fed's policy stance. On July 9, 1990, Treasury Secretary Nicholas Brady, in chiding the Fed to ease after a six month period of an unchanged Fed policy stance, argued: "[i]n the U.S., it seems to me, it's not a wise idea to emphasize an undying forever attack on inflation if it jeopardizes growth." Secretary Brady added that troubles with savings and loans and real estate "are becoming more apparent" and that "[i]t's quite clear that they would be helped by lower interest rates."

On July 10, Chairman Greenspan met with GOP Senators to hear their constituents' complaints about high interest rates and bank loan stringency. Then, on July 11, President Bush repeated his call for lower interest rates at a news conference at the conclusion of the Economic Summit in Houston, Texas. On July 12, Chairman Greenspan in Congressional testimony observed that a Fed easing step to counter increased bank loan stringency might be in order. On the following day, July 13, 1990, the Greenspan Fed acted to ease its policy stance.

In his January 29, 1991, State of the Union Address, President Bush made a unique political request of Fed Chairman Greenspan combining *both* monetary and fiscal policy considerations. The President not only pointedly called again for lower interest rates "now," as might have been expected; but he also unexpectedly requested that Chairman Greenspan enter the fiscal arena to head a study of the Bush Administration's politically controversial proposal for a cut in the capital gains tax rate. (Reportedly, this request was relayed to Greenspan through Treasury Secretary Brady only a matter of hours before the State of the Union Address.) For Greenspan, this unusual fiscal task, suddenly thrust upon him by President Bush, could pose major political danger that might harm his objectivity and credibility as Fed Chairman. In essense, this fiscal project could represent a political minefield for Chairman Greenspan not unlike that through which former Fed Chairman Arthur Burns walked as head of President Nixon's Interest and Dividends Committee (arising out of the imposition of price controls in 1971).

The President's Council of Economic Advisers (CEA), established by the Employment Act of 1946, is another arm of the Executive Branch that has exerted a steady bias for easier money. Note in Table 6.1, based on an analysis of CEA memos to the President in the Kennedy, Johnson, Nixon, and Ford administrations, that most often the CEA's advice to the President was that monetary policy was too tight. Most remarkably, there was not a single CEA memo over the

Table 6.1. CEA Advice to the President on Monetary Policy 1960–1974

	Monetary Policy Is:		
	Too Tight	Just Right	Too Easy
Kennedy	16	8	0
Johnson	19	29	0
Nixon*	11	4	0
Ford	1	3	0

*1969–1971 only.

Source: Donald F. Kettl, *Leadership at the Fed* (New Haven, CT: Yale University Press, 1986), p. 138.

14-year period examined that argued that the Fed's policy stance was too easy. Needless to say, the same CEA easy-money "tilt" continues to prevail to this day.

FED INDEPENDENCE

By common understanding, the concept of Fed independence that has evolved since the 1951 Treasury—Fed Accord is that the Fed is independent within government rather than independent of government.[8] It must be remembered, in this connection, that the Federal Reserve System was created by Congress and is responsible to the people through Congress.[9] Consequently, the Fed's broad policy goals should be generally consistent with those of the Congress and the Administration. But it is also true that money management is best left to independent experts because it is a highly technical, full-time job. It involves the continuous observation and interpretation of incoming economic and financial data, followed by frequent adjustments in the Fed's policy stance. Moreover, if money management is to be impartially and effectively handled, it must be divorced from partisan politics.

Currently, Fed officials seek through informal meetings

to maintain the appropriate balance between their policy independence and their pursuit of policy goals consistent with those of the Administration.[10] These include weekly (Thursday) breakfast meetings between the Fed Chairman and the Secretary of the Treasury (following in the tradition of weekly meetings between the Fed Chairman and the Treasury Secretary begun in 1936 by Chairman Eccles and Secretary Morgenthau). Also, there are regular monthly meetings between the Fed Board and members of the President's Council of Economic Advisers. Not to be overlooked on the recreational front is the fact that Fed Chairman Greenspan occasionally also plays tennis with CEA Chairman Michael Boskin and golf with Treasury Secretary Nicholas Brady.

POPULIST TRADITION

The political vein that Fed critics, such as Representative Patman, have traditionally tapped is populism.[11] Fed anti-inflation policies, so the argument goes, result in tight (hard) money conditions and high interest rates which harm the small individual debtor (e.g., sturdy, self-reliant farmers, small, industrious entrepreneurs, God-fearing blue-collar workers, etc.). These tight money Fed policies, it is further argued, favor "big, bad" creditor banks, railroads, and other "untrustworthy" large corporations. The refrain of the populist politicians dates back to the 1800s. In 1830 Andrew Jackson, a popular man of the common people if there ever was one, attacked Biddle's "Monster Bank"; in 1896, populist William Jennings Bryan delivered his famous "cross of gold" Presidential campaign speech. Bryan argued that the small, hard-working debtor was being crucified on a cross of gold by the big, hard-money lenders. To help the indebted common folk, Bryan favored, in effect, more inflation—in the form of free silver.

The populist argument (and that of many modern-day

political liberals as well) is that the best policies for the country today would be easy (soft) money conditions and low interest rates, even if these policies threaten, from time to time, some acceleration in inflationary pressures. Indeed the lingering political appeal of this easy money argument is dramatically evidenced by the fact that even President Bush, a moderate Republican no less, has recently observed that "all Presidents want lower interest rates."

In a modern-day context, liberal politicians have also continued in the populist tradition by wrongly attempting to blame the Fed for the enduring historical struggle between the "haves" and the "have nots." These well-meaning, but off-the-mark liberals should instead be criticizing the redistributive shortcomings of fiscal tax and spending policies; but it is apparently more convenient for these critics to wrongly blame monetary policy for every social ill imaginable.

The main point is that to judge the outcome of Fed policy, it is necessary to first know the Fed's basic objective. Specifically, the Greenspan Fed's primary desire was to reconcile the objectives of reduced inflation and sustained growth so as to benefit the many, not just the few.

To be sure, some will be hurt when the Fed aggressively tightens money to fight inflation, as in the case of Volcker's move to tighten during the period from late 1979 through early 1982. But, in fact, those who got hurt the most from this absolutely necessary and widely acclaimed Fed anti-inflation battle in the early 1980s were, for the most part, the same ones who benefited the most from the earlier dangerously accelerating inflationary pressures; they were the big and small speculators in land, commodities, real estate, and resources.[12] Most important, what the populist/liberal critics of the Fed seem to ignore is that the Fed's successful taming of inflation in the early 1980s set the stage for the longest peacetime expansion on record (December 1982 to July 1990), one in which approximately 20 million jobs were created, again helping the many, not just the few.

Part Three

Confidence in the Financial System

Confidence is the wellspring of the financial system. Without it there would be a breakdown in the intricate web of financial relationships that facilitate the global matching of ultimate lenders (or investors) with borrowers (both public and private). A smoothly functioning financial system and efficient payments mechanism is essential for healthy global economic growth, trade, and development. It goes without saying that all financial market participants expect that payments for goods, services, and financial transactions will be processed efficiently with little risk.

In particular, confidence is the necesssary ingredient of banking, enabling banks to intermediate funds by taking in funds mainly through deposits, and short-term borrowings on one hand, and lending or investing these funds mostly on a longer-term basis on the other. The First RepublicBank of

Dallas (which is the focus of Chapter 7) learned the lesson of how important confidence can be the hard way, as it suffered a loss of confidence and a huge resulting run on its deposits in March 1988. This necessitated a temporary but costly takeover by government regulators (FDIC), followed by the bank's eventual sale to an out-of-state bank (NCNB).

A similar lesson was learned by Drexel Burnham, Lambert, the brash but highly profitable investment bank of the 1980s, which was forced to declare a shockingly spectacular bankruptcy in early 1990. Though there were many factors contributing to the collapse, the immediate cause of the downfall of this once feared, if not respected, investment banking firm came from a very simple source—a loss of confidence on the part of investors in its short-term commercial paper. When banks and regulators failed to come to the rescue with back-up credit lines, Drexel was forced to declare bankruptcy. In essence, this ill-fated investment bank suffered the same fate as many weakened commercial banks or other troubled financial intermediaries; Drexel (or more precisely, the parent company) got caught borrowing short in order to fund shaky loans and illiquid longer-term investments. In this case, Drexel was impaled on bridge loans, the repayment of which had been stalled by unsuccessful LBOs, and a rapidly depreciating "junk" bond portfolio.

Viewing the financial excesses of the "roaring" 1980s in a broader context, the Drexel experience was only one example of a remarkable decade characterized by self-indulgence and instant gratification. In search of quick profits, commercial banks and thrifts made risky loans in many areas including speculative land deals and commercial real estate projects. Likewise, in the spirit of the times, most investment bankers favored big, impersonal, quick-money transactions over the more traditional longer-term customer advisory and underwriting relationships. In the heady financial environment, big individual "producers" were paid big bonuses and too many financial institutions paid too little heed to the use of retained earnings to strengthen their capital positions. The 1980s saw the clash of big egos, particularly among corporate raiders, and the building of shamelessly large fortunes by heretofore unknown players on the takeover stage such as Henry Kravis, Ronald Perelman, and Nelson Peltz.

In the wake of the financial excesses of the 1980s, there has been a mounting crescendo of banking, thrift, and insurance company difficulties, not to mention Drexel's dramatic downfall. In an effort to rid themselves of the unwanted vestiges of the past decade, commercial banks, thrifts, insurance companies, and investment banks alike have attempted, as the decade of the 1990s begins, to purge (through secondary markets) their asset holdings of "bad" paper (junk bonds, bridge loans, shaky real estate loans, foreign loans, etc.). Similarly, regulators have forced thrifts to trim their junk bond holdings. This purging process has largely represented financial institutions' attempts to try to avoid (not always successfully) a downgrading of their short-term commercial paper or longer-term debt by the credit rating agencies. To say the least, the 1990s are starting on a weakened and unstable financial footing.

CHAPTER 7

Confidence: The Foundation of Banking

Confidence in the financial viability of a bank is hard to build, easy to lose, and, once lost, usually extremely difficult to regain. During the 1980s, banks faced a baffling array of either unfamiliar or unfavorable forces, including banking deregulation, unexpected interest rate volatility, and sudden downturns in such key domestic sectors as energy, farming, and real estate. Above all else, however, the story of the 1980s is a story of resiliency as well as one of financial excess and distress, and of "rolling readjustment" across major economic sectors and regions of the country that helped sustain a peacetime expansion of record duration (nearly eight years). It is also a story of some temporary cracks in depositor confidence in individual institutions, but, remarkably, never a complete breakdown of depositor confidence in the banking system as a whole.

The recurring shocks to the banking system in the 1980s led to loan problems and recurring "liquidity scares" which afflicted many individual banking and thrift institutions, especially in the Southwest, and, more recently, the Northeast. Adding to banking problems was a mounting Third World debt crisis. In these circumstances, nervous, though hardly ever panicky depositors were prone to shift funds from weak to strong financial institutions. For many of the nation's thrift institutions, in particular, financial conditions had deteriorated by the end of the decade to a point that forced the Bush Administration to design massive thrift assistance legislation in 1989. This large-scale government effort to shore up weakened financial institutions represented perhaps the most important and hopeful factor lessening the potential negative economic impact of these financial difficulties; this government support contrasts markedly with the experience in the Great Depression when inadequate government assistance to depositors meant that financial collapse would inevitably lead to economic collapse.

"SILENT" CREDIT SQUEEZE

All the same, the past decade's traumatic financial developments have had major deflationary implications for the early 1990s. At a time of great economic vulnerability, an unusual and ominous "silent" bank-induced credit squeeze or "drought" has emerged.[1] Congress, still smarting from the negative publicity associated with the S&L crisis, has tried to shift the blame to government regulators of financial institutions. In turn, these regulators have toughened bank capital requirements and have exerted pressure on their bank examiners to redouble their efforts to find bad loans. Bank examiners have reacted, as might have been expected, by exerting tremendous pressure on bank management. The management of many individual banks have, in turn, responded by downsizing their balance sheets and putting pressure on its loan officers to avoid making risky loans at all costs.

The upshot is that lenders have become exceedingly cautious, favoring liquidity over new credit risk, or, in some cases, favoring the contraction of asset and liability footings over expansion, in order to improve their capital ratios and avoid debt downgradings. This lender caution, combined with tighter thrift lending rules to individual borrowers, has had the effect of reducing the availability and increasing the cost of credit to many borrowers. Suffering the most have been local home builders and developers, large merger/LBO borrowers, and smaller businesses that might be viewed as potentially risky borrowers. (The latter, it should be noted, are in many cases the same smaller businesses that created the bulk of the whopping 20 million jobs generated in the record-long 1982–90 economic expansion.)

More significantly, this credit stringency represented a private or "silent" bank-induced tightening, rather than a Fed-induced one. Uniquely, the bank loan restraint was spreading from the grassroots, or from the bottom up rather than from the top (Fed policy level) down. Such a silent but sudden bank-induced credit squeeze affected some regions more than others. For example, in 1990, overly zealous national bank examiners swept out of the Southwest into the Northeast, forcing banks in that latter region to classify loans as nonperforming if there was even the slightest hint that the borrower might be suffering financial strains. These examiners, smarting from criticism of their inadequate examination procedures in the 1980s and from all the negative political fallout from the thrift crisis, did not want to be blamed for any undiscovered bad loans. Thus, banks not only had to add to loan-loss reserves and take a hit on profits because of nonperforming loans but they also had to start worrying about a new loan category—"nonperforming, performing loans." As regulators toughened their loan evaluations particularly in the hard-pressed real estate category, some banks began to re-evaluate all their customer relationships. In essence, banks tightened their loan terms relative to their cost of funds. Specifically, banks raised loan rates, required more collateral as backing for loans, or established other more restrictive covenants on back-up credit lines. And some banks went so far as to cut back on or even completely terminate certain borrowers' credit lines.

Of course, the precise extent of the bank credit squeeze from the supply side is difficult to measure with accuracy because it has occurred at a time when the demand for credit is also weakening. But the squeeze on the supply of credit is nonetheless powerful and unique as a major cause of the current recession; the credit squeeze is founded on the bank psychology of restraint and shaken confidence. Moreover the constraints on the supply of credit apply not only to bank loan stringency, but also to the supply of credit from non-bank sources ranging from commercial paper to junk bonds.

Of course, the extent of the depressing impact on economic activity of the silent credit squeeze depended on whether disappointed customers could find new money from other bank lenders in the affected region or in other regions of the country or in the credit markets. The State of Massachusetts actually set up a telephone hotline to facilitate this search. As matters turned out, the silent credit stringency spread from thrifts to banks and across much of the country, exerting a major depressing impact on economic activity.

It should be noted that the silent bank-induced credit squeeze or "drought" is very different from the traditional credit "crunch." The old-fashioned credit crunch was triggered by Fed tightening actions; the current credit "drought," in contrast, came at a time of Fed easing actions. Moreover, the credit crunch usually was typified, at least when Regulation Q ceilings on time deposit rates previously prevailed, by a predictable disintermediation process in which Fed tightening moves pushed money market interest rates above bank time deposit rate ceilings causing savers to shift funds out of depository institutions into money market instruments carrying relatively more attractive yields. This precipitated a credit crunch in the sense that the supply of credit (provided at that time mostly by depository institutions) was severely constrained relative to demands in key areas such as mortgage lending. By way of contrast, the current bank-induced credit "drought" was for many borrowers in various regions sudden, arbitrary and unpredictable.

In order to try to arrest the spreading of the psychology of a silent credit squeeze among banks, the top bank regulators—the head of the FDIC, the Comptroller of the Currency (who arranged the meeting), and the Fed Chairman—attended an unprecedented meeting on May 10, 1990, with the top bankers of the country. The regulators encouraged banks to continue to make prudent loans to financially sound consumer and business borrowers. But in fact these supposedly high-quality borrowers were at that time actually reducing their credit demands in view out of fear of a weakening in economic activity. The regulators feared that some regional pockets of credit restraint affecting some types of borrowers might spread more widely, particularly at a time when lenders were growing more concerned over a possible near-term weakening in economic activity. However, the bankers present at this highly unusual meeting generally distrusted the regulators' urgings; the dominant bank view was that regulators would go back on their word and classify as nonperforming most new loans made in the prevailing uncertain economic environment.

Subsequently, on November 14, 1990, President Bush met with bank regulators and other Administration economic officials to discuss whether a bank-induced credit squeeze was stifling economic activity. Commerce Secretary Robert Mosbacher and White House Chief of Staff John Sununu argued that the tough attitude of bank regulators was restricting the flow of credit needed to keep the economy healthy. Treasury Secretary Nicholas Brady and Fed Chairman Alan Greenspan countered that much of the slowdown in bank lending reflected market forces, not regulatory overkill.

More recently, however, Treasury Secretary Brady seemed to convert to the side of those fearing a bank-induced credit squeeze. In a speech on November 21, 1990, he urged banks to keep lending to good customers. Brady also asked regulators to avoid using unrealistically negative scenarios in evaluating loans. Chairman Greenspan seemed to undergo a similar conversion. In his February 9, 1991, remarks to the National Association of Manufacturers, Greenspan stated, in effect, that he saw no convincing signs that the credit stringency was ending. He said that Federal bank examiners played a significant role in making banks reluctant to lend. These regulatory officials, according to Chairman Greenspan, failed to recognize the special role of banks in society; banks are, in effect, in the business of establishing long-term credit lifelines for borrowers. Yet too many regulators take the short term view.

In his January 29, 1991 State of the Union address President Bush directly confronted the bank-induced credit squeeze by stating that "[s]ound banks should be making more sound loans, now." These blunt Presidential admonitions served as precursors to a Bush Administration package aimed at countering bank credit stringency measures. Unveiled at the end of February 1991, this modest package included about half a dozen interpretations of accounting rules for dealing with shaky loans. In some cases these measures allowed banks to reduce the reserves they must hold against nonperforming loans which could potentially boost bank profits.

BAILOUT EFFORTS

The severity of the past decade's banking problems was ominously foreshadowed in 1984 by the sudden depositor run on the largest money center bank to get in trouble so far, Continental Illinois. (The ten largest insolvent institutions can be seen in Table 7.1.) In response, the FDIC mounted a costly rescue effort, which, though unforeseen at the time,

Table 7.1. The Ten Largest Insolvent Institutions

Institutions	Assets (Billions of $)	Date
1. Continental Illinois Corp., Chicago	$41.0	May 1984
2. First Republicbank Corp., Dallas	32.7	Jul. 1988
3. American Savings, Stockton, CA.	30.1	Dec. 1988
4. Bank of New England Corp., Boston	22.0*	Jan. 1991
5. Mcorp, Dallas	15.4	Mar. 1990
6. First City Bancorp., Houston	11.2	Apr. 1988
7. Imperial Federal Savings Association, San Diego	9.6	Feb. 1990
8. Franklin Savings Association, Ottawa, KS	9.3	Feb. 1990
9. City Savings Bank, Bedminster, NJ	8.9	Dec. 1989
10. Empire of America, F.S.B., Buffalo, NY	8.2	Jan. 1990

*Assets as of Sept. 30, 1990.

Source: Reuters

was to set the precedent for a flurry of massive and costly regulator bailout efforts for both commercial banks and saving and loan associations as the 1980s came to a close.

The Fed's precedent-setting policy response to the Continental Bank crisis was to advance reserves directly to the bank in difficulty through the extended credit facility of the discount window. However, in order to maintain unchanged overall reserve pressures, the monetary authorities moved to offset the extra reserve injection through the extended credit facility of the discount window with a commensurate amount of open market reserve-draining actions.

During 1987–91 in particular, massive financial institution rescue efforts were mounted. The major government protectors of financial institutions—the Federal Deposit Insurance Corporation (FDIC) which insured the deposits of savings banks and commercial banks and the Federal Savings and Loan Insurance Corporation (FSLIC) which insured the deposits of savings and loan associations—were required to bail out the depositors in a host of insolvent financial institutions. These payouts to insured depositors were so large that the very solvency of both the FSLIC and FDIC eventually came into question. The FSLIC was bailed out by the Bush Administration's thrift plan (FIRREA) in 1989; but the solvency of the FDIC was still being debated without an agreed upon plan of action well into 1991. A major issue in connection with proposed legislation was how to replenish the FDIC's badly depleted deposit insurance fund. Bankers offered their own plan, proportedly not costing the taxpayers anything. Other plans emphasized increased borrowing from the Treasury and a large increase in bank deposit insurance assessments.[2]

SAVINGS AND LOAN DEBACLE

The savings and loan crisis took a while to capture the public's attention. However, the late-1988 crescendo of federally assisted takeovers of faltering savings and loan associations began to capture the news headlines. Remarkably, for just the single year 1988, the FSLIC alone liquidated, sold, or took over a record 222 ailing savings and loan associations.

Subsequently, in February 1989, the Bush Administration warned that there could be additional closings of at least 500 more insolvent savings and loan associations (some later estimates pushed this figure as high as 1,000) as part of its massive proposed thrift assistance plan, called the Financial Institutions Reform, Regulation, and Enforcement Act (FIRREA). At the time of its final passage in August 1989, this plan was initially estimated to cost $257 billion (with subsequent estimates ranging as high as $500 billion), including the FSLIC bailouts in 1988, and taking into account interest payments on the additional government debt required to fund the plan over 30 years. (Moreover, in early 1990, as if to underscore the monumental dimensions of thrift problems, the Bush administration estimated that it needed in the second quarter of that year an additional $45.7 billion and in the third quarter $34 billion in temporary working capital to help finance the assets of government-acquired savings and loan associations and to replace their maturing high-yield CDs, at least until these troubled S&Ls or their assets could be sold off.) Among its other features, the Bush thrift assistance legislation sharply increased capital requirements for S&L associations.

In passing, some misguided Congressional regulatory policies should be noted. Legislative actions of dubious merit in 1980 and 1982, in addition to liberalizing thrift lending and investment activities, raised the maximum ceiling for insured deposits to $100,000 from $40,000 (this latter action being taken without public hearings). These largely indefensible actions ushered in a new era of brokered deposits, bad loans, and outright thrift management fraud. These liberalizing regulatory actions had the effect of providing an all win, no lose situation for the financial institutions deciding to take on excessive risk under the liberalized regulatory guidelines (such as speculation in high risk corporate "junk" bonds, in high risk real estate development projects, or even in raw land). This new breed of risk-seeking thrift institutions could rake in all the potential profits, while leaving government deposit insurance funds (and ultimately U.S. taxpayers) holding the bag for the considerable potential losses.

Moreover, the initial FIRREA regulation that limited thrift loans to any one borrower to 15% of the institution's unimpaired capital (which excludes good will) had the effect of completely cutting off credit to certain types of borrowers. Especially hard-hit were local residential builders and developers.

COMMERCIAL BANK PROBLEMS

At the same time, commercial banks faced increased capital requirements applied on a global basis. Specifically, the Bank for International Settlements (BIS) laid down the requirement that bank ratios of capital to assets be increased to 8% by December 1992. As a result, many banks contemplated downsizing their balance sheets in an effort to meet these future tougher capital requirements.

In the case of commercial banks, the FDIC's problems have been less numerous but more spectacular, especially in the case of the major Texas banks. Indeed, during the brief but tumultuous 1987–89 period, all of the five major Texas banks, once considered among the nation's strongest and most aggressive, were either temporarily taken over by the government or sold directly to out-of-state banking interests.

A particularly vivid example of one Texas bank's "brush with death" and remarkable resurrection was the tale of First RepublicBank, a commercial bank headquartered in Dallas, Texas. This institution suffered a massive March 1988 deposit outflow triggered largely by depositor concerns over loan problems that were widely publicized in a March 1988 series of *Wall Street Journal* articles on the bank's plight. The sudden March 1988 run on the bank forced the FDIC to move quickly (within the same month) to put together a bailout package; it included an immediate Federal infusion of $1 billion of capital into the troubled bank, and the official promise, first offered by the FDIC in the 1984 Continental Illinois collapse, to insure all First Republic deposits (including those above the prevailing legally insured maximum of $100,000).

The FDIC's promise to insure *all* the deposits (including those exceeding the $100,000 insured limit) of certain large troubled financial institutions, including Continental and First RepublicBank is highly controversial. In February 1990, bank regulators belatedly began to publicly question this "too big to fail" approach; but the concept still applied to the Bank of New England seized by government regulators in January 1991. Regulators viewed the Bank of New England as essential to meeting the financial needs of the local economy and to preserving the soundness of local banks. The bottom line was that the demise of the Bank of New England was unacceptable because it was thought to pose too much systemic risk.

Initially, in March 1988, the FDIC named Albert Casey (former Chairman of American Airlines) as temporary Chairman and Chief Executive Officer of First RepublicBank. Subsequently, in July 1988, the FDIC also seized all the assets of First RepublicBank's 40 banking units. Ultimately, in August 1988, the FDIC orchestrated and assisted the sale of First RepublicBank to North Carolina National Bank (NCNB). All in all, the failure of First RepublicBank cost the FDIC—and ultimately U.S. taxpayers—an estimated $3 billion, making it the most expensive bank failure to date.

ANATOMY OF A LIQUIDITY CRISIS

The highlights of the story of the First RepublicBank liquidity crisis are provided in the following list:[3]

1. First RepublicBank was formed in 1987 through the merger (not initially federally assisted) of two large and prestigious regional Dallas banks, InterFirst Corp., and Republic Bank. The assets of the combined banks totaled about $36 billion.
2. Both banks were in a weakened state when merged, largely as a result of bad loans related to a depressed Texas economy. Conditions were depressed in major sectors including energy, farming, and real estate (the latter accounting for a hefty 40% of the merged bank's loan portfolio). In addition, intensifying Third World debt problems added to the woes

of Republic Bank which had attempted to diversify its lending activities beyond Texas to Third World countries.

3. From its beginning, the massive provisions of reserves for bad debts served to depress the profits of First RepublicBank. However, the bank had substantial core operating profits (fees and interest received less interest paid) even though the final quarter of 1987; and, most remarkably, the bank nearly broke even, at least in terms of core operating profits, in the first quarter of 1988. Bank officials, just before the March 1988 run on the bank, had developed a restructuring plan, based on projected deposit flows and asset write-offs, that could, they thought, bring this still solvent bank back to financial health.
4. The negative publicity surrounding the bank's provision of reserves for bad loans had caused many foreign depositors to withdraw funds in an orderly way starting about six months prior to the March 1988 run on the bank. The erosion of foreign deposits was, however, steady and predictable, at least prior to the bank's March 1988 liquidity crisis.
5. The March 1988 run on First RepublicBank was, at least according to the bank's own funding officers, attributable mainly to a series of articles detailing the precarious financial condition of the bank by reporters Leonard M. Apcar, Richard B. Schmitt, and Robert E. Taylor in the *Wall Street Journal.* These articles—the most important of which were published on March 3, March 10, March 15, March 16, and March 17, 1988—were factually correct in most aspects. However, these articles implied, most alarmingly, that First RepublicBank's efforts to avoid financial collapse were extremely urgent if not desperate. Thus, it was the frantic tone of these articles, inadequately refuted by First Republic,

rather than anything particularly new or revealing that apparently triggered the crisis of depositor confidence and the resulting run on the bank. For example, reporter Apcar asserted the First RepublicBank was urgently seeking to begin to work with bank regulators at a time of growing bad debt and liquidity problems. In fact, First Republic without fanfare had sought the assistance of bank regulators well before the March 1988 liquidity crisis, contrary to Apcar's assertion. One agitated bank funding officer said, "All I ask is for five minutes in a back alley with reporter Apcar to impress on him the damage his articles have done to my bank."

6. Promptly after the March articles appeared in the *Wall Street Journal*, corporate depositors, especially those in the middle and upper-middle size categories, began to pull their deposits. Interestingly, the largest corporate depositors did not immediately withdraw their funds, although they indicated their concern with the negative publicity.
7. The crisis of confidence in the bank's financial viability was compounded most innocently by weekly Federal Reserve statistics on Dallas district bank deposits and Federal Reserve discount window borrowings. Those statistics had been routinely provided on a weekly basis for many years. Enterprising reporters were quickly able to determine the massive dimensions of the run on First Republic. On Wednesday, March 9, however, the Dallas Fed abruptly discontinued its weekly deposit report. This came a week after this report showed that First Republic suffered an unusually sharp $600 million drop in deposits. Reflecting the growing First Republic liquidity crisis, discount window borrowings in the Dallas Fed district, which continued to be published, surged to $2.8 billion on March 16, up sharply from $371 million on March 9. On

balance, the statistics suggest that the run on the bank may have amounted to upward of $4 billion in deposit outflows in only a few weeks.

8. In short order, there was a flurry of additional press reports, again inadequately countered by the besieged bank, of increasing FDIC regulatory scrutiny of First Republic. This unsettling news triggered the final massive hemorrhage of the largest corporate deposits. The death spiral of shattered confidence and rapidly declining deposits was finally completely out of control. It was a full blown liquidity crisis.
9. The FDIC's growing regulatory demands on First Republic may have actually made the problem worse.

   a. The basic FDIC objective was to shrink the asset and liability footings of the Bank and to sharply curtail the bank's interbank borrowing in the Eurodollar market. The aim was to shrink the bank perhaps $20–25 billion in assets from $32.7 billion in July 1988.
   b. To shrink assets, the bank's highest quality and most marketable loans were sold off.
   c. The FDIC imposed a cutback on interbank lending that had the most unfortunate effect of eliminating a low-risk source of core operating earnings.
   d. The FDIC examiners rushed to classify loans that might have been paid off if given more time, especially in view of indications that the Texas economy was beginning to recover in many areas. The FDIC apparently wanted to be sure that it was not blamed for any additional bad loans found at the bank.
   e. The negative publicity associated with growing FDIC involvement in the bank's activities caused

a sharp increase in the premium First Republic had to pay for CD funds. This virtually guaranteed a sharp drop in core earnings and more bad publicity over the remaining quarters of 1988, if not beyond.

f. In a highly controversial move, the FDIC seized the assets of all 40 First Republic banking units, wiping out its bond holders and leaving few assets to settle creditor claims. (Some belated relief came, however, on February 12, 1991, when a Federal bankruptcy judge approved a settlement of legal claims and counterclaims that amounted to nearly complete repayment for holders of senior debt at the First RepublicBank Corporation.)

10. In the wake of the flood of bad publicity, someone called depositors of First Republic's valley bank unit and misrepresented himself as being from the bank. The impostor said that the depositors should pull their funds immediately because the FDIC was about to shut down the bank. This triggered, in a manner reminiscent of the 1930s bank failures, a run on the bank by smaller depositors. First Republic officials had to rush to the valley bank with cash hurriedly acquired from the Dallas Federal Reserve. First Republic officials asked the FBI to investigate, but the impostor was never found.

11. Once depositor confidence is shattered, not even oral FDIC promises to insure all deposits (including those above the prevailing legal limit of $100,000) may be fully believed. For example, First Republic lost a massive amount of large depositor funds in just the three days between the time when the FDIC orally guaranteed all of First Republic's deposits and the time when First Republic finally got the FDIC's deposit guarantee in writing. Apparently, large depositors were mostly looking for an excuse to pull their funds out of First Republic. They asked First Republic officials whether the initial FDIC deposit guarantee was in writing; when First Republic, faced with the FDIC's bureaucratic delays and indecisiveness, had to say "not yet," the large depositors fled the bank. Also tending to shake large depositor confidence was the legal opinion by a prestigious Texas law firm, Fulbright and Jaworski, that the FDIC has no legal authority to insure all bank deposits (specifically those above the current, legally insured maximum of $100,000).

LESSONS

The main lesson of the First Republic downfall is that overzealous regulators may sometimes seize an institution too soon or can make a bad situation even worse and unnecessarily costly. This is especially true if excessively aggressive bank regulators downsize a bank in difficulty too quickly (as in the case of First Republic) or force bankers to increase loan-loss reserves for loans (especially real estate) that are still current on interest payments, just on the chance that the borrowers might suffer future financial difficulties. Obviously, over-eager regulators could easily make this a self-fulfilling prophesy; specifically, real estate prices fall, bank examiners threaten to classify performing real estate loans as nonperforming, banks cut back further on real estate lending, and real estate prices fall further in a self-reinforcing process.

A broader lesson is that the ill-advised Congressional increase in 1980 of government deposit insurance to cover deposits of $100,000 in maximum size from $40,000 presents some major moral hazzards. In effect, this action went a long way toward shifting bank loan and investment risks from bank management and shareholders, where they belong, to U.S. taxpayers, where they don't belong. It is simply inappropriate to place future bank risks on the shoulders of taxpayers. However, the efforts to correct this problem and to strengthen the banking system come at a very delicate time. The danger is that government proposals to limit the number of individual deposit accounts subject to the $100,000 deposit insurance guarantee and to increase risk-based capital standards, come at a time when bad loans abound, real estate prices are collapsing, depositors are nervous and the economy is sinking into recession. Thus, the unfortunte timing of these remedies could actually make the problem worse by intensifying the current bank loan stringency and perhaps triggering depositor runs on banks.

Another important lesson of this harrowing experience is that there must be new "tools of the trade" for those in charge of funding a large regional or money center bank and maintaining the confidence of large and small depositors. In the current age of instant communications and abundant information, senior bank officers must possess more than a mere understanding of funds sources, capital ratios, return on assets, and credit risks. Indeed, when a bank, as in the case of First Republic, is about to receive a dose of bad publicity, it is perhaps most important for senior bank officers, if they wish to avoid a fatal run on their deposits or the loss of other sources of short-term funds, to simply carry in their wallets the telephone numbers of their key depositors and of other large creditors and investors. This would allow the bank's senior officers in charge of funding to act without delay to personally get in touch with large corporate depositors in order to kill rumors and shore up their confidence in the bank, as well as that of other creditors and investors.[4]

Ideally, this confidence-building public relations effort should be undertaken in the days before a negative press story on the bank is to be printed. In this way the bank's senior officers can instantly inform key depositors, creditors, and investors of management's positive goals for the bank, including promising areas of financial services specialization and potential profitability. And, regarding the prospect of sudden negative publicity, the senior bank officers should be in a position to inform key depositors, creditors, and investors that the bank's loan or funding problems are not as urgent as may be portrayed in the impending press account. At that time, the senior bank officers can also inform their valued depositors, creditors, and investors that the appropriate steps to remedy the problems are being taken. Thus, in order to head off a deadly liquidity crisis, the need for good public relations to build and sustain the confidence of major depositors, creditors, and investors in this age of instant communications and bountiful information has seemingly been raised to a par with the more traditional requirements of good bank lending and liability management practices.

POSTSCRIPT

In its new incarnation, First Republic, now named NCNB Texas, has been surprisingly successful. To an important extent, this success stemmed from the high visibility and good public relations of the acquiring North Carolina National Bank (NCNB). In addition, there was, of course, the fact that the FDIC offered extremely favorable terms[5] to NCNB (North Carolina), and this was reflected promptly in a healthy initial increase in the price of this bank's stock. (In a good loan–bad loan strategy, the FDIC took over the risks of all of First Republic's bad loans, leaving NCNB in the favorable position of selectively acquiring only First Republic's good loans, but all of its deposits.)

Meanwhile, it is no coincidence that NCNB Texas has been able to acquire with ease deposits in the depressed Texas thrift and banking markets. Without question, this deposit-gathering ability has been greatly enhanced by not only the competitive CD rates offered by NCNB Texas but also by renewed depositor confidence stemming from the newly christened Texas bank's association, officially blessed by the FDIC, with the high-profile North Carolina banking organization. As a result, NCNB Texas has been able to begin to rebuild its loan and deposit footings and to establish a successful and potentially profitable nitch in the Texas banking market. Indeed, beginning as soon as the third quarter of 1989, the newly incarnated NCNB Texas began to contribute significantly to the profits of the acquiring North Carolina National Bank Corporation. By mid-1990, NCNB Texas, in the midst of purchasing a large batch of failed thrifts from the government, had grown to a statewide network of 250 branches with $33 billion in assets, making it the largest subsidiary of the NCNB Corporation. And, of course, the August 1990 oil price shock further brightened prospects for the previously depressed energy sector and the Texas economy.

CHAPTER 8

The Corporate Takeover Frenzy

The 1980s saw a frenzy of corporate mergers and acquisitions (M&A) activity. This takeover craze represented, not unlike the Gilded Age of the late nineteenth century and the Roaring Twenties,[1] an era of galloping greed, incipient capitalist anarchy encouraged by inadequate antitrust restraints, market manipulation, the accumulation of staggering personal fortunes, and clashing corporate raider egos.

However, in contrast with the two earlier periods, the United States was on the decline relative to the other major industrial economies of the world in the 1980s; it was suffering from too much "paper entrepreneurialism." Specifically, the nation was mostly rearranging corporate assets and borrowing more than it built. Although the financial pursuits of repackaging, remortgaging, or dismantling of Fortune 500 companies paid handsomely, this corporate paper shuffling did little to promote long-term capital spending. This was more the stuff of steamy novels or Hollywood movies than of staid business finance texts or reasoned discourses.

It is, of course, inappropriate to characterize the corporate takeover frenzy of the 1980s as simply a time when a bunch of greedy corporate heads, investment bankers, and Wall Street lawyers happened to get together and make mischief. Actually, the corporate takeover frenzy was nurtured by a special set of favorable conditions. Perhaps most important, as in the late nineteenth century, the government's antitrust restraints on corporate mergers were next to nonexistant. Moreover, despite some periods of extreme monetary restraint such as in the early 1980s, the decade of the 1980s, and especially the 1984–89 period of most intense takeover activity, saw generally accommodative monetary conditions. In addition, debt expansion during the period was encouraged by the lax attitudes of both bank and nonbank (SEC) government regulators and by tax laws which favored the expansion of debt over equity.

Whether this latest spasm of corporate balance sheet excess has proven to be a force for good (increased productivity) or evil (a declining standard of living and reduced world standing) remains to be seen. Certainly, many overleveraged U.S. corporations have been rendered more vulnerable to cyclical downturn. This is underscored by the fact that during the five-year period from 1983–88 alone U.S. corporations increased their debt by an astonishing $1.5 trillion and retired about $500 billion in equity. The ultimate test is whether the past decade's outburst of M&A activity has made U.S. businesses more or less productive and competitive in domestic and global markets (and so far the results are less than impressive).

In the first half of the past decade, corporate M&A activity grew at a fairly orderly pace and was generally based on sound economic grounds (taking advantage of cost reduction through economies of scale or increased productivity through restructuring). However, this restructuring activity began to accelerate at a dangerously rapid pace in the second half of the 1980s before reaching a crescendo (measured in dollar amounts) in 1988 (see Table 8.1). The problem in the second half of the 1980s was that takeover deals were hurriedly assembled, typically using financial criteria (i.e., the amount of funds that could be raised at the time in the junk bond market) rather than economic criteria. Moreover, the hectic pace of M&A activity came to be dominated in the last half of the past decade by the clash of egos among an aggressive new breed of corporate raiders and fee-hungry Wall Street investment bankers and lawyers. This unholy alliance spawned a rash of mega-sized LBOs (leveraged buyouts). In total, the past decade's massive restructuring of corporate America involved some 31,200 completed mergers and acquisitions totaling in dollar value a hefty $1.4 trillion.[2]

THE CASE FOR CORPORATE RESTRUCTURING

The basic case for the restructuring of U.S. business during the past decade was a sound one. In the early 1980s,

Table 8.1. Corporate Mergers and Aquisitions Activity 1980–89

Year	Number	Dollar Value (Billions of $)
1980	1,800	45
1981	2,200	55
1982	2,200	53
1983	2,500	51
1984	3,200	135
1985	3,500	150
1986	4,400	215
1987	4,000	190
1988	4,000	230
1989	3,400	230

Source: The 1990 *Business Week* 1000 (Special Issue).

U.S. businesses were faced with a strengthening dollar, mounting international competition, and the need to improve productivity. Many U.S. corporate conglomerates began to favor restructuring as a means of thinning down and focusing only on product lines in which they had some advantage. This corporate attempt to get "leaner and meaner" represented a reversal of the trend toward multibusiness conglomerates begun in the 1960s. The new idea was to focus on only the few profitable product lines where the greatest cost reductions or productivity increases could be achieved.[3] Inevitably, this new focus involved not only the selling off of unrelated and unprofitable subsidiaries but also the possible acquisition of complementary and cost-efficient business lines.

In the early 1980s, many companies found the market value of their stock trading below its intrinsic (break-up) value. At the same time, the Fed was easing monetary conditions and interest rates were declining. Moreover, Federal tax laws favored debt (on which interest payments were exempted from taxes) over equity (on which dividends were subject to taxation).

The past decade's takeover frenzy was actually pioneered in the "oil patch" by a diminutive country boy Texan named T. Boone Pickens. His first big target was Gulf Oil in late 1983 and then, roughly a year later, Phillips Petroleum. The idea was to target firms whose stock prices were languishing under entrenched and unimaginative management. Pickens chastised management who held proportionately little of their own company's stock and were more interested in their own perks and longevity than the well-being of the company's shareholders. Pickens' simple idea was to form a small group of investors, to borrow heavily (using the target company's stock as collateral) and use the borrowed funds to buy controlling interest in the company.[4]

A "strike-fast" technique was soon refined by Pickens and others. In the typical case where a firm's stock price had dropped below its estimated break up value, a group of investors would suddenly and unexpectedly buy a block of stock and thus put the company in play. And even if unsuccessful in taking the company over or selling the shares at a profit to a competing bidder, this group of investors could, through greenmail, force the company to buy its shares back at a handsome profit to the raiders. (In many ways, these activities of the modern-day corporate raiders were difficult to distinguish from the illegal investment pools of the Roaring Twenties.) Among the most notorious practitioners of this questionable but highly profitable pasttime were the high profile New York investment groups of Gollust, Tierny & Oliver (Coniston partners), Wasserstein Perella & Co., and, of course, the granddaddy of them all, Kohlberg, Kravis, and Roberts. Also prominent in the takeover game were the Belzbergs (Canadian financiers), Carl Icahn, Irwin Jacobs, Saul Steinberg, Asher Adleman, Ivan Boesky (who went to jail for his activities), and Ronald Perelman. (In June 1990, after running out of companies to raid, Coniston partners, victims of a new wave of corporate financial conservatism, announced that it planned to dissolve its $700 million investment pool and return the money to its limited partners.)

LBO CRAZE

The LBO is not a new concept. But the LBO was tailor-made for the takeover frenzy of the 1980s. In an LBO, a small group of investors that generally includes senior management borrows heavily and uses the borrowed funds to buy a company from public shareholders and take the company private. The debt is to be rapidly repaid (or so it is assumed) from the company's own cash flow or from sales of its assets.

Proponents of LBOs argue that they are good for U.S. business competitiveness and thus are good for America. Fat corporations with too many management layers and inefficient and costly production facilities are forced by the LBO to cut costs and improve productivity. By placing ownership in the hands of a small group of investors and managers with a powerful debt-driven incentive to improve productivity, so the argument goes, the revitalized companies can't help but trim down and shape up. One notable LBO success story that performed according to this script was Duracell, the battery company. In 1988, an investment group led by Kohlberg, Kravis, and Roberts took the company private, using more of the investment group's own equity than usual for such a deal. Thus far the new owners have a successful performance record; new product development is flourishing, earnings are better than planned, and debt is being retired ahead of schedule without asset sales. And, most impressively, Duracell's longer-term capital spending plans are substantially higher under the new ownership compared with the pre-LBO plans.[5]

The emergence of the high yield (junk) bond market in the 1980s was the primary force behind mushrooming LBO activity. Drexel Burnham, Lambert took the lead in underwriting and distributing junk bond debt issued in connection with increasing LBO activity. These junk bonds, which are the debt obligations of companies with low credit that traditionally could only borrow from banks, were sold mainly to insurance companies, mutual funds, and savings and loan associations, the latter of which raised the funds to buy the junk bonds by issuing deposits insured by the Federal government (and ultimately U.S. taxpayers). The amount of junk bonds outstanding soared to $200 billion in the late 1980s before this market fell on hard times.

The mushrooming of corporate debt, especially in the 1984–88 period (see Table 8.2), was accompanied by a pay down in outstanding equity shares. In essence, the increasingly popular LBO involved the reshuffling of corporate assets on a massive scale. Investment bankers have characterized this as a noble-sounding effort to "unlock the intrin-

Table 8.2. Domestic Private Sector Nonfinancial Debt (Percentage Change—SAAR)

	Pvt. Non-fin.	— Households — Total	Home Mtges.	Consumer Credit	Nonfinancial Business Total	Long Term	Short Term
			Annual (Percent)				
1977	13.1	16.2	17.0	15.9	12.4	11.2	14.7
1978	14.2	17.0	17.5	16.9	13.2	10.6	18.1
1979	13.5	15.1	16.2	13.0	13.6	9.9	20.3
1980	8.9	8.9	11.3	0.7	9.9	9.1	11.2
1981	9.4	8.0	7.8	4.8	11.5	7.9	17.2
1982	6.9	5.4	4.5	4.4	7.8	7.7	8.1
1983	9.6	11.4	11.0	12.6	8.3	9.3	6.9
1984	13.7	12.9	11.7	18.7	15.6	13.4	18.9
1985	13.6	14.1	11.9	15.9	11.4	14.2	7.5
1986	11.9	12.8	14.9	9.6	12.0	14.4	8.4
1987	9.3	11.6	14.0	5.1	7.0	8.2	5.1
1988	9.5	10.9	12.2	7.2	8.2	8.2	8.3
1989	7.5	8.9	10.5	5.3	6.7	5.7	8.2
			Quarterly (Percent, SAAR)				
1986 — I	9.4	9.6	10.9	10.6	11.4	16.1	4.1
II	10.9	11.8	12.9	9.4	10.1	13.7	4.4
III	12.1	14.0	16.7	8.9	10.6	13.0	6.7
IV	13.4	13.2	15.8	8.3	14.1	12.1	17.4
1987 — I	7.6	9.8	14.5	–.4	5.3	9.6	–1.6
II	10.1	13.3	14.6	5.0	7.6	7.6	7.6
III	9.4	10.8	12.3	7.8	7.4	8.0	6.5
IV	8.8	11.0	12.2	7.6	6.8	6.3	7.8
1988 — I	9.1	10.1	10.3	8.2	8.6	7.5	10.5
II	10.4	12.3	14.8	7.1	8.9	9.0	8.8
III	9.0	10.4	11.5	5.9	7.8	7.8	7.7
IV	8.1	9.2	10.1	7.0	6.7	7.6	5.2
1989 — I	8.6	9.2	10.6	5.1	8.4	6.7	11.2
II	7.9	8.0	9.7	4.9	8.3	6.7	10.9

Table 8.2. Continued

	Pvt. Non-fin.	— Households — Total	Home Mtges.	Con-sumer Credit	Nonfinancial Business Total	Long Term	Short Term
III	6.9	8.7	10.2	4.8	5.6	4.5	7.4
IV	5.9	8.5	9.6	5.7	3.8	4.5	2.5
1990 — I	6.8	8.6	10.2	1.8	6.0	4.7	8.2
II	5.2	7.6	9.4	1.2	3.2	3.3	3.1
III	5.4	7.8	8.4	3.5	3.4	2.1	5.4

sic value of corporate assets." But, just the same, it produced a decline in corporate net worth, both relative to GNP and absolutely, thus rendering the corporate sector unusually vulnerable to future economic recessions. During this period, corporate holdings of financial assets relative to GNP remained unchanged. However, most disturbingly, corporate tangible assets, such as new plant and equipment, declined relative to GNP, a troubling sign of deteriorating incentives for longer-term capital investment.[6]

The LBO was a means of instant gratification, at least for some. The big LBO winners were typically corporate management, investment bankers, Wall Street lawyers and existing stock holders, all of whom fattened their pockets handsomely. In contrast, the big losers were existing bond holders, who suffered major capital losses from the downgrading of the corporation's debt rating owing to the typically huge additional offerings of lower quality bond offerings associated with the LBO. Additional losers were the future share-holders of the company who faced the risk that the company could not generate sufficient future cash flow to service the company's new heavier debt burden, resulting in potential bankruptcy.

PITFALLS

As abuses mounted in the second half of the 1980s, the corporate takeover craze, and especially the LBO explosion, began to dominate real business strategies and spending, rather than supporting them. No company seemed too large to escape the takeover threat; for many companies, especially those not making maximum use of their capital, the fear was that if they didn't restructure themselves some hostile outsider would do it for them. For some languishing companies, of course, restructuring may have been the right answer; but for the vast majority it was a destructive threat. Moreover, it seemed that once a company was put in play, its fate was sealed—it would be taken over, broken up, or restructured in one way or the other. Corporate management became obsessed with short-term financial considerations rather than with long-term measures enhancing future competitiveness, growth, and long-term profitability. They were preoccupied with defending themselves from takeover or with taking over someone else (the notion being that the best defense is a good offense).

The main problem was that LBO "fever" not only occupied an inordinate amount of corporate management's time but the LBO also represented an inherent conflict of interest for management. Corporate management was more often than not preoccupied with the LBO as a get-rich-quick scheme for themselves when they should have been focusing instead on the more vital objectives of future new product development, distribution, and marketing. Even more disturbing, companies saddled by heavy debt burdens as a result of LBOs have been forced to scale back plans for new capital spending and research and development (R&D).

Even companies that successfully employed antitakeover measures during this feeding frenzy by raider "sharks" often found themselves choking on debt from defensive recapitalization packages, and often on the verge of bankruptcy. A perfect example was Interco, the conservatively run furniture and footwear company headquartered in the heartland city of St. Louis, Missouri.[7] In this case, the takeover threat—which arrived via fax machine—was posed in 1988 by Steven and Mitchell Rales of Washington, D.C., brothers who were only in their 30s. They were novices in Interco's businesses, but investors took them seriously because these upstart raiders were backed by Drexel Burnham, Lambert—the junk bond powerhouse.

To help ward off this takeover bid, Interco sought the counsel of the high-profile New York investment banking boutique, Wasserstein Perella & Co. These New York takeover experts, formerly with First Boston, suggested that Interco fight the Rales brothers with a recapitalization package worth an estimated $76 a share, but leaving Interco staggering under $1.8 billion of debt. By the spring of 1990, this ill-fated recapitalization package, owing mainly to miscalculations, was worth as low as $42 a share and Interco was on the verge of bankruptcy. As matters turned out, Wasserstein Perella & Co.'s recapitalization plan, as approved by the Interco Board of Directors, had grossly overestimated what Interco assets could bring at auction. (Wasserstein Perella originally valued Interco's Ethan Allen division at $587 million; it was eventually sold for $388 million.) In addition the plan overestimated how much the company's Lane and Broyhill furniture units and its Converse sneaker and Florsheim shoe operations could earn. Finally, the plan also erred fatally on how much debt Interco could tolerate. On January 24, 1991, Interco sought bankruptcy court protection and sued its former investment banker, Wasserstein Perella & Co., for negligence.

Not surprisingly, one of the greatest threats posed by the LBO was overleveraging. The suddenly easy access to an abundance of funds raised through short-term bank HLT loans or longer-term junk bond borrowings created an environment of quick transactions and easy morality. Accordingly, a management and investor group taking a company private through an LBO typically overpaid and overborrowed. Nevertheless, they often paid themselves fat salaries, bonuses, and dividends while making only meager capital investments to improve the company's future competitiveness. A classic example of overborrowing occurred in the famous case of the Campeau Corp.'s acquisition for $3.6 billion of Allied Stores Corporation in 1986.[8] (Allied profits and the market value of its stock at that time were 30 times and 10 times, respectively, larger than those of the acquiring Campeau Corp.) And, as if Campeau Corp.'s first mistake were not big enough, it turned around and purchased Federated Department Store Inc. in 1988 for $6.5 billion. Real estate developer Robert Campeau, a volatile personality who borrowed heavily in the junk bond market to accomplish this dream of building a department store empire, was unable to generate sufficient earnings to service his huge debt burden. As a result he was forced to declare bankruptcy on January 15, 1990.

An example of using abundant borrowed funds in an LBO to overpay for a company occurred in the case of Australian financier Alan Bond's $1.3 billion LBO of Heileman Brewing Co. in 1987.[9] (In July 1990, Bond was forced by his creditors to step down as head of his crumbling worldwide financial empire.) Bond paid between two and three times what the brewing company was worth. Even though Heileman's still had an operating profit in the first half of its 1990 fiscal year, it suffered, as increasingly has been the experience with LBOs, a net loss after interest payments. In an increasingly common post-LBO ritual, Heileman was forced to meet with its bankers to try to restructure its debt. Some analysts compared Heileman's bank debt to the debt of Third World countries because it appeared that its bank loans can't be paid in full out of income. (Heileman is presently in bankruptcy.)

Another LBO example from the late 1980s demonstrates how damaging, indeed deadly, LBOs can be for the international competitiveness of basic U.S. industries. In this case, management and a group of investors led by Citicorp Capital Investors Ltd., Drexel Burnham, Lambert and the Bass brothers took the nation's number two stainless steel maker, J&L Specialty Products Corp., private in a 1986 leveraged buyout.[10] (J&L's management and these investors financed the deal with $159.3 million in bank debt and paper and only $800,000 in cash.) During the next 3½ years, J&L's owners spent little on capital improvements and research. At the same time the top nine managers paid themselves up to $3.8 million in cash and bonuses annually. For the fiscal year ending September 1988 management paid itself and other investors a $120 million cash dividend. A year later J&L issued $200 million in junk bonds and took on more bank debt, with the proceeds used to pay J&L's investors and management $200 million. In March 1990, J&L was sold to a large French steel company, Usinor Sacilor, for an estimated $270 million in cash and the assumption of $290 million in debt. In effect, the LBO produced for J&L's management and investors a tidy profit of nearly $600 million on an initial cash investment of only $800,000.

The historic climax of this frantic period of LBO activity came in early 1989 with the whopping $24.7 billion leveraged buyout of RJR Nabisco by the big LBO firm of Kohlberg, Kravis, and Roberts. This widely touted deal involved drama, intrigue, the clash of powerful egos and the participation, some on the winning side, some on the losing side, of nearly every major investment bank and deal-oriented commercial bank in the nation. In the end, the investment group led by Kohlberg, Kravis, and Roberts beat management's rival bid for the company.[11]

Illustrative of the short-sighted nature of most LBOs, the new debt-burdened RJR Nabisco owners, in mid-1990, slashed their own original 1990 capital spending plans by 45%. The new RJR Nabisco owners also promptly announced price increases for many of the consumer product company's product lines. While these product price increases increased short-term operating profits, they created major uncertainties about the company's future share of highly competitive consumer product lines, thus potentially dampening its longer-term growth and profitability.

MARKET DISCIPLINE REASSERTS ITSELF

Two major shocks signaled an end to the flurry of financially, rather than economically based takeover activity. First, there was the October 13, 1989, stock market collapse. This plunge of 190 points in the Dow-Jones industrial average was triggered by the failure of a United Airlines management and pilots takeover scheme. Second, there was the spectacular February 1990 bankruptcy of Drexel Burnham, Lambert. The Drexel bankruptcy served to severely disrupt the junk bond market which had been so vital in fueling the LBO explosion.

These symptoms of an unwinding of the financial excesses of the 1980s presented Fed policymakers with a dilemma. As long as there was an orderly contraction in such financial excesses, it seemed to be inappropriate for the monetary authorities to supply additional liquidity. Indeed, it is necessary for these 1980s financial excesses (e.g., speculative stock price increases, financially based takeover activity, excessive junk bond debt expansion, etc.) to be unwound before a new sounder base for future economic expansion in the 1990s could be established. However, there is, at the same time, the danger that the financial contraction might pass over a fine line and become disorderly, threatening a chain-reaction involving major financial institution failures or corporate bankruptcies that could push the economy over the edge into a deep recession or even depression.

Actually, the October 1989 stock price collapse produced a split within Fed policy ranks. Acting without Chairman Greenspan's approval and against his better judgment, Vice Chairman Johnson leaked to the *New York Times* and the *Washington Post* that the Fed was prepared, in response to the 1989 stock price collapse, to again supply the necessary liquidity to the financial system (*see* Chapter 5). But it was the opposing view of Chairman Greenspan, apparently supported by New York Fed President Gerald Corrigan, that the October 13, 1989, stock price plunge merely reflected the appropriate correction of financial takeover excesses and thus was not deserving of the special provision of an additional Fed liquidity. (This conflict between Johnson and Greenspan, along with the conflict between Johnson and the U.S. Treasury over dollar intervention policy (*see* Chapter 1) may have contributed, together with personal financial considerations, to Johnson's decision to resign effective August 3, 1990.)

In the same vein, in February 1990, Fed Chairman Greenspan and New York Fed President Corrigan—along with SEC Chairman Richard Breeden and Treasury Secretary Nicholas Brady—decided that the outmoded concept of "too big to fail" did not apply to Drexel Burnham, Lambert, which at the time desperately needed bank loans to back up its rapidly contracting commercial paper debt footings (which were being assaulted by a crisis of investor confidence). These regulators reasoned that as long as this firm's bankruptcy neither impaired the workings of the U.S. payments system, nor posed a threat to the financial stability of other national or regional financial institutions, it should be allowed to go under.

DREXEL'S DOWNFALL

Nothing better symbolized the fast-paced, transactions-oriented, short-term gain character of the corporate takeover frenzy of the 1980s than the saga of Drexel Burnham, Lambert. Indeed, this firm, which always seemed to operate on the margin of propriety, was perhaps more closely tied to the 1980s takeover roller coaster than any other, first riding to the great heights of success and unimaginable riches and then plunging to the depths of utter despair and failure. In December 1988, Drexel pleaded guilty to six felony counts of mail and securities fraud, and agreed to fire Michael R. Milken, its junk bond king. Also, Drexel agreed to pay a hefty fine of $650 million for these crimes. Most observers cite this event as the beginning of the end for Drexel in setting off a chain of events that eventually culminated in Drexel's declaration of bankruptcy in February 1990. After Drexel's guilty plea, for instance, employee morale plummeted, and CEO Fred Joseph was forced to offer huge bonuses to key employees, greedily fighting among themselves for the top dollar, in order to keep them from resigning.

The ingredients of Drexel Burnham, Lambert's flashy but short-lived success are legion. Drexel became a titan by pioneering the sale of junk bonds or corporate obligations of companies with low credit. Michael R. Milken, an obscure Wharton graduate who started his career as a run-of-the-mill fixed-income analyst, became the Drexel evangelist for junk bonds. In this role, he was catapulted to the exulted status of being America's highest paid executive, earning more than half a billion dollars in 1987. Milken, whom his sentencing judge declared followed a "gospel of greed," succeeded in persuading investors that the extra high interest rates on junk bonds more than compensated for the risk that they might not be paid (a premise later found to be in error).

Drexel was the primary medium for the corporate takeover frenzy of the 1980s. Key employee Milken manipulated junk bond and stock underwritings (relying in part on secret investment pools among his colleagues) and built a huge distribution network in part consisting of a daisy chain of captive insurance companies (such as Executive Life) and savings and loan associations (such as Columbia S&L). In April 1990, Milken followed the lead of his company and pleaded guilty to six counts of securities fraud and conspiracy in the junk bond market he had crafted. Milken himself agreed to pay a whopping $600 million fine, nearly as large as that which started his company on the road to ruin. In November 1990, after a lengthy and highly publicized pre-sentencing hearing, Federal Judge Kimba Wood sentenced Milken to ten years in prison and to 1,800 hours of community service during *each* of three additional years of probation.[12]

Part Four

International Financial Relationships

A new element bursting on the U.S. financial scene is the growing integration of global financial markets. For example, beginning in late 1989 and continuing through early 1990, there was a surge in German bond rates reflecting prospects in a united Germany and capitalistic Eastern Europe for stepped-up investment-led economic growth, supported by a huge expected jump in credit demands (both public and private). This increase in German bond rates spilled over into upward pressure on U.S. long-term rates helping to push the 30-year Treasury bond yield slightly above 9% by the end of April 1990 from 7⅞% in December 1989. Similarly, there were sharp increases in Japanese long-term rates during this period as well.

As U.S. investors found bond rates increasingly attractive, U.S. stock prices declined sharply at times during early

1990. Likewise, against the background of rising Japanese bond rates, Japanese stock prices also nose-dived during the first four months of 1990, before rebounding in May. The increase in Japanese bond rates reflected fears over a decline in the yen, especially in terms of the D-mark, and worries over a modest though increasing rate of inflation in Japan. Subsequently, the August 2, 1990, Iraqi invasion and occupation of Kuwait triggered soaring oil prices, fears of renewed worldwide inflation, rising longer-term interest rates, and plunging stock prices, to varying degrees in the United States, Japan, and Germany.

The growing influence of foreign interest rates on U.S. longer-term rates is likely to persist in the 1990s, except in periods when the U.S. dollar suddenly strengthens. When the dollar rebounds, there will tend to be a decoupling of foreign and U.S. longer-term interest rates. This is because the appreciating dollar, especially at a time of foreign political uncertainties, will continue to attract private foreign investors into U.S. fixed-income securities as a safe haven thereby temporarily stabilizing U.S. longer-term rates, despite further increases in foreign interest rates.

A major international monetary policy issue of the early 1990s is what form the new central banking framework supporting European Monetary Union (EMU) will take. In Chapter 10, it is argued that the historical evolution of the Federal Reserve System can provide important guidance in shaping new European central banking arrangements. The new European monetary institution comprising monetary representatives from the 12 member states' central banks and an executive managing board, should exercise the full responsibility for monetary policy. This single European central banking institution's main task is to maintain price stability; without prejudice to this objective, the new European central bank will support the general economic policy of the European Community (EC).

CHAPTER 9

The Coupling and Decoupling of U.S. and Foreign Interest Rates

The U.S. bond market was jolted in the early months of 1990 by an unexpected influence—rising foreign interest rates. During the brief period from the end of December 1989 through the end of April 1990, the yield on 30-year Treasury bonds rose from 7⅞% to slightly above 9%. The same four-month period saw similar upward pressure on longer-term interest rates in both Germany and Japan. These dramatic parallel movements in U.S. and foreign long-term interest rates reflected the increased integration of global financial markets, together with strong expected credit demands in Germany. In essence, this upward pressure on U.S. and foreign long-term interest rates reflected the increased demands relative to the supply of global capital. Another striking example of parallel movements in U.S. and foreign interest rates occurred in August 1990 when renewed inflation fears, ignited by a new oil price shock, sparked sharp increases in U.S., German, and Japanese longer-term rates. At the onset of war in the Persian Gulf in January 1991, early hopes of a quick and complete military victory by the United States and its allies triggered a plunge in oil prices, declining long-term interest rates, and a global stock market rally.

THE COUPLING OF U.S. AND FOREIGN RATES

In late 1989, a sea-change occurred in global politics. A pronounced easing in political tension between the United States and the Soviet Union triggered an unimaginable and shockingly fast-paced series of political and economic changes in Germany and Eastern Europe. In November 1989, the seemingly forever-standing and impenetrable wall between East and West Germany came tumbling down and the winds of freedom and representative democracy swept through Eastern Europe blowing away the last vestiges of communism, as fallen leaves borne on the winds of a winter storm.

With these rapid-fire political changes came prompt steps in 1990 toward the reunification of East and West Germany. In addition, there were throughout Eastern Europe major economic reforms favoring economic incentives and moves toward the establishment of private enterprise capitalism and market-oriented economies and the scrapping of the old centrally controlled socialist economies.

By early 1990, participants in the major world capital markets were beginning to recognize the potential for massive German credit demands to finance the rebuilding of the public infrastructure of East Germany and to help finance private investment-led growth. (One early estimate of German reunification costs, including the rebuilding of East German infrastructure, was $600 billion over ten years.) Reflecting these looming massive credit demands, German nominal (and real) longer-term interest rates began to rise sharply in early 1990. Also adding to the upward pressure on German interest rates, both nominal and real, were expectations of a mismatch between Bundesbank monetary restraint and fiscal stimulus. Real interest rates are defined as nominal interest rates less inflationary expectations.

In this environment the D-mark strengthened during the final two months of 1989 and the first two months of 1990, both in terms of the dollar and the Japanese yen. Global investors were increasingly attracted to German currency holdings. The early 1990 increase in German bond rates was paralleled by increases in U.S. and Japanese longer-term rates as competition for global savings intensified (*see* Exhibit 9.1).

The conditions of a "coupling" of U.S. and foreign long-

Exhibit 9.1. Selected Global Bond Yields (ten-year maturity: Japan, United States, and Germany, weekly 1989–90)

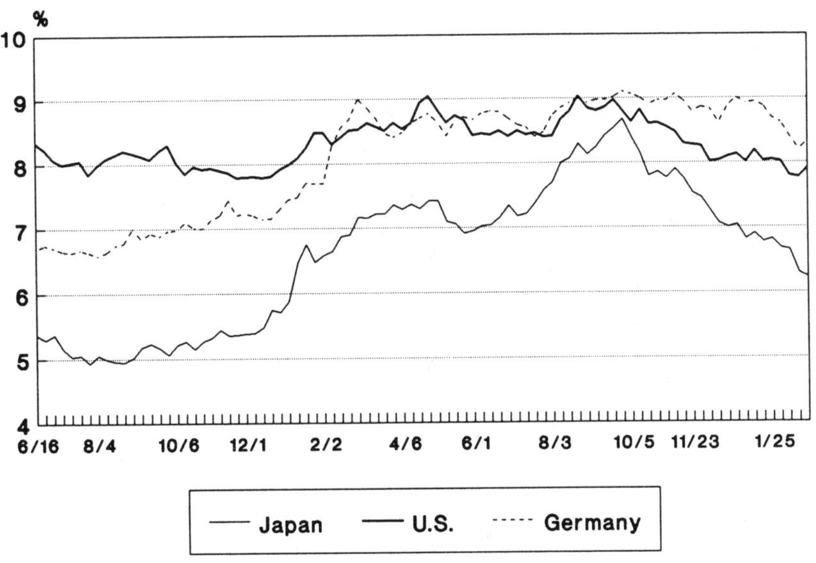

Source: DRI, Bloomberg

er-term interest rates were thus established. These coupling conditions exist when under conditions of globally integrated financial markets stepped-up investment-led growth and a related surge in credit demands relative to supply operate in any given country to increase its real interest rates (nominal rates less inflationary expectations) relative to real rates in other countries. As foreign investors are attracted to the country's securities carrying relatively high real rates, other major countries must increase their own nominal (and real) longer-term interest rates in order to remain competitive in this environment of increased global demand for savings relative to its supply.

In addition, as a result of the increased integration of international financial markets, U.S. and foreign interest rates may move more or less together in response to major international crises. This was the case, for example, when U.S. and foreign longer-term rates climbed, though to varying degrees, in the wake of August 1990 Middle East hostilities and the related oil price shock. Likewise, these longer-term rates fell together following the successful Allied attack on Iraq in January 1991.

THE DECOUPLING OF U.S. AND FOREIGN RATES

To be sure, there are some circumstances in which U.S. longer-term rates will not be held hostage to rising foreign rates. For example, U.S. rates will be "decoupled" from foreign rates when foreign interest rates are being pushed higher by political instability in foreign countries. In this case, the politically stable U.S. may be considered a safe haven.

For example, in the late-March, early-April 1990 period, both the U.S. stock and bond markets were at least briefly decoupled from the weakening Japanese stock and bond markets (*see* Exhibits 9.2 and 9.3). In Japan, continued political instability following the mid-February elections and uncertainties over the extent to which the Ministry of Finance would allow the Bank of Japan to tighten in defense of the yen and to maintain price stability, caused a harrowing plunge in Japanese stock prices and a sharp increase in nominal Japanese Government Bond (JGB) rates with real rates lagging behind. Generally, these Japanese conditions were viewed as a special case.

The August 1990 oil price shock, pushed longer-term Japanese interest rates more sharply higher than U.S. or German long-term rates. This was partly because of special economic and inflation fears owing to Japan's heavy dependence on Persian Gulf oil supplies. This triggered a further dramatic plunge in Japanese stock prices that was mirrored by stock price declines of varying magnitudes in the U.S. and Germany. The surge in nominal (and to a lesser extent real) Japanese long-term rates moved them up to levels more closely in line with U.S. nominal and real longer-term rates. In these conditions Japanese investors found dollar investments relatively less attractive (*see* Exhibit 9.2).

Looking ahead, the 1990s may see temporary periods of decoupling of U.S. and foreign longer-term rates, but this is likely to be the exception rather than the rule. The trend in the 1990s is instead likely to be one in which U.S. longer-term rates are increasingly linked to longer-term foreign rates, especially under conditions where world investment demands are increasing relative to the pool of world savings and liquidity.

This coupling of U.S. and foreign longer-term interest rates can occur on the downside as well as the upside. In mid-May 1990 for example, fears of a Fed tightening move were allayed by second quarter signs of a weakening in real economic activity and some hints of reduced price pressures. This sparked a strong rally on the U.S. bond and stock markets. At the same time, however, the prospect of lower real U.S. interest rates triggered a sharp mid-May decline in the dollar, especially in terms of the yen. The yen also

Exhibit 9.2. Yen and D-Mark Exchange Rates (weekly 1989–91)

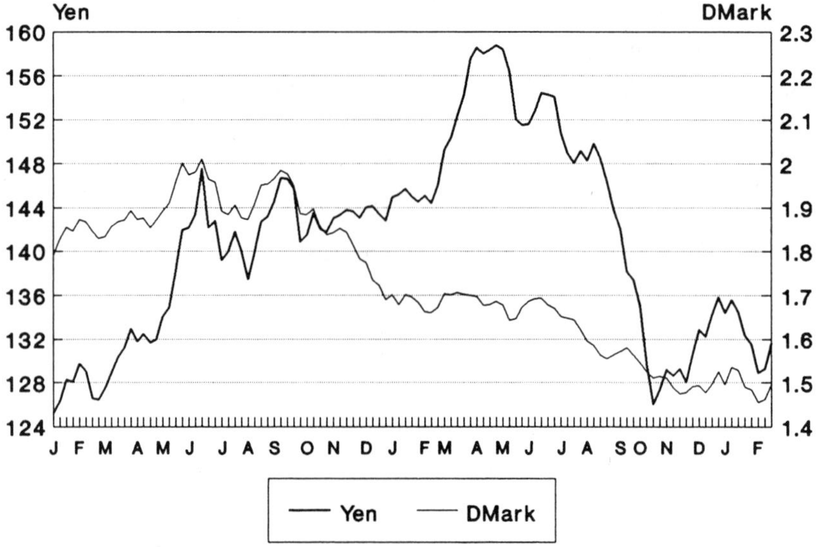

Sources: Wall Street Journal, Aubrey G. Lanston & Co. Inc.

strengthened in terms of the D-mark in mid-May. The D-mark was depressed by increased jitters over the slow pace of monetary union in East and West Germany and fears of rising political instability in Eastern Europe and the Soviet Union. The strengthening yen reduced the chances of any near-term Bank of Japan tightening in monetary conditions, resulting in Japanese bond and stock market rallies.

In August 1990, the Iraqi invasion and occupation of Kuwait triggered an oil price shock and renewed worldwide inflation fears. As a result, longer-term interest rates in the United States, Japan, and Germany, recorded increases of varying magnitudes and stock prices plummeted in each of these nations (*see* Exhibits 9.3, 9.4, and 9.5). The increase in interest rates and stock market decline were most pronounced in Japan largely owing to its heavy dependence on Persian Gulf oil. In this crisis, the German D-mark seemed to

Exhibit 9.3. Japan Nikkei Dow Index (weekly 1989–91)

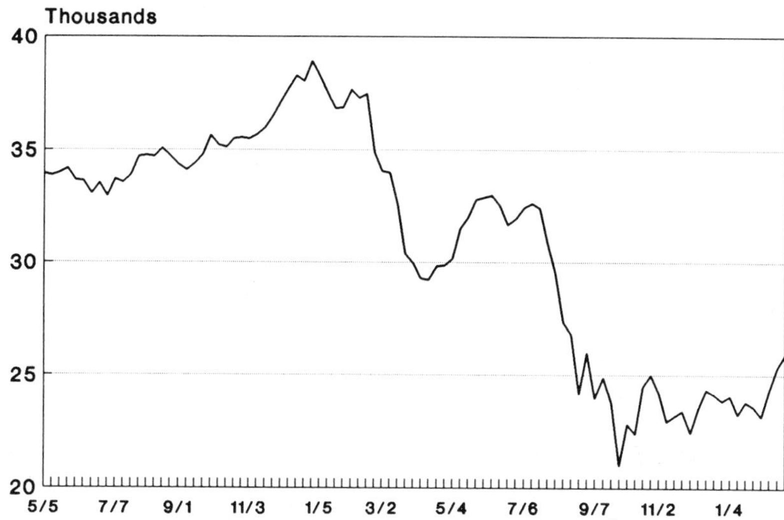

Exhibit 9.4. German Dax Stock Index (weekly May 1989–Jan 1991)

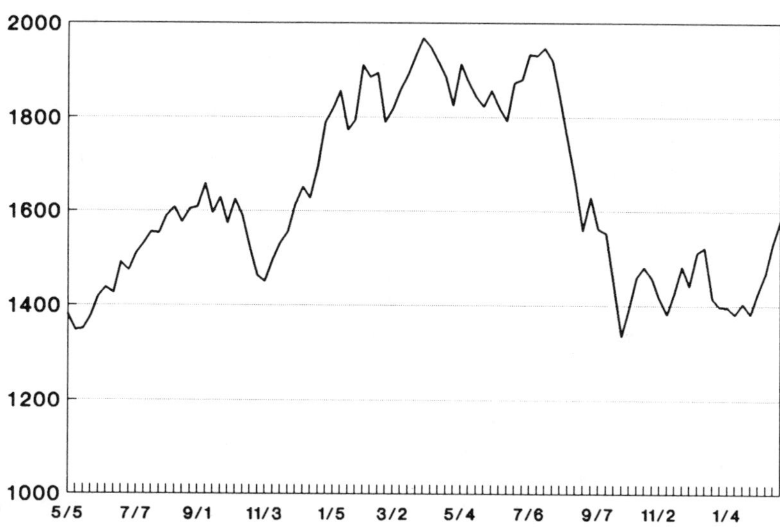

Source: DRI

Exhibit 9.5. U.S. Dow-Jones Stock Index (weekly 1989–91)

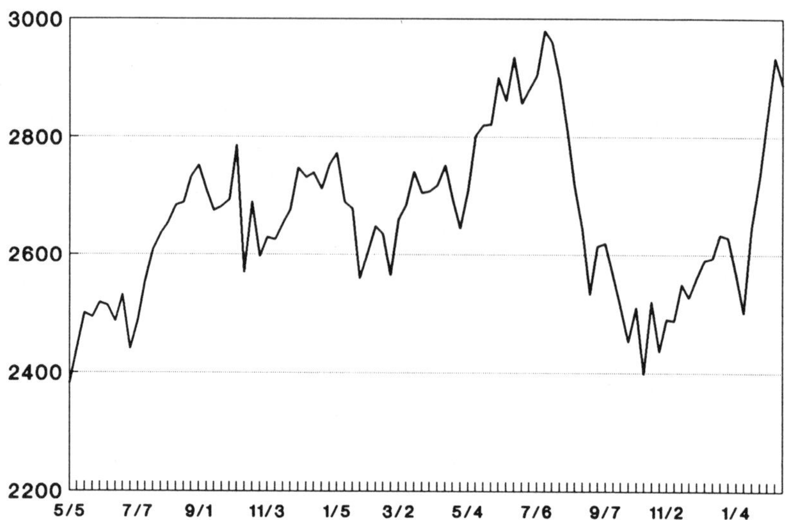

be the favored safe-haven currency, apparently nudging the declining dollar out of this role. This partly reflected attractive real rates on D-mark investment and partly the easing of tensions between the United States and the Soviet Union, which lifted the cloud of a threatened Soviet invasion that had hung over D-mark investments. (The safe-haven role for the German D-mark was short lived, however, as political instability increased in February-March 1991 in both East Germany and the Soviet Union.)

On the evening of January 16, 1991, combined United States and allied forces attacked Iraq. Initial reports of great military success on the part of the international coalition sparked a plunge in oil prices and euphoric rallies in global bond and stock markets. Within two days of the international coalition's successful first night air attack against Iraq, oil prices fell below $20 per barrel for the first time since July 1990. Treasury bonds rallied pushing yields down to just over 8% from just under 8½% accompanied by foreign bond market rallies, and U.S. stock prices initially soared by over 100 points.

Within the first month of the Persian Gulf war the gains in the U.S. Dow-Jones Industrial stock average had been extended to over 400 points (from about 2,500 to just under 3,000). Market opinion was buoyed by the expectation that the U.S. and allied forces would sweep to a quick and complete victory and that Persian Gulf oil supplies would not be significantly affected. It was felt that this outcome would trigger a further decline in oil prices, which, against the background of U.S. recessionary conditions, would result in a lowering of investor inflationary expectations and further substantial declines in U.S. long-term interest rates. Stock market investors thus formed grounds for considerable optimism with the expected decline in yields on alternative bond investments declining and with prospects that this decline in longer-term interest rates (in concert with expected further aggressive Federal Reserve easing moves) would eventually produce rebounds in economic activity and in corporate earnings.

On a more immediate technical level, stock traders followed a more straight-forward rule—Don't fight the Fed. Specifically, when the Fed is easing (and particularly when these Fed easing moves are aggressive, involving a string of two or more discount rate cuts), the resulting sharp decline in short-term rates on money market investment signals that investors should make immediate adjustments. They should trim their large pools of liquid short-term instruments carrying increasingly less attractive rates and shift their funds into either bonds, or (if longer-term rates are also declining) into stocks.

The brief ground war phase of the Persian Gulf war began at 8:00 P.M. (EST) on February 23, 1991, and ended when a victorious President Bush declared a cease fire at 12:00 midnight (EST) on February 27, 1991. During this period U.S. Treasury bond yields continued to hover around 8% and stocks turned in a mixed performance. The consensus market view was that this brief war would bring about a short and shallow recession. This expected outcome dashed hope for future Fed easing moves.

It is important to note, that, despite the increasingly close relationship between U.S. and foreign longer-term rates, the Federal Reserve (and other foreign central banks as well) can continue to exert the dominant influence on shorter-term rates in their respective countries. Note in Exhibit 9.6, for example, that in the second half of 1989, Fed easing moves pushed short-term Eurodollar rates lower, while contrasting tightening moves by the Bank of Japan and the Bundesbank pushed the respective Euroyen and Euromark rates higher.

The contrast between tightening and easing international monetary policy actions became even more striking in late 1990 and early 1991, especially in the case of Germany and the U.S. On January 20, 1991, the G-7 countries held a meeting supposedly aimed at coordinating international economic policies. But only 10 days later, on January 30, 1991, the German Bundesbank moved with unexpected

Exhibit 9.6. Selected 3-month Eurocurrency Rates (weekly 1989–91)

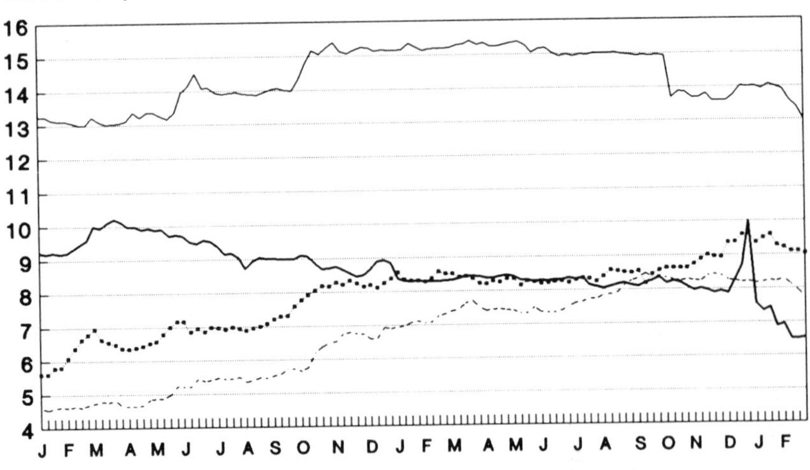

suddenness to tighten by increasing its Lombard and discount rates. Then, on the very next day (February 1, 1991), the Federal Reserve moved with equally surprising suddenness in the opposite direction to ease aggressively by cutting its discount rate to 6% from 6½%, paralleled by a pronounced decline in the Federal funds rate to 6¼% from 6¾%. As could easily have been foreseen, the dollar broke into full retreat leaving the G-7 countries with the unenviable task of trying to pick up the pieces through largely unsuccessful direct dollar support operations.

COUNTRY COMPARISONS

Viewing conditions in a longer-term prospective, Germany, at the beginning of the 1990s, is experiencing fiscal stimulus and huge public and private credit demands, potentially clashing against monetary restraint, somewhat like the conditions in the United States in the early 1980s. Moreover, the United States is facing potential rising export growth, such as Japan was at the beginning of the 1980s. Furthermore, Japan, at the beginning of the 1990s, could be moving toward a more mature condition with mounting environmental problems and labor shortages, not unlike Germany's situation at the beginning of the 1980s.

To spell out these country comparisons more fully, Germany in the early 1990s, just like the United States in the early 1980s, will likely experience strong economic growth, soaring credit demands (both public and private), and a mismatch between monetary restraint (aimed at curtailing inflationary pressures) and fiscal stimulus, as government spending requirements mount in connection with the unification of East and West Germany. For Germany, in the early 1990s, again as in the United States in the early 1980s, the likely outcome will be high real interest rates and depending on the degree of political instability in Germany and the Soviet Union, sharply appreciating D-mark. In addition, Germany in the early 1990s will be the locomotive for U.S.

growth (in the form of rising U.S. exports to Germany) representing a reversal of the conditions in which the United States was the locomotive for German growth in the early 1980s. In these conditions the German trade surplus should decline as imports rise while export growth is constrained by inadequate productive capacity.

The United States, in the early 1990s, like Japan at the beginning of the 1980s, has the potential for increased savings and investment and for export-led growth (especially in the case of European demands for U.S. exports). In contrast, Japan at the beginning of the 1990s, like Germany at the beginning of the 1980s, has the earmarks of a maturing economy with its potential economic growth constrained by growing labor shortages and environmental problems. At the same time, Japan will experience a further shift in favor of more cyclically pronounced (and interest-sensitive) sources of domestically generated growth (paced by public construction, housing, and consumption) and away from export-led growth. This shift toward Japanese domestically generated growth and higher imports is what the United States has urged on Japan in its negotiations on structural trade initiatives.

However, continued Japanese trade with, and direct investment in, other Asian newly industrialized economies (NIEs)—especially the emerging economic stars of the 1990s including Thailand, Malaysia, Indonesia, and the Philippines, along with such already blossoming economic powers as Hong Kong, Taiwan, South Korea, and Singapore—is likely to continue to be an important source of regional growth in the 1990s. It is estimated that GNP growth for the Asian NIEs will moderate to a slower but still strong 6 to 7% pace in the first half of the 1990s, compared with a peak growth rate of 9.2% during the 1984–88 period. This expected moderation in Asia NIE growth reflects moderating demand for their exports, particularly in the case of the oil-shock-depressed industrialized countries. Also, for some Asian NIEs there may be mounting internal problems such as accelerating wage and price pressures, labor disruptions, and pollution problems.

In 1989 and 1990, the Bank of Japan was forced to tighten money conditions to support the yen and to contain inflationary pressures. The Bank of Japan tightened in five steps, beginning in May 1989 and continuing through August 1990, pushing its discount rate up from 2.50% to an August 1990 level of 6.00%. Previously, the Bank of Japan had pursued an extended period of monetary ease (lowering its discount rate in ten steps from 9% in March 1980 to 2.5% in February 1987 and then holding the discount rate at this low level until May 1989). This prolonged period of Japanese monetary ease resulted in a huge build-up in liquidity and kicked off raging asset inflation, as reflected in soaring Japanese stock prices and real estate values.

Against the background of the Bank of Japan's belated tightening moves in 1989 and 1990, Japanese bond yields increased and there was a sharp decline in Japanese stock prices. However, in May 1990, the yen suddenly strengthened in terms of the D-mark (as well as the dollar), kicking off a strong rally in Japanese bonds and stocks. In contrast, the latest oil price shock in August 1990 triggered inflation fears (owing to Japan's heavy dependence on Persian Gulf oil), and this in turn sparked sharp increases in Japanese longer-term interest rates and a panicky plunge in Japanese stock prices. Subsequently, another pronounced strengthening in the yen in the late-September, early-October 1990 period triggered yet another rebound in Japanese bond and stock prices.

The sudden 1990 spurt in Japanese longer-term bond yields triggered a flight by Japanese lenders and investors away from foreign securities into Japanese yen holdings. To accomplish this shift favoring yen investments, large Japanese insurance companies and other institutional investors sharply reduced their new investment in foreign securities, including U.S. government securities. This shift was encouraged as the gap by which U.S. interest rates exceeded

Japanese rates closed. Furthermore, Japanese institutional investors found that the increasingly attractive yen investments had the added advantage of eliminating foreign exchange risk. Moreover, within their declining share of foreign currency holdings these private Japanese investors were induced to diversify their declining holdings in favor of German fixed-income securities carrying relatively more attractive real interest rates (nominal interest rates less inflationary expectations). In early 1990, for example, German real interest rates on ten-year D-mark bonds were about 6%. In contrast, real rates on U.S. fixed-income securities of a similar maturity were about 4% while comparable real rates on Japanese bonds were about 4.5%.

CHAPTER 10

A New Central Bank for Europe

One of the major international monetary policy issues of the early 1990s is how to shape European Monetary Union (EMU). The primary aim is to establish a European central bank committed to price stability, independent of governments, and issuing a single currency (ECUs) no less strong than the ultimately disappearing German D-mark. It is precisely this task that greeted the first session of the European Intergovernmental Conference meeting in Rome on December 14, 1990, as it considered changes in the original Treaty of Rome (which established the initial European Economic Community of six countries in 1958).[1]

Of particular interest is the nature of the new central banking framework that must evolve in order to ensure the success of EMU. An effectively organized European central bank that successfully pursues the primary objective of curtailing inflation is absolutely essential to the success of the EMU effort.

The best model for the creation of a new European central bank is, most intriguingly, the Federal Reserve System framework. The primary task in the creation of both central banking systems is remarkably similar—the balancing of interests between a Board which has sufficient centralized powers to carry out flexible but effective monetary policies appropriate for changing financial and economic circumstances. At the same time the new European central banking system must allow for sufficient voice but not domination by the 12 EC (European Common market) member nations. Precisely the same issue confronted the newly emerging Federal Reserve System regarding the balance of power between the Board of Governors and the 12 district Federal Reserve banks.

DELORS PLAN

The three-stage Delors Plan sets out a timetable for adopting one European currency managed by one independent central bank.[2] This plan was proposed in April 1989 by a special committee headed by Jacques Delors, former French Finance Minister, now president of the European Commission. Under the first stage of this plan, which began on July 1, 1990, the now enlarged group of 12 European Community (EC) countries (Germany, Spain, Ireland, Portugal, Greece, France, Itlay, Belgium, Denmark, Netherlands, United Kingdom, and Luxembourg) agreed to eliminate restraints on the free movement of capital among their respective countries and to coordinate their monetary policies more closely.

Stage two of the Delors Plan, originally scheduled to start in January 1993, envisions a progressive narrowing of the margins of fluctuation around each EC country's central exchange rate and reduced recourse to realignments within the European currency "bands." This would represent in effect a more rigid and tightly aligned version of the prevailing currency bands or Exchange Rate Mechanism (ERM) of the European Monetary System (EMS), forcing anti-inflation discipline on the EC countries participating in ERM, together with an eventual convergence in EC interest rates. Also, in its second stage, the Delors Plan envisions the creation of a new European central bank that would seek to achieve still more coordination of monetary policies, though in this transitional stage monetary sovereignty would still rest with each of the national central banks.

The United Kingdom finally joined the ERM of the EMS on October 8, 1990, adding a third major internationally traded currency to the German D-mark and the increasingly important French franc. The pound sterling will initially be allowed to fluctuate up to 6% on either side of its bilateral central parity rate against other currencies participating in the ERM. All other currencies, with the exception of the Spanish peseta, have fluctuation margins of 2.25% on either side of their central parity rates. All 12 EC countries are members of the EMS; with the United Kingdom's decision to join, there are now 10 countries in the ERM. Portugal and Greece are currently members of the EMS but not of the ERM.

After a transitional stage two, which some visualize as being relatively brief, stage three of the Delors Plan proposes the surrendering of all national monetary sovereignty to the new European central bank and the permanent fixing of all exchange rates. According to the Delors Plan, a single currency would be adopted as legal tender for all economic and financial transactions within and among the EC's 12 member countries.

SUGGESTED MODIFICATIONS

On a microeconomic level, a single European currency has much to recommend it. Most obviously, there would be no more transaction costs for changing from one currency to another as people and goods cross borders. Furthermore, there would be no more worries that exchange rates between EC countries might unexpectedly change in the future. Indeed, in this sense, it might be argued that it would be impossible to reap the full rewards of EC economic and monetary union until individual currencies, the ultimate non-tariff barriers to trade, are done away with. (Certainly the United States has benefited hugely from having a dollar currency rather than dozens of currencies.)

More ammunition for advocates of speedy monetary union was provided by a year long study of its potential benefits by the European Commission. This thorough but somewhat self-serving study, released on October 19, 1990, asserted that seven EC members (Germany, France, Belgium, Netherlands, Luxembourg, Denmark, and Ireland) are now ready to move to the final stage of monetary union, and three (the United Kingdom, Italy, and Spain) are nearly ready. Only Greece and Portugal, with more intractable economic problems, require major adjustments.[3] The study went on to state that the creation of a single currency and the elimination of the cost of change of currencies for travel or conducting business would save $17.9 billion to $26.1 billion per year. Moreover, the resulting lower inflation and more stable prices could increase annual EC real economic growth by .3%. Finally, eliminating the risk of exchange rate fluctuations would encourage investors to accept a lower rate of return on capital investments in the EC.

Another plan of monetary union was advanced on June 20, 1990, by John Major, the United Kingdom's Chancellor of the Exchequer but more recently elevated to Prime Minister. Alone among the leaders of the EC countries, the United Kingdom's Prime Minister Margaret Thatcher had viewed the Major Plan as consistent with stage three of the Delors Plan. Some moderation in the United Kingdom's hard-line position was suggested by the United Kingdom's subsequent October decision to join the ERM of the EMS though Mrs. Thatcher vowed that a further erosion of the United Kingdom's monetary sovereignty was not acceptable. (Prime Minister Thatcher unexpectedly announced her resignation on November 22, 1990, and later in the same month the Conservative Party voted in John Major as their leader and new Prime Minister.)

The Major Plan advocated a "hard ECU" that conceivably might co-exist with the currently prevailing European Unit of Account (ECU). The current ECU is defined as a basket of specified amounts of each EC currency. The new hard ECU was designed by Major to be no weaker than the strongest currency, the German D-Mark (which accounts for a lion's share—35% of the present ECU); as such, Major's new ECU was offered as the centerpiece of progress toward monetary union.

The new ECU would, according to the Major Plan, be issued by the European Monetary Fund (EMF). The EMF, a version of the Delors European central bank, would exchange the new ECU for deposits of national currency by whoever wanted the new hard currency. The new ECU would be managed so as never to be devalued against any EC currency. The EMF could use its not inconsiderable powers to demand that any profiligate-seeming national central bank buy back deposits of its own currency from the EMF with other hard currencies, say dollars or yen. The EMF would also require each central bank to compensate the EMF for any losses caused by a devaluation of its currency. Obviously, the more that people chose to hold the hard ECUs, the more draconian these EMF powers to crack down on any inflation-prone central bank would be.

Under the Major Plan, the EMF would gain credibility managing a currency poised to evolve into Europe's money. Moreover, the Major Plan would give EC countries a taste of the discipline needed to achieve ultimate anti-inflation goals. In this way the Major Plan could be viewed (whatever the objections of former Prime Minister Thatcher) as a substitute for or at least a guide for modifying the short and somewhat fuzzy stage two of the Delors Plan, making the final stage of this plan less of a leap of faith.

The possible blending of Major's hard ECU into the

Delors approach was envisioned in the late summer of 1990 by Carlos Solchaga, the Spanish Finance Minister. Mr. Solchaga also called for stage two to be delayed a year, starting in January 1994. In sympathy with the Majors Plan, the Spanish Finance Minister foresaw the EMF issuing hard ECUs in stage two, thereby disciplining national monetary policies. But contrary to the Delors concept of a relatively brief phase two, Spain's Solchaga envisioned a long stage two lasting five or six years. It would take that long, he argued, to break the inflationary habits of some countries. Furthermore, in stage three when the hard ECU would become the single EC currency, the Spanish Finance Minister wants to increase EC regional aid to ease the adjustment pain of stage three for the poorer EC members.

In another initial challenge to the Delors Plan, the German Bundesbank argued as recently as September 19, 1990, against setting specific dates for EMU's future stages; the timing, the German central bank asserted, should depend on the EC's progress in reaching a sufficient degree of economic convergence. More specifically, Bundesbank President Karl-Otto Poehl advocated a "two-speed" approach in which a hard core of seven or eight EC countries create monetary union first (Germany, France, Belgium, Holland, Luxembourg, Denmark, and perhaps Italy or even Ireland), followed by other countries when their inflationary rates are both lower and more stable. Subsequently, however, in mid-October 1990, German Chancellor Helmut Kohl threw his weight behind the EC plan to create a single currency and a new European central bank by in effect overruling his Bundesbank head and announcing that he favored as a compromise starting the second stage on January 1, 1994, a year later than originally proposed in the Delors Plan.

Still more recently, at a two-day summit of the 12 EC leaders in Rome at the end of October 1990, it was agreed in principle, over protests by then-British Prime Minister Thatcher, that stage two should indeed come into existence on January 1, 1994. The EC leaders also mapped out a timetable that could result in a single EC currency during the latter 1990s.

Subsequently, on November 9, 1990, Bundesbank President Poehl announced that he did not like the Major Plan to introduce an alternative hard ECU. Poehl proposed instead hardening the existing ECU. The existing ECU could be hardened, according to Poehl, by dispensing with basket revisions and by not devaluing the ECU in future realignments. In a subsequent dramatic warning on March 19, 1991, the still disaffected Poehl proclaimed that the excessively rapid German monetary union was a "disaster" that should serve as a "drastic illustration" of mistakes the European Community must avoid as it moves toward a single currency and a new central bank.

FED MODEL

Any modifications to the Treaty of Rome covering European economic and monetary union (which requires unanimous EC consent) must inevitably start with the right institutional arrangements for a new European central bank. The simple fact is that any set of appropriately anti-inflationary monetary arrangements must necessarily hinge on the proper institutional structure, independence, and effectiveness of the new European central bank. The new central bank institution must command the respect and confidence of all 12 EC nations in order to effectively discipline EC monetary growth and curtail inflation.

Fortunately, the evolution of the Federal Reserve System can shed some constructive light on the process of building a new European central bank. The main lesson lies in how power was eventually centralized in the Board of Governors in Washington, D.C., subject to the continued influence of the 12 district Reserve Banks.[4] An analogous allocation of power can be envisioned between the governing board of the new European central bank and the influence of the monetary officials of the 12 member nations (paralleling the 12

Federal Reserve districts). The difficulties associated with the Federal Reserve Act's initially unclear delegation of powers to the Board highlights the need for greater clarity in the new constitution establishing the Eurofed. It suggests that once chosen, the governing board of the new European central bank should promptly seek to centralize decision making and to acquire sufficient explicitly defined powers to effectively formulate monetary policy and carry it out while still giving adequate voice to all 12 member nations.

It is noteworthy that the process of investigation, discussion and compromise leading up to President Woodrow Wilson's signing of the Federal Reserve Act on December 23, 1913, took fully five years. And, following the signing into law of the Federal Reserve Act, it took no less than another two decades or so to organize an effective U.S. central banking system with sufficient power centralized in the Board of Governors so that it could develop new policies and tools to meet the changing needs of the economy. The obvious lesson is that the road to an effective central banking structure can be a fairly long one if governing board powers are not clearly defined at the outset.

On the heels of the Panic of 1907, the Aldrich-Vreeland Act of 1908 created the bipartisan U.S. National Monetary Commission headed by Senator Nelson Aldrich (Republican—Rhode Island). The commission's recommendations were formalized in a bill, generally known as the Aldrich Plan, calling for 1 central bank and 15 branches. The Aldrich Plan stirred deep-seated distrust of the centralization of power, however, eventually stimulating an outpouring of alternative plans that proposed a more equal balance between central and regional control. The major forthcoming plans provided for governing bodies ranging in size from 7 to 45 members. These plans envisioned functions of the central bank ranging from issuing national currency to setting the discount rate and overseeing foreign exchange operations (see Table 10.1). The final blueprint for the Federal Reserve System was forged by Representative (later Senator) Carter Glass (Democrat—Virginia) and Senator Robert Owen (Re-

Table 10.1. Major Plans for a Federal Reserve Governing Body for the Central Banking System

Plan, bill, or act		Governing body				
Name	Date	Name	Number of members	Term of office (years)	Composition	Function
Warburg Plan	November, 1907; revised April 1908	Board of Managers	42	1, or until their successors qualify	Secretary of Treasury; Comptroller of the Currency; U.S. Treasurer; 6 members of Congress; 20 chairmen of branches; 12 others voted by stockholding member banks; a salaried board governor	Issue notes based on commercial bills and gold; fix the discount rate and rediscount short-term commercial paper; maintain central cash reserve; establish branches; manage and supervise activities of 20 regional bank associations
Fowler Plan	February 1908	Court of Finance	17	Serve until age 72, unless majority of Court extends appointment	6 members from Atlantic coast; 6 from Mississippi region; 4 from Pacific Coast; all experienced in business and banking; one at-large appointee to preside over court; all appointed by the President	Issue notes based on secured bank assets; consider appeals from member banks not satisfied with rulings from regional associations; manage central gold reserve

Table 10.1. Continued

Plan, bill, or act		Governing body				
Name	Date	Name	Number of members	Term of office (years)	Composition	Function
Aldrich Plan	January 1911	Reserve Association Board	45	3	Secretaries of Treasury, Commerce, Labor and Agriculture; Comptroller to the Currency; 14 members elected by boards of branches; 12 representing stockholding interests; 12 representing agriculture, commerce and industry; governor and deputy governor	Act as fiscal agent for government; determine discount rate for short-term commercial paper, bills of exchange, and so on; engage in open market purchases
Owen Bill	May 1913	Board of Governors of the National Currency	7	Serve at the pleasure of the President	Secretaries of Treasury and Agriculture; Comptroller of the Currency; 4 governors appointed by the President: 1 knowledgable in commerce, 1 in manufacturing, 1 in transportation, and	Exercise general supervision over reserve banks and examine accounts of national and reserve banks; act as fiscal agent for government; adjust boundaries and districts of reserve banks if necessary;

					1 in banking and credit	supervise issuance of national currency; suspend for no more than 30 days reserve requirements specified in bill; approve reserve bank accounts in foreign countries; oversee foreign exchange operations
Glass Bill	June 1913	Federal Reserve Board	7	8	Secretaries of Treasury and Agriculture; Comptroller of the Currency; 4 board members appointed by the President, at least 1 experienced in banking	Examine accounts of reserve banks; require or permit reserve banks to discount paper of any other reserve bank; establish mandatory weekly discount rates upon each class of paper; suspend for no more than 30 days reserve requirements specified in bill; supervise and regulate the issuance of notes to reserve banks; prescribe rules for reserve banks to engage in open market operations

Table 10.1. Continued

Plan, bill, or act		Governing body				
Name	Date	Name	Number of members	Term of office (years)	Composition	Function
Vanderlip Plan	November 1913	Governing Board	7	14; staggered expiration	7 members appointed by the President; nonpartisan, government board	Approve rediscounting; oversee clearinghouse operations; issue bank notes
Federal Reserve Act (Glass-Owen Bill)	December 1913	Federal Reserve Board	7	10	Secretary of Treasury; Comptroller of the Currency; 5 members appointed by the President with due regard to commercial, industrial and geographical representation, with at least 2 members experienced in banking and finance	Supervise and regulate the issuance and retirement of Federal Reserve notes; reclassify Reserve Districts and add Reserve Banks if appropriate; supervise the activities and audit accounts of Reserve Banks; select 3 directors, including chairman, of each Reserve Bank board; require or permit Reserve Banks to rediscount paper of other Reserve Banks; approve discount rates set by Reserve Banks; issue

						regulations regarding Reserve Bank open market operations
Federal Reserve Act amended	June 1922	Federal Reserve Board	8	10	Secretary of Treasury; Comptroller of the Currency; 6 appointive members; added agricultural representative and eliminated requirement for 2 members to be experienced in banking and finance	Same as above
Federal Reserve Act amended (Banking Act of 1935)	August 1935	Board of Governors of the Federal Reserve System	7	14	7 members appointed by the President, representing financial, agricultural, industrial and commercial interests, and geographical divisions of the country; removed Secretary of Treasury and Comptroller of the Currency from Board	Exercise authority over national monetary and credit policies and, as part of the Federal Open Market Committee, help set open market policy

publican—Oklahoma); it was known as the Federal Reserve Act (or Glass-Owen Bill).

The Federal Reserve Act provided that members of the Federal Reserve Board of Governors should be presidential appointees. This was done in order to keep the Federal Reserve System under a centralized public authority so as to balance it against the power of private money interests. The Aldrich Plan, in contrast, had given private banking interests effective control over the Federal Reserve System.

Furthermore, in order to broaden representation on the Federal Reserve Board of Governors and to help ensure that it would not be dominated by any one interest group or region, the Federal Reserve Act provided that no more than one member was to be selected from any one Federal Reserve District and that the President, in choosing the Fed Reserve Board members, should have "due regard to a fair representation of the different commercial, industrial, and geographical divisions of the country." In addition, at least two Board members were to be "persons experienced in banking or finance" so that the Federal Reserve System would be governed by sound and scientific principles in addressing the commercial and financial needs of the nation. In a further attempt to insulate the Federal Reserve Board from partisan politics, the Federal Reserve Act originally provided for 10-year terms (lengthened to 14 years in the Banking Act of 1935), longer than the terms of elected members of the House of Representatives which were 2 years, the U.S. Senate, 6 years, or for any other executive appointees except for those of the Federal judiciary, which were lifetime appointments, and the Controller General which was for 15 years.

The Federal Reserve Act originally established an excessively decentralized Federal Reserve System. The 12 regional Reserve Banks were to have considerable authority to set the terms for credit provision and regulate member banks in their districts. The Board in Washington was assigned responsibility to oversee the activities of the Reserve Banks.

The problem was that the Board's functions were in

some cases presented vaguely and indirectly. For example, each Reserve Bank's power to establish discount rates was "subject to review and determination of the Federal Reserve Board." But what "determination" meant was not clear so that the line between the Reserve Banks' power and the Board's power was left ill-defined.

Likewise, there was considerable uncertainty with regard to who would speak for the Federal Reserve System in international policy matters. Some members of the Reserve Bank Organization Committee, a Committee established by the Federal Reserve Act to designate Federal Reserve cities and districts, favored the New York Reserve Bank, since its head, Benjamin Strong, was well known to central bankers in Europe. Others favored the Board as the international spokesman. In practice, the New York Reserve Bank became the principal representative in international affairs during the early years of the System because of its superior knowledge and experience in international finance. This principal of specialization might be applied to the new European central bank. For example, under the guidance of the Executive Board of Eurofed, the German monetary officials might carry out domestic open market monetary operations, the U.K. monetary authorities might carry out foreign exchange intervention, and the French monetary authorities might carry out the regulatory and supervision functions of the new European central bank.

The centralization of power in the Federal Reserve Board was given a boost early on (1914) by Attorney General T. W. Gregory who rendered the opinion that the Board was an independent board or government body separate from the Treasury and was "not merely supervisory, but . . . a distinctly administrative board with extensive powers." However, the question remained as to whether the Board was to be the " . . . partly automatic regulator of an organization that was generally passive except when an emergency required it to accommodate commerce and business"; or whether the Board was to be "the central policymaker in a system that actively participated in regulating the economy through managing the availability of money and credit." Needless to say, the Board eventually evolved in the direction of the latter role, and this should be the case for the new Eurofed as well.

The Board initially found it difficult to maintain control over the Governors (later named Presidents) of the various Reserve Banks. In October 1914, the Board called an initial meeting in Washington of the Governors and other officers of the Reserve Banks to deal with practical items that required uniformity and cooperation among the Reserve Banks such as a check-clearing and check-collection system and a common method of accounting. Buoyed by the success of this initial meeting, Benjamin Strong of the New York Reserve Bank and Alfred L. Aiken of the Boston Reserve Bank took the lead in urging that a conference of Governors be established. This conference of Governors proved to be such a success that it began to meet in different places several times a year. However, the Governors Conference, as it became known, began to challenge the Board's authority by issuing resolutions on System policies and criticizing rulings and orders from the Board. In January 1916, the Board decided that it must move to check the authority of the Governors Conference by refusing to approve its expenses for a secretary and for travel not undertaken at the behest of the Board. The Board also insisted that any meetings of the Governors Conference take place in Washington at a time designated by the Board.

At times in its early evolution, the authority of the Federal Reserve System as a whole was challenged by private interests. For example, the Fed's establishment of a universal par check-clearing system was opposed by many member banks, particularly those in small towns that depended heavily on their check "exchange charges" or processing fees. To the lasting benefit of the Federal Reserve System, its authority was greatly enhanced by the Supreme Court in a 1923 decision which affirmed the right of a Reserve Bank to collect checks within its District for other Reserve Banks, for member banks, and for affiliated nonmember banks without paying an exchange charge.

Perhaps the greatest early challenge to the Federal Reserve's general monetary policy-making powers came soon after World War I. As early as December 1918, members of the Board began to stress the connection between low discount rates and the excessive expansion of credit, and accelerating inflation. In April 1919, the Board discussed at length requests by several Reserve Banks to raise the discount rate. But the Board decided to keep the discount rate low to discourage competition with Treasury Victory bonds and to assist the Treasury in keeping the Treasury's interest payments low.

By 1920, however, the wholesale price index had soared to more than twice its 1914 level. In January of that year the Reserve Banks, with the approval of the Board, raised the discount rate to 6% from 4¾%. Subsequently, in May, the Board approved another Reserve Bank discount rate increase to 7%. These discount increases triggered a brief but severe recession in business activity and a deflationary collapse in prices in 1920–21. The agricultural sector was particularly hard hit. Farmers who had incurred large mortgage obligations when farm prices were high found debt carrying-costs beyond their means when farm prices plummeted. Farm mortgages became uncollectable, and in 1921 more than 500 banks failed. For the public at large, Liberty and Victory bond holders (including future President Harry Truman) suffered major capital losses. Some members of Congress claimed that in its anti-inflationary tightening actions the Federal Reserve System had discriminated against certain sectors, especially agriculture.

In an effort to resolve this controversy, the Federal Reserve Board requested a Congressional investigation. The Joint Congressional Commission of Agricultural Inquiry started hearings on August 1921 and submitted a report to Congress on January 1922. The commission concluded that the Federal Reserve System had erred in not acting sooner to raise interest rates. It also determined that the charges of discrimination against agriculture had no basis. Most important, the Commission helped the Board establish independence from the Treasury by asserting that the Federal Reserve should answer to Congress, not to the Treasury.

This gradual but inevitable transfer of power to the Board was crystallized in the Banking Act of 1935. Under the terms of this legislation, the Board's membership was set at 7 members (the same as in the original 1913 Federal Reserve Act) but their terms of office were increased to 14 years from 10 years to lessen the influence of partisan politics. Moreover, the Banking Act of 1935 greatly increased the Federal Reserve System's independence from the Treasury by removing the Secretary of the Treasury and the Comptroller of the Currency from ex officio Board membership and replacing them with two additional members appointed by the President with the advice and consent of the Senate. This legislation also increased the Board's powers to exercise authority over monetary and credit policies and, as part of the Federal Open Market Committee (FOMC), to help direct open market operations. Also, the Board's power to vary reserve requirements was enlarged. Other powers gained by the Board included control over interest rates on time deposits, control over the percentage of bank capital and surplus that could be represented by security loans, and the policing of the prohibition of interest on demand deposits.

INSTITUTIONAL FRAMEWORK

Following the example of the Federal Reserve System, the new European central bank should be independent from direct control by national governments and EC authorities. The European central bank should be composed of a 6-member Executive Board chaired by the Eurofed President and a Deputy President (all chosen at large from member EC countries by virtue of their monetary experience and ability), and the 12 Governors of the EC member central banks. The European central bank's President, Deputy President, and other members of the Executive Board, should be appointed for 10-year terms by the European Council (composed of the Heads of State of the 12 member countries) after consultation with the European Parliament. The President of the European central bank should report to both the European Parliament and the European Council annually.

The key policy-making body of the European central bank might be called the Council. Headed by the President of the Executive Board it should consist of the 6 members of the Executive Board plus 4 voting members chosen annually on a rotating basis from among the 12 Governors of the member central banks. The Council of the European central bank, which should meet every four to six weeks, would establish monetary policy for EMU on the basis of majority vote.

The European central bank should have the full responsibility for the formulation and implementation of monetary policy across Europe. The sole object of monetary policy should be price stability. The European central bank would be charged with influencing European interest rates and with disciplining European monetary growth. European central bank intervention in the markets for foreign exchange and the daily management of its foreign exchange reserves could be controlled on the basis of instructions from the European central bank's Council.

PROPOSED ARRANGEMENT

Conceivably, the best arrangement would be for the second stage of the Delors Plan to begin on January 1, 1994, and last four years. The duration of this second phase should be fairly long because it involves the transformation of habits, accounting procedures, and organizational structures as well as the desired convergence of widely differing inflation rates among the 12 EC countries. The third and final stage of this plan, in which a single European currency is managed by an independent European central bank, should thus ideally begin on January 1, 1998.

The second stage of the Delors Plan might appropriately incorporate the important money discipline principles of the Major Plan. To ensure that individual governments do not simply finance their budget deficits by printing money, this transition phase might involve a system of specific penalties for inflation-prone central banks. This would give EC countries a taste of the discipline needed in a future stage three when the new European central bank is in full force and European monetary policy is indivisible.

Also in the second phase, the first President of the European central bank should be chosen from the major hard currency country—Germany—and the first Deputy President should be chosen from the traditional money center—the United Kingdom. The new Council of the European central bank should consist of the 6-member Executive Board plus 4 voting members chosen annually on a rotating basis from among the 12 Governors of member central banks. The Council of the European central bank should come into being two years after phase two begins, or on January 1, 1996.

The Council of the European central bank should formulate European monetary policy, and the new central bank's Executive Board should have the centralized powers sufficient to fully implement these monetary policy decisions. Taking a lesson from the history of the too long delayed centralization of power in the Federal Reserve Board of Governors, the centralization of power in the Executive Board of the European central bank, along with its singular anti-inflation aim, should be immediate and clearly defined by legal statute. Also, the make-up of the Federal Reserve System's Federal Open Market Committee (FOMC) provides a good model for the Council of the new central bank. (The FOMC is the key Federal Reserve policy-making body in charge of open market operations, which is the Federal Reserve Systems' primary tool.) Specifically, in order to preserve a "two-tier" system, the Council of the European central bank should involve all 12 Governors of the EC member country central banks (though only 4 might actually vote), just as all 12 district Reserve Bank Presidents participate in each FOMC meeting (though only 5 actually vote).

CHAPTER 11

Conclusions

The primary conclusion of this analysis of contemporary Fed money management and related financial developments is that the monetary authorities should look ahead to the 1990s with only one long-term objective in mind—to curtail inflationary pressures. Following the lead of Congressman Stephen Neal (Democrat—North Carolina), perhaps this ideal Fed aim should be included in new legislation. Fortunately, the Federal Reserve System has developed the tools and techniques for an effective anti-inflationary monetary policy. However, some shortening of the Fed's currently unwieldy list of intermediate policy indicators may be called for in the 1990s.

During the 1980s, U.S. monetary policy clearly bested fiscal policy as the government's most effective economic weapon. Accordingly, the Fed Chairman has become at times the second most powerful person in our government. The Federal Reserve System, though still accountable to the legislative branch, has gained an appropriately large measure of political independence. As a rule, the greater the degree of independence of a country's central bank from partisan political influence, the greater the soundness of its currency.

Some have wrongly characterized Federal Reserve policymakers as resembling a religious order or priesthood that meets secretly in a temple and somehow conspires against the good of society.[1] But a more apt characterization of the Federal Reserve as an institution is judical, not religious. The Fed is, at its core, the Supreme Court of the U.S. finance. It is both the lender and the macro-policymaker of last resort. The central bank is to financial and economic policy what the Supreme Court is to law. Both of these institutions, which are appointive rather than elective, are critically important to the success of our political and economic systems; however, in order to continue to command public respect they must each show continuity, stability, and a measure of predictability in their actions. Ideally, the Fed should consist of competent professionals who rise above partisan politics in making judgments about the appropriate degree of monetary restraint required to achieve sustained, noninflationary economic growth.[2] At the same time, however, Fed officials, like the Supreme Court Justices, can never be oblivious to the myriad of political pressures that lurk about them.

The best Fed leaders, not unlike the most influential among those serving on the Supreme Court, are cool-headed and highly professional in analyzing problems and crafting solutions to them. They recognize that any monetary course of action, just as any legal decision handed down, will inevitably help some and hurt others. But central bankers must try to gain the high ground of consistency and objectivity in deciding on the appropriate course of policy action that is best for the common good. As in the case of the increasingly intense scrutiny of Supreme Court nominees,

Presidential policy advisers and Congress should launch an upgrading effort by redoubling their efforts to choose high-quality (professional and experienced) nominees for all the membership slots on the Federal Reserve Board. Currently, only the Fed Chairman position gets adequate scrutiny.

The ideal outcome would be for Fed policymakers to reconcile their primary objective of stabilizing inflationary pressures with a secondary countercyclical objective of achieving acceptable and sustained economic growth. Of course, this job is made more difficult by the fact that other forces besides monetary policy may affect the latter objective. Former Fed Chairman Paul Volcker has observed that the risk of an economic downturn can be laid to "massive imbalances domestically and internationally, low savings, sluggish investment, unsustainable dependence on foreign capital, and slow productivity growth."[3]

From early 1988 through early 1990, the Greenspan Fed attempted a delicate balancing act at a time of near full employment and still undesirably high price pressures, by experimenting with a soft-landing policy approach. Specifically, the Greenspan Fed attempted to nudge real GNP growth on to a downward glide path that leveled out. At a pace that was slightly but not too far below the economy's longer-term potential real growth path (estimated at about 2½% per year). Needless to say, the Fed faced a difficult task in keeping the economy poised in this no man's land between expansion and contraction, while encouraging an orderly unwinding of the financial excesses of the 1980s. The Fed's soft-landing experiment was brought into question in the second half of 1990, however, when an intensifying bank-induced credit squeeze, Gulf War fears, and a related oil price shock helped push the economy into recession.

In pursuit of the goal of reducing inflationary pressures, the Volcker Fed (1979–87) tightened aggressively in the early 1980s to conquer soaring two-digit price pressures and to shatter deeply ingrained inflationary expectations. The initially harsh outcome of this Fed anti-inflation effort was to help contribute to the deepest recession in 1981–82 since the Great Depression. But the backs of inflation and, most important, of inflationary psychology were broken. This helped set the stage for the longest U.S. peacetime economic expansion on record.

Most important, the Fed should avoid other more politically appealing objectives such as single mindedly attempting to reduce the unemployment rate. In the 1970s, these excessively stimulative Fed efforts to push the unemployment rate lower brought about mounting demand pressures on labor and capital resources and accelerating price pressures. Even more dangerously, this Fed preoccupation with reducing the unemployment rate created an easy money environment that fostered an outbreak of mounting consumer and business inflation psychology and escalating worker wage demands. This explosive condition of soaring inflationary expectations can usually be defused only by a Fed dose of extremely aggressive monetary restraint and a deep recession, as was the case in 1981–82.

The 1980s has seen the rapidly evolving forces of deregulation, financial innovation, and increased international integration. Against this unsettled background, Fed officials have become increasingly uncertain over the relationship between money and economic activity. As a result, Chairman Greenspan and his fellow monetary authorities began to focus directly on measures of inflation and economic activity and have de-emphasized the role of money as an intermediate policy target except when sluggish monetary growth appeared to be a symptom of intensifying bank loan stringency. Indeed, in contrast with the Volcker Fed which focused primarily on the monetary aggregates as intermediate policy targets, the Greenspan Fed has cast the net wide to encompass a host of intermediate policy variables, including, in addition to the monetary and credit aggregates, quarterly real GNP growth, monthly industrial production, employment, corporate purchasing managers' index, the balance of inventory stocks in relation to sales, unfilled orders, and resource utilization rates. In addition, the Fed scrutinized wage pressures, commodity prices, the foreign exchange value of the dollar, bond yields, equity prices, and the spread between short- and long-term interest rates.

Unfortunately, Greenspan Fed officials have sometimes found appropriately timed policy shifts more difficult, owing to the fact that such a wide array of intermediate policy variables often gave off conflicting or misleading signals. Moreover, while it officially recognized the unusual bank-induced credit crunch as early as the July 2–3, 1990, FOMC meeting, the Greenspan Fed failed to give adequate weight to this major economic depressant, perhaps because they paid too little attention to anecdotal evidence or were trying to watch too many other signals. These problems were compounded by the fact that Chairman Greenspan may at times have been too democratic in his leadership approach leading to periodic policy paralysis, policy leaks, a deepening split between policy hawks and doves, and sometimes unclear Fed communications with the domestic and foreign financial markets.

As a prescription for the 1990s, future Fed Chairmen should be effective communicators, decisive policymakers, and intellectually persuasive advocates, both inside and outside Fed policymaking circles. Among the brightest and the best contemporary Chairmen have been Eccles, Martin, Volcker, and Greenspan. However, future Fed Chairmen would be well-advised to whittle down the Greenspan Fed's currently unmanageable list of intermediate policy indicators. A short list of such intermediate indicators on which Fed officials should focus most of their attention might include the credit aggregate (domestic nonfinancial debt), the average level of interest rates on 1 to 10 year government securities (representing the average cost of credit), the spread between the Federal funds rate and the 30-year Treasury bond yield and the foreign exchange value of the dollar.

In this way, Fed policymakers can maintain a healthy balance between domestic and foreign intermediate policy indicators. On the domestic side, the monetary authorities might appropriately focus on the availability and cost of credit (both bank and nonbank). In addition, to help determine the impact of Fed policy shifts on bond investor inflationary expectations another useful intermediate policy indicator would be the spread between short- and long-term interest rates.

The growth of the credit aggregate moved closely in line with nominal GNP growth during the 1972–81 period as evidenced by the fact that the average annual increase in the velocity of credit, GNP/Credit, was a negligible .06%. However, owing mainly to an explosion in government debt and the massive substitution of debt for equity in the business sector, credit velocity declined at an annual average 3.6% pace during the abnormal 1982–89 period. Fortunately, the relationship between credit and nominal GNP growth appears to be returning to normal, as the 1990s begin (see Exhibit 11.1).

On the international side, movements in the dollar might serve as a good intermediate policy indicator for Fed adjustments in reserve pressures. Specifically, Fed tightening moves that are convincingly anti-inflationary will be reflected, other things being equal, in a stronger dollar;

Exhibit 11.1. Velocity of Credit (domestic nonfinancial debt)

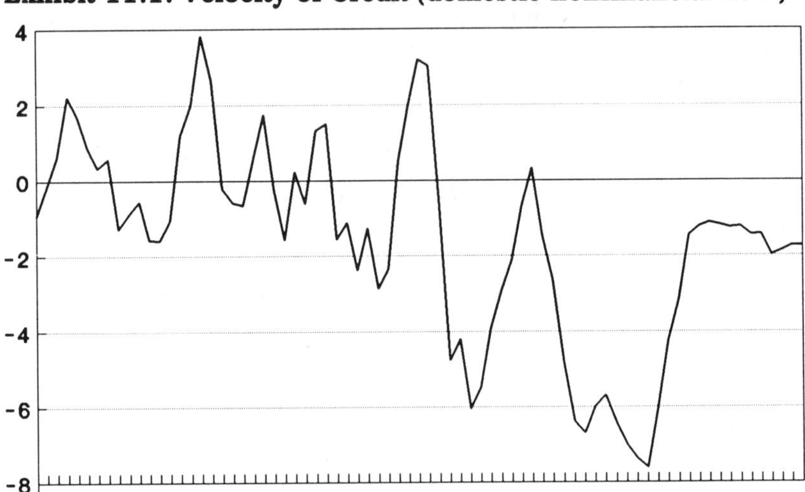

conversely, excessive Fed ease will be evidenced by a declining dollar.

As the means to achieve its primary objectives, the Fed uses two primary policy tools—open market operations and the discount rate. Thus, if inflationary pressures are accelerating at a time of high labor and capital utilization rates, the monetary authorities will move to tighen reserve pressures through open market operations and to push the Federal funds rate and other money market rates higher. In order to avoid cumulative policy errors at a time of unusual uncertainty concerning monetary and economic relationships, the Greenspan Fed has preferred, in contrast with the more dramatic bent of the preceding Volcker Fed, to make small and frequent adjustments in its policy stance that could be easily reversed if necessary. However, Fed policymakers may decide that their efforts to reduce inflationary pressures (or stimulate economic growth) require a separate publicly emphasized "exclamation point"; in this case, the Fed will use its second policy tool—a discount rate hike (or reduction). Both policy tools were used during the period from March 1988 through February 1989, when the Fed acted in response to accelerating inflationary pressures, at a time of high rates of resource utilization, to tighten its policy stance in small and frequent steps through open market operations, backed up by two highly visible half point discount rate increases in August 1988 and February 1989. (Both policy tools—along with a cut in reserve requirements—were also used in the second half of 1990 and early 1991 at a time when the Fed was moving in the opposite direction to ease its policy stance to fight the recession.)

As Fed tightening moves push short-term rates up more sharply than long-term rates, the yield curve will flatten (or even become inverted), thus squeezing bank profit margins and reducing incentive to lend to consumer and business borrowers. With funds becoming scarcer and more costly, spending will be curtailed and economic activity will slow, eventually resulting in a reduction in inflationary pressures.

It is important to note that because of the deregulation of interest rates and foreign exchange rates as well as the greater integration of world financial markets, the channels of monetary policy influence have changed. For example, the elimination of deposit interest rate ceilings and the emergence of secondary mortgage markets have weakened the depressing impact of tighter monetary policy on housing activity. But at the same time, it appears that the rising indebtedness of corporations in the 1980s may have made business spending more sensitive to interest rate fluctuations. Moreover, the increased openness of the U.S. economy may have made the exchange rate a more important channel of monetary policy influence. Certainly a strong dollar loomed large as a cyclical influence when it helped produce a huge trade deficit (by making exports more expensive and imports less expensive) that nearly brought the U.S. economy to its knees in 1986.

Fed policymakers must remain independent of undue political influences. However, it must be remembered that the Fed is a creature of Congress and responsible to the people through Congress; the Fed is thus independent within government, rather than independent of government. Former Fed Chairman Volcker has stated that "[a]n effective central bank must be a strong central bank, with substantial autonomy in its operations and with insulation from partisan and passing political pressures." However, this can not imply isolation since "a central bank operating in an open democratic society will need to develop and sustain its basic policies within some broad range of public understanding and acceptability."[4]

Populist and liberal politicians like to blame the Fed for all of society's ills. But it should be emphasized that the age-old struggle between the "haves" and "have nots" is best addressed not through monetary policy but through the redistributive powers of fiscal tax and spending policies. Actually, a new bout of fiscal policy activism in the 1990s could operate to complicate the Fed's dominant policy role established in the 1980s. Indeed, monetary policy could be at times subordinated to fiscal policy shifts, as in the Fed's easing step on October 29, 1990.

Nevertheless, Fed officials should be free to pursue, over the long term, their appropriate primary objective of curtailing inflationary pressures, thereby setting the stage for sustained economic growth. Of course, the Fed's anti-inflation strategy may be made more difficult at times of supply shocks, as in August 1990, when the sudden move by Iraq to invade Kuwait led to temporary fears of an interruption of Persian Gulf oil supplies. The resulting surge in oil prices triggered renewed fears of inflation and sharply rising interest rates. Unfortunately, this uncertainty and related decline in consumer confidence came at a time when the U.S. economy already seemed to be on the verge of a recession.

Contributing importantly to the emerging weakness in economic activity in 1990 was a bank-induced or silent credit squeeze. A unique combination of factors contributed to this bank lending restraint, including tougher capital standards, overzealous bank examiners, declining commercial and residential real estate prices in major regions of the country. These developments reflected in part the huge S&L crisis, bad loan experience, the downgrading of bank debt by credit rating agencies and concerns over a potential weakening in economic activity. In these circumstances, many banks in the affected regions have been reevaluating all their customer relationships. These banks have at a minimum asked borrowers for more collateral or other assurances, and in some cases banks have cut back on, or even completely terminated, certain borrowers' credit lines.

This silent or grassroots credit tightening was unusual in the sense that it was bank-induced rather than Fed-induced; it emerged from the grassroots or "bottom up" rather than the monetary policy level or "top down." This new version of a credit drought was sudden, arbitrary, and unpredictable. Whatever its origin, this bank-induced loan squeeze posed a dangerously depressing threat to already sluggish economic activity at that time. This threatened a prolonged period of bank loan stringency accompanied by the deflation of corporate assets, real estate, stock, and other financial assets. The Fed's July 1990 easing step through open market operations and its December 1990 reserve requirement cut were aimed specifically at countering the bank-induced credit squeeze.

A new and important influence on U.S. long-term interest rates that is largely independent of Fed actions is the growing integration of global financial markets. In early 1990, for instance, there was a surge in German bond rates reflecting prospects that a united Germany and a reformed Eastern Europe would sharply boost investment and growth, producing a related surge in public and private credit demands relative to supply. This rise in German bond rates helped push U.S. longer-term rates sharply higher. Adding to global credit demands are the mounting post-Persian Gulf War rebuilding costs in the Middle East. The growing influence of foreign interest rates on U.S. long-term rates is likely to persist in the 1990s.

The upshot is that Fed policymakers can still control U.S. short-term rates and thereby influence economic activity in the short run and U.S. inflationary pressures in the long run; but the influence of the monetary authorities on longer-term U.S. interest rates has been rendered less exact in the 1990s by international influences. This highlights the need for greater international policy cooperation and coordination and adds to the sense of urgency in designing new central banking arrangements appropriate for European monetary union.

Notes

Preface

[1]Paul Volcker, *Statement before the U.S. Congress, Joint Economic Committee* (June 14, 1982), p. 2.

Introduction

[1]A senior Fed staff member has stated:

> Realistically, policy cannot afford to lose any information about the complex relationships in the economy. Signals from financial and foreign exchange markets and from the domestic economy and foreign economies, all need to be filtered for clues about where the economy and the price level are headed relative to the objectives for policy. Casting the net wide is especially important when the underlying relationships among financial and economic

variables seem to be evolving in ways that are not easy to predict.

See: Donald L. Kohn, "Policy Targets and Operating Procedures in the 1990s," in *Monetary Policy Issues in the 1990s*, A Symposium Sponsored by the Federal Reserve Bank of Kansas City (Jackson Hole, Wyoming, August 30–September 1, 1989), p. 139.

Chapter 1

[1]Under the terms of the Banking Act of 1935, a new and strengthened Federal Open Market Committee (FOMC) was established to oversee Federal Reserve open market operations. The newly constituted FOMC, which was to become the key policy-making body of the Federal Reserve System, was comprised of the seven members of the Board of Governors plus five voting representatives of the Federal Reserve banks. Initially, the FOMC was to meet at least four times a year at the request of either the Chairman of the Board of Governors or any three Committee members. Furthermore, the Banking Act of 1935 required for the first time that the new FOMC maintain an accurate record of its transactions and of the votes cast on every open market policy issue. Further, the Banking Act of 1935 provided that the Federal Reserve Board submit to the Congress annually a full report of all such decisions.

[2]The 5 voting Reserve Bank Presidents include the New York Reserve Bank President who has a permanent vote on the FOMC (as Vice Chairman of the FOMC) and 4 additional voting Reserve Bank Presidents chosen from among the remaining 11 Reserve Banks on a rotating basis. The rotation is for a one-year term (currently changing each year on January 1): one representative, as originally stipulated by the Banking Act of 1935 (section 12A), is elected annually from the

Board of Directors of the Federal Reserve Banks of Boston, Philadelphia, and Richmond; one by the Board of Directors of the Federal Reserve Banks of Cleveland and Chicago; one by the Board of Directors of the Federal Reserve Banks of Atlanta, Dallas, and St. Louis, and one by the Board of Directors of the Federal Reserve Bank of Minneapolis, Kansas City, and San Francisco.

[3]*See* Fed Governor David Mullins' remarks to the American Bankers Association on October 21, 1990.

[4]*See* Dallas Reserve Bank President Robert Boykin's remarks to a Pension Fund Conference on Real Estate Investment on November 6, 1990.

[5]An informative look at the agenda and inner workings of a typical FOMC meeting can be found in: Ann-Marie Meulendyke, *U.S. Monetary Policy and Financial Markets* (New York: Federal Reserve Bank of New York, 1989), pp. 106–22.

[6]In Congressional testimony on November 28, 1990, Fed Chairman Greenspan became the first top Washington policy official to suggest that real economic activity was actually contracting in the final quarter of 1990. Chairman Greenspan noted that the "downturn" (he said it was too early to tell whether the slide would last long enough to amount to a recession) was mainly caused by three factors. He stated that "a significant part or even a major part" of the decline was related to the Middle East crisis. The Fed Chairman cited two factors in this connection, including both rising oil prices and "the enormous uncertainty about how and when the tensions in the Persian Gulf will be resolved." Chairman Greenspan noted that "there is no policy initiative that can in the end prevent the transfer of wealth and cut in our standard of living that stems-from higher prices for imported oil." A third factor

serving to depress the economy is, according to Chairman Greenspan, the tightening of credit by banks. The Fed Chairman said he had considerable "anecdotal evidence," though little hard data, that the bank-induced credit crunch had worsened since summer.

[7]As might have been expected, the organization of the 12 Federal Reserve districts and the choice of Federal Reserve cities was not entirely free of politics. For example, Cincinnati and Pittsburgh were rejected as Federal Reserve cities in favor of Cleveland, hometown of President Wilson's influential Secretary of War, Newton D. Baker. Similarly, Baltimore lost to Richmond, capital of Representative (later Senator) Carter Glass's home state of Virginia. Although the deliniation of the boundaries of Federal Reserve districts at least seemed a reasonable representation of the nation's primary economic regions at that time, there was one notable exception—Missouri. While dozens of other states fought for the honor and lost, Missouri won the jackpot of 2 Federal Reserve cities—St. Louis and Kansas City. It was no coincidence that the Speaker of the House of Representatives, Champ Clark, was from Missouri.

See: William Greider, *Secrets of the Temple: How the Federal Reserve System Runs the Country* (New York: Simon & Schuster, 1987), p. 292.

[8]Reserve requirements are another Federal Reserve policy tool. The Federal Reserve Act of 1913 lowered reserve requirements and provided that banks hold all reserves either as vault cash or deposits at district Reserve Banks.

Subsequently, the Banking Act of 1935 gave the Board of Governors authority, within prescribed limits, to set minimum ratios for the reserves that member banks must hold against their demand and time deposits. From 1935 through 1979, the Federal Reserve Board actively used reserve requirement adjustments as a policy tool. When the Board of Governors engages in a *restrictive* action to increase required reserve ratios, the amount of banking system deposits that a given supply of reserves can support is reduced. Conversely, when the Board of Governors takes *expansive* action to reduce required reserve ratios, the volume of liabilities and credit that the banking system can support on a given reserve supply is increased. This can be seen in the conventional statement of the reserve-deposit multiplier:

$$D^* = \mathrm{R} \cdot \frac{l}{r} = \frac{R}{r}$$

where D^* = the maximum deposit level the banking system can support
R = total reserves
r = the legal ratio of required reserves to deposits

Perhaps the most insightful contemporary analysis of reserve requirements as a policy tool was made by Professor Warren L. Smith in the mid-1960s. He concluded, most appropriately, that there appear to be few if any circumstances in normal times when reserve requirement changes are clearly superior to open market operations as a means of disciplining money and credit growth. He noted that although reserve requirement changes have "announcement effects," they can be produced more effectively by other methods. In addition, he noted that it is not certain that reserve requirement changes affect business conditions more promptly than open market operations. Finally, in view of the superior administrative efficiency of open market operations, together with the unpopularity among banks of frequent two-way adjustments of reserve requirements, "there is much to be said for relying exclusively on open market operations under normal circumstances."

The Depository Institutions Deregulation and Monetary Control Act of 1980 (MCA) imposed uniform reserve requirements across all depository institutions holding transaction accounts. Commercial banks and other depository institutions accepting accounts against which third-party payments can be made must maintain a percentage of these deposits as reserves in the form of either cash held in their vaults or deposits at their district Federal Reserve Banks (*see* Appendix F). The MCA also specified a schedule for implementing and subsequently reducing the new reserve requirements. The MCA gave the Board of Governors of the Federal Reserve authority to alter reserve requirements without regard to the designated phase-in schedule if necessary for the successful execution of monetary policy; but the monetary authorities chose not to exercise this authority during the phase-in period. Indeed, the Fed made no reserve requirement adjustments for monetary policy purposes during the entire decade of the 1980s.

For a general discussion of reserve requirements as a Fed policy tool *see*: Warren L. Smith, "The General Instruments of Monetary Control," in *Readings in Money, National Income and Stabilization Policy*, eds. Warren L. Smith and Ronald L. Teigen (Homewood, IL: Irwin, 1965), pp. 231–36; Federal Reserve Board of Governors, *Federal Reserve System: Purposes and Functions*, 6th Ed. (Washington, D.C.: September 1974), pp. 78–83; and Ann-Marie Meulendyke, *U.S. Monetary Policy and Financial Markets*, p. 9.

[9]An excellent short history of the evolution of the Federal Reserve's tools and techniques in formulating and implementing monetary policy from 1913 through 1989 can be found in: Ann-Marie Meulendyke, *U.S. Monetary Policy and Financial Markets*, pp. 18–47.

See also: Robert Heller, "Implementing Monetary Policy," in *Federal Reserve Bulletin*, July 1988, pp. 419–29.

Chapter 2

[1]According to Stuart Eizenstat, President Carter's domestic policy advisor, President Carter's fateful choice of Paul Volcker as Fed Chairman was dictated largely by the financial markets. According to Eizenstat, "Volcker was selected because he was the candidate of Wall Street. This was their price, in effect. What was known about him? That he was able and bright and it was also known that he was conservative. What wasn't known was that he was going to impose some very dramatic changes."

On the morning of the same day that the White House announced the appointment of Volcker as Fed Chairman, Bert Lance, President Carter's Georgia banker friend (who had been forced to resign from his Budget Director's job in the Carter Administration because of scandals surrounding his private banking affairs), called White House aide Gerald Rafshoon and cautioned, "I don't know who the President is thinking of for Fed Chairman, but I want you to tell him something for me. He should not appoint Paul Volcker. If he appoints Volcker, he [President Carter] will be mortgaging his re-election to the Federal Reserve." *See*: William Greider, *Secrets of the Temple*, pp. 47, 570–74; *see also*, William A. Niskanen, *Reaganomics: An Insider's Account of the Policies and the People* (New York: Oxford University Press, 1988), p. 171.

[2]An excellent analysis of the sources of power of the Fed Chairman and this leader's key role in shaping the Federal Reserve System's money management techniques can be found in: Donald F. Kettl, *Leadership at the Fed* (New Haven, CT: Yale University Press, 1986), pp. 13–17.

[3]For an authoritative contemporary description of how the monetary authorities estimate the impact of market factors on bank reserve availability see: Ann-Marie Meulendyke, *U.S. Monetary Policy and Financial Markets*, pp. 124–47.

[4]The Fed's use of the yield spread as a policy guideline is grounded in a neo-Wicksellian theoretical approach. Specifically, the theories of Swedish economist Knut Wicksell (1851–1926) have led modern central bankers to consult the market price of money (i.e., interest rates) to decide whether monetary policy is on the right track. The central tenet of Wicksellian theory is to distinguish between the "bank rate" and the "natural rate" of interest. The bank rate is similar to today's Federal funds rate. The natural rate of interest is the hypothetical cost of capital that would balance savings and investment in the economy at stable prices. In the neo-Wicksellian's view, the long-term Treasury bond yield is the best approximation of the theoretical natural rate. The Wicksellian theory holds that so long as the bank rate is close to the natural rate, the rate of increase in prices will be stable or declining.

To gauge inflationary expectations and to see if they conform to movements in the yield curve, neo-Wicksellians also follow commodity prices. Thus, monetary policy may be viewed as too loose or excessively accommodative, in Wicksellian terms, whenever the Federal funds rate moves significantly below the long-term bond yield and commodity prices are rising. Conversely, monetary policy can be viewed as overly restrictive or too tight if the Federal funds rate climbs above the long-term bond yield and commodity prices are falling. Thus, following this neo-Wicksellian approach, the modern Fed's aim is to adjust the Federal funds rate in a manner that brings it roughly in line with (or slightly below) the long-term bond yield in order to achieve a stable or declining rate of inflation. For a recent discussion of neo-Wicksellian theory, *see*:

"Dr. Wicksell, We Presume," *The Economist*, April 28, 1990, pp. 84–86. *See also*: Manuel H. Johnson, "Perspectives on the Implementation of Monetary Policy," Remarks to American Enterprise Institute Conference, Washington, D.C. (November 16, 1988); and Manuel H. Johnson, "Recent Economic Developments and Indicators of Monetary Policy," Remarks to the Money Marketeers of New York University (March 15, 1988). In addition, *see* Knut Wicksell, *Value, Capital, and Rents* (Stockholm, 1893).

[5]Contemporary research has found that the spread between the commercial paper rate and Treasury bill rate appears to be the best predictor of future fluctuations in economic activity—although this predictive power has weakened recently. This particular interest rate spread is so informative in part because it contains information about default risk and in part because it seems to reflect shifts in monetary policy. Indeed, recent research has shown that the spread between the commercial paper rate and the Treasury bill rate has been related in a more "clear-cut" manner to shifts in monetary policy than to variations in default risk. (This problem with default risk may arise in part because the commercial paper rate reflects the borrowing pressures of primarily high-quality borrowers—approximately 85% of commercial paper borrowers are of the highest credit quality—rather than more accurately reflecting the higher rates paid by lesser rated borrowers, especially at times of rising default risks.) The commercial paper–Treasury bill rate spread also predicts well because it registers developments in both the nonmonetary and monetary sectors of the economy. *See*: Ben S. Bernanke, "On the Predictive Power of Interest Rates and Interest Rate Spreads," *New England Economic Review*, November/December 1990, pp. 51–66.

[6]For an excellent contemporary analysis of the channels of monetary policy and how it effects economic activity

see: Benjamin M. Friedman, "Changing Effects of Monetary Policy on Real Economic Activity," in *Monetary Policy Issues in the 1990s*, A Symposium sponsored by the Federal Reserve Bank of Kansas City (Jackson Hole, Wyoming, August 30–September 1, 1989), pp. 55–111. Another outstanding analysis of the channels by which monetary policy influences economic activity can be found in Eileen Mauskopf, "The Transmission Channels of Monetary Policy: How Have They Changed?," *Federal Reserve Bulletin* (December 1990), pp. 985–1008. This latter study confirms Benjamin Friedman's results that the effect of monetary policy on housing activity (owing to the development of a secondary mortgage market and the removal of bank time deposit rate ceilings) was weakened in the 1980s, relative to the 1960s and 1970s, and that exchange rates have become a more important channel of monetary policy influences.

Chapter 3

[1]This chapter represents an expanded and updated version of my article, "Grading Greenspan," *The International Economy*, April/May 1990, pp. 74–77.

[2]For an excellent discussion of economic forecasting opportunities and limitations, *see*: Alan Greenspan, "Economic Forecasting in the Private and Public Sector," *Business Economics*, January 1991, pp. 52–55.

[3]The publisher of *Barron's*, Robert M. Bleiberg, has commented, "To be a central banker, one needn't be a flim-flam man, but it helps," See: *Barron's*, July 16, 1990, p. 12.

[4]Philosopher Ayn Rand was a Russian emigre who came to the United States in 1926 and became one of the foremost proponents of capitalism. Alan Greenspan was a member of her inner circle of supporters. This close knit group of disciples was called "the children" or the "class of '43." Greenspan's former

wife, Joan Mitchell, was also in this inner circle as was Mitchell's girlhood friend Barbara Branden and her husband Nathaniel Branden, who was one of the chief communicators of Ayn Rand's ideas. Greenspan contributed articles and reviews to Ayn Rand's newsletter, *The Objectivist Newsletter*. Greenspan also contributed an article to: Ayn Rand, *Capitalism: The Unknown Ideal* (New York: New American Library, 1966), which was a collection of essays on the moral aspects of capitalism. For additional recent information on Ayn Rand, *see*: Mimi Gladstein, *The Ayn Rand Companion* (Westport, CT: Glenwood Press, 1984); Barbara Brandon, *The Passion of Ayn Rand* (Garden City, NY: Doubleday, 1986); and Nathaniel Branden, *Judgment Day: My Years With Ayn Rand* (Boston: Houghton Mifflin, 1989).

[5]Former Reagan Administration domestic policy adviser Martin Anderson has stated that "Alan Greenspan has probably been a key player in more Republican presidential campaigns [including President Reagan's campaign], and Republican party platforms and Republican Administrations, than any other economist in the country." *See*: Martin Anderson, *Revolution* (New York: Harcourt Brace Jovanovich, 1988).

[6]A discussion of the fact that financial market participants considered the Fed's July 13 easing step to be at least partly political can be found in *Barron's*, July 16, 1990, p. 44.

[7]*See*: Marriner S. Eccles, "The Lessons of Monetary Experience," *Essays in Honor of Irving Fisher* (New York: Farrar and Rinehart, 1937).

[8]*See*: Sidney Hyman, *Marriner S. Eccles, Private Entrepreneur and Public Servant* (Stanford, CA: Stanford University Graduate School of Business, 1976); and *see also* Marriner S. Eccles, *Beckoning Frontiers* (New York: Knopf, 1951). For a knowledgable discus-

sion of the Treasury-Fed Accord *see*: Allan Sproul, "The Accord-A Landmark in the First Fifty years of the Federal Reserve System," in *Selected Papers of Allan Sproul*, ed. Lawrence S. Ritter (New York: Federal Reserve Bank of New York, 1980), pp. 51–73.

[9]Burns' high political visibility was damaging to his Fed Chairmanship. Perhaps most damaging to Burns were two totally unsubstantiated stories that he could not shake despite repeated denials. In the July 1974 issue of *Fortune*, Sanford Rose cited an incident (refuted by virtually everyone directly involved) in which Burns was supposed to have angrily stalked out of an FOMC meeting in 1972, after his aggressive easing initiatives were rejected by his fellow policymakers. He then supposedly returned saying, "I have just talked to the White House." This statement, according to the unsubstantiated tale, supposedly electrified the FOMC and caused them to agree to Burns' desires to ease policy more aggressively than had been originally contemplated. (Former Fed Governors Brimmer and Holland, among others, have refuted this story.) In another incident, earlier in 1971, Nixon staff assistant Charles Colson apparently played a dirty trick on Burns. Specifically, Colson leaked to the *Wall Street Journal* the story that Fed Chairman Burns had proposed, in the midst of his public campaign for wage and price controls, an increase in his own Fed Chairman's salary to the level of cabinet members. Burns looked on this unfounded pay raise leak as being vicious and mean.

Apart from these unsubstantiated stories, perhaps Burns' most controversial political decision was to become head of Nixon's interest and dividends committee in 1971. This position posed a clear conflict of interest. Acting in this capacity, Burns tried to limit the more restrictive inclinations of his fellow Fed policymakers in order to keep interest rates from rising. Apparently, Burns decided to serve as head of the interest and dividends committee to keep Treasury Secretary Connelly from getting this job. In any case, it unquestionably compromised Burn's objectivity. *See*: Donald F. Kettl, *Leadership at the Fed*, pp. 127–28; Andrew F. Brimmer, *Politics and Monetary Policy: The Federal Reserve and the Nixon White House*, a paper presented to the Eastern Economic Association, March 16, 1984; and John T. Woolley, *Monetary Politics: The Federal Reserve and the Politics of Monetary Policy* (Cambridge: Cambridge University Press, 1984), pp. 161–66.

[10]At his first Federal Reserve Board meeting in 1978, Chairman Miller placed a small sign on the large rectangular table around which the Board members were seated. The sign stated "Thank You for Not Smoking." His fellow Board members were not amused. *See*: William Greider, *Secrets of the Temple*, p. 66.

[11]*See*: Cary Reich, "Inside the Fed," *Institutional Investor*, May 1984, p. 139.

[12]The term "Saturday Night Special" was coined in the discussion of Volcker's surprise October 6, 1979, actions in: William C. Melton, *Inside the Fed: Making Monetary Policy* (Homewood, IL.: Dow Jones-Irwin, 1985), p. 43. See also, William R. Neikirk, *Volcker: Portrait of the Money Man* (New York and Chicago: Congdon & Weed, 1987), pp. 31–42.

Chapter 4

[1]For a discussion of this incident, *see*: William Greider, *Secrets of the Temple*, pp. 700–01; William R. Neikirk, *Volcker*, pp. 190–193; Rowland Evans and Robert Novak, "Backstage at the Fed," *Washington Post*, March 17, 1986; Paul Blustein and Allan Murray, "Vote

on Discount Rate Cut Was a Defeat for Volcker By Reagan Appointee," *Wall Street Journal*, March 18, 1986; and John M. Berry, "Board Discount Rate Cut Followed Tortuous Trail," *Washington Post*, March 19, 1986. This account is also based on conversations with a participant at the February 24, 1986, meeting.

[2]In an examination of FOMC decisions during the 1960s and 1970s, political scientist John T. Woolley found that 90% of the dissents cast by Reserve Bank presidents were in favor of tighter money. In contrast, the members of the Board of Governors cast 60% of their dissents in favor of an easier policy. On balance, Reserve Bank Presidents seemed to persist more doggedly in the anti-inflation fight than the politically sensitive Board members located in Washington.

Woolley also found that Fed Governors appointed by Democrats tended to be slightly more inclined toward easier money than Governors appointed by Republicans. Specifically, only 13.8% of Fed Governors appointed by Democrats dissented in favor of firmer policy while a whopping 86.2% dissented in favor of easier policy. In contrast, a substantial 57.1% of governors appointed by Republicans dissented in favor of firmer policy, while 42.9% dissented in favor of easier policy. *See*: John T. Woolley, *Monetary Politics: The Federal Reserve and the Politics of Monetary Policy*, p. 63. For a somewhat more controversial analysis of the predictability of the partisan political reliability of appointees to the Federal Reserve Board of Governors, *see*: Thomas Havrilesky and John Gildea, "Packing the Board of Governors," *Challenge*, March–April 1990, pp. 52–55.

Chapter 5

[1]For an in-depth and up-to-date examination of a typical day at the New York Reserve Bank's domestic trad-

ing desk at which Federal Reserve System open market operations are carried out. *See*: Ann-Marie Meulendyke, *U.S. Monetary Policy and Financial Markets*, pp. 157–77.

[2]*See*: Peter D. Sternlight, "Monetary Policy and Open Market Operations During 1989," *Quarterly Review*, Federal Reserve Bank of New York, Spring, 1990.

Chapter 6

[1]In a broader political context, the Fed has been called "a lightning rod for groups unhappy with the state of the economy." *See*: Donald F. Kettl, *Leadership at the Fed*, p. 205.

[2]The concept of the Fed as a scapegoat was advanced in: Edward J. Kane, "External Pressure and the Operation of the Fed," in *Political Economy of International and Domestic Monetary Relations*, eds. Raymond E. Lombra and Willard E. Witte (Ames: Iowa State University Press, 1982), pp. 211–32.

[3]In 1990, Fed officials appeared a total of 40 times before Congress. The Chairman appeared 23 times before Congress, other Board members and Board staff appeared 12 times, and Reserve Bank Presidents appeared 5 times. In 1989, Fed officials appeared a total of 36 times before Congress, with the Chairman appearing 15 times, other Board members and Board staff appearing 16 times, and Reserve Bank Presidents appearing 5 times.

[4]For a discussion of the delicate political balance between the Greenspan Fed and Congress and how this relationship was affected by the proposed Hamilton legislation *see*: Paul Starobin, "Why Fed's Shades Still Closed," *National Journal*, November 25, 1989.

[5]*Ibid.*

[6]*See*: Cathy Kristiansen, "Richmond Fed's Black Battles Inflation With FOMC Vote," *Knight Ridder Money Center News Wire*, January 15, 1991.

[7]In testimony before the Joint Economic Committee in early 1982, Treasury Secretary Regan complained that, "The erratic pattern of money growth that occurred in 1980 and 1981 contributed to the onset of the current downturn." He noted that there was almost no money growth in most of 1981, but beginning in October the money growth spurted ahead. Secretary Regan further observed "They [the FOMC] don't seem to be able to be very precise about what they are doing." *See*: Donald F. Kettl, *Leadership at the Fed*, p. 181.

[8]Perhaps the best way to view Fed independence is to picture the Fed as "independent" *within* government but not *from* government. The appropriateness of Fed independence from the U.S. Treasury (*within* government) rests on the realistic assessment of history that Treasury officials seem to be inherently inflationary in their biases. (To reduce their cost of borrowing, the Treasury officials invariably press the Fed for lower interest rates.) But the Fed should *not* be independent *from* government. Without question, the Fed should be accountable to Congress. Under the Federal Reserve Act of 1913 the Fed was, after all, established as an independent agency of Congress; and Congress could change the make-up of the Federal Reserve System through new legislation any time it might choose. Moreover, the Fed should not use its independence to negate the economic goals of the President. Fed officials can exchange policy ideas in informal sessions with the President's Council of Economic Advisors, Treasury officials and the Office of Management and the Budget (OMB). *See*: George L. Bach, "Federal Reserve Organization and Policymaking," in

Readings in Money, National Income, and Stabilization Policy, eds. Warren L. Smith and Ronald L. Teigen (Homewood, IL: Irwin, 1965), pp. 238–44. Another excellent statement on Fed independence can be found in: U.S. Treasury Department, "Treasury Views on Independence of the Federal Reserve," in *The Federal Reserve and the Treasury: Answers to Questions from the Commission on Money and Credit* (Englewood Cliffs, NJ: Prentice Hall, 1963), pp. 250–52.

[9]William McChesney Martin, Jr., in particular, was always careful in framing his concept of Fed independence. In his Fed confirmation hearings, he stated "that it was intended the Federal Reserve should be independent and not responsible directly to the executive branch of the Government, but should be accountable to the Congress." He went on to argue, "I like to think of a trustee relationship to see that the Treasury does not engage in the natural temptation to depreciate the currency or engage in practices that would harm the general welfare." *See*: William McChesney Martin, Jr., U.S. Senate, Committee on Banking and Currency, *Hearings on Nomination of William McChesney Martin, Jr.* 84th Cong. 2nd sess, 1956, p. 5.

[10]Among the precedent-setting historical arrangements for Fed–White House consultation was President Roosevelt's creation, in 1938, of a Monetary and Fiscal Advisory Board, composed of the Secretary of the Treasury (Chairman), the Fed Chairman, the Director of the Budget, and the Chairman of the Advisory Committee on Natural Resources. Subsequently, during the Eisenhower Administration, Fed Chairman Martin began meeting regularly with Treasury Secretary Humphrey. Later, when Raymond J. Saulnier succeeded Arthur Burns as Chairman of the

President's Council of Economic Advisers, Saulnier lunched every two weeks at the Fed with Chairman Martin and Vice Chairman C. Canby Balderston.

In 1961, the Kennedy Administration formed the *Quadriad*, consisting of the Chairman of the President's Council of Economic Advisors (CEA), the Secretary of the Treasury, the Fed Chairman, and the Director of the Budget. This group met every two months at the call of then Chairman of the CEA, Walter Heller. *See*: Donald F. Kettl, *Leadership at the Fed*, pp. 91–93.

[11]*See*: William Greider, *Secrets of the Temple*, pp. 243–47.

[12]*See*: David M. Jones, Book Review of *Secrets of the Temple*, *America*, May 14, 1988.

Chapter 7

[1]A major shortcoming in measuring the extent of the bank-induced credit crunch has been a lack of hard evidence. One important source of information is the Federal Reserve Board's quarterly survey of senior loan officers. For example, *The October 1990 Senior Loan Officer Opinion Survey on Bank Lending Practices* noted that respondents "generally painted a picture of increased credit restraint, with agencies and branches of foreign banks reporting more tightening than domestic banks." The bank "pullback" in lending was "clearest" in commercial real estate lending, a category for which a large majority of respondents continued to raise their credit standards. Sizable shares of domestic respondents reported tightening their credit standards on nonmerger-related commercial and industrial (C&I) loans to large (about one-half), middle market (nearly one-half), and small (two-fifths) firms. Each of these figures was up noticeably from the preceding survey.

[2]In testimony on January 29, 1981 before the Senate Banking Committee, the Bush Administration's budget director, Robert Reischauer, projected that the Federal Deposit Insurance Corporation's Bank Insurance Fund, which backs $2.2 trillion in bank deposits, could run out of money in 1992. He warned that the assets of this fund were expected to drop to $4 billion by the end of 1991, down from $9 billion at the end of 1990, and $13.2 billion at the end of 1989. Budget director Reischauer recommended that the fund borrow about $11 billion from the Treasury to get it through the wave of bank failures expected during the recession and that bank deposit insurance premiums be raised to 30 cents per $100 of domestic deposits from 19.5 cents.

[3]This account is based largely on an interview with a senior bank funding officer.

[4]There has emerged a contemporary public relations boom aimed at killing rumors before they kill companies. Stopping damaging rumors is especially important for financial companies which depend on public confidence. One system for zapping rumors rests on a foundation of common sense: facts fully disclosed both inside and outside the firm; figures, and optimist rhetoric, preferably published in ads. *See*: Larry Light, "Killing a Rumor Before It Kills a Company," *Business Week*, December 24, 1990, p. 23.

[5]The initial NCNB Texas deal was considered one of the sweetest ever struck with regulators. In essence, the bad loans were transferred to the government, while NCNB Texas got all First Republicbank deposits, its choice loans, and some $2.8 billion in tax benefits that would allow NCNB Texas to operate virtually tax free for another three to five years.

Chapter 8

[1]*See*: Kevin Phillips, *The Politics of Rich and Poor: Wealth and the American Electorate in the Reagan Administration* (New York: Random House, 1990).

[2]Judith H. Dobrzynski, "The Top Two Hundred Deals," *Business Week*, January 1990, pp. 34–62.

[3]Lindley H. Clark, Jr., "De-Diversification: Aid to Productivity," *Wall Street Journal*, May 14, 1990.

[4]Thomas Boone Pickens, *Boone* (Boston: Houghton Mifflin, 1987).

[5]Alan Farnham, "What's Sparking Duracell," *Fortune*, July 16, 1990, p. 74.

[6]These figures were cited by Professor Benjamin M. Friedman at a Research Department Seminar at the International Monetary Fund's Visitors Center on March 15, 1990. *See*: "U.S. Corporate Debt Buildup Threatens Price Stability," *IMF Survey*, April 2, 1990, p. 97. For a general discussion of the dangerously mounting debt burden of the 1980s, *see* Benjamin M. Friedman, *A Day of Reckoning* (New York: Random House, 1988), pp. 99–102.

[7]George Anders and Francine Schwadel, "Wall Streeters Helped Interco Defeat Raiders But at a Heavy Price," *Wall Street Journal*, July 11, 1990.

[8]Carol J. Loomis, "The Biggest Looniest Deal Ever," *Fortune*, June 18, 1990, pp. 48–72.

[9]Marj Charlier, "Heileman Brewing Unit of Bond Corp. Acts on Huge Debt," *Wall Street Journal*, April 19, 1990.

[10]Gregory L. Miles, "This Steel Sale Seems Far from Stainless," *Business Week*, April 2, 1990, p. 36.

[11]For a fascinating inside look at the high drama of the bitterly fought takeover battle for RJR Nabisco with all its intrigue, back stabbing, deceit, high stakes, and clashes of big egos, *see*: Bryan Burrough and John Helyar, *Barbarians at the Gate* (New York: Harper & Row, 1990).

[12]For an examination of Drexel's downfall and Milken's erroneous theory that "investors obtained better returns on low-grade issues than on high-grade issues," *see*: Christopher Byron, "Drexel's Final Days," *Best of Business Quarterly*, Fall 1990, pp. 26–32; George Anders and Constance Mitchell, "Milken Sales Pitch on High-Yield Bonds Is Contradicted By Data", *Wall Street Journal*, November 20, 1990; and Carol J. Loomis, "How Drexel Rigged a Stock," *Fortune*, November 19, 1990, pp. 85–88.

Chapter 10

[1]Fulfilling the dream of French economist Jean Monet, the original six countries (Belgium, West Germany, France, Italy, Luxembourg, and the Netherlands) signed the Treaty of Rome establishing the European Economic Community in March 1957, and it went into effect on January 1, 1958. Subsequently, the United Kingdom, Ireland, and Denmark joined under the Treaties of Accession signed on January 22, 1972 and January 1, 1973. More recently, on January 1, 1981, Greece became the tenth member of the European Community. Finally, Spain and Portugal became the eleventh and twelfth members of the Community on January 1, 1986.

The institutional system of the European Community (EC) is more than a simple intergovernmental arrangement. It has special legal status and extensive powers of its own. At the same time, however, the EC is not a true federation to which national parliaments and governments are completely subordinate.

The government of the EC is composed of four principal institutions. The *Council* is composed of ministers from each of the 12 member states and is the final EC decision-making body. (The Council legislates on policy on the basis of Commission proposals.) Participants at Council meetings change according to subject matter. The senior council is composed of the 12 EC Foreign Ministers; but if the theme of a Council meeting is, for example, finance, the 12 EC finance ministers would attend the meeting. The *Commission*, consisting of 17 members appointed by agreement between member countries for four-year terms is the EC's executive body. The Commission is the only EC body that can initiate EC policy. The Council can not take decisions on specific policy issues without a Commission proposal. The Commission is responsible for implementing decisions taken by the Council. The Commission has responsibility for enforcing EC treaties and the legislation derived from them. The *European Parliament* is the EC's only directly elected body. It is composed of 518 members, elected every five years by voters in all member countries. The Parliament scrutinizes draft EC legislation, questions the Commission and the Council of Ministers on their conduct of EC affairs and debates topical issues. Most pieces of draft legislation cannot be formally adopted by the Council until they have received the Parliament's opinion. Currently, the European parliament has much less legislative authority than the national parliaments of member countries, though this relationship is changing. The European Parliament can dismiss the Commission (a power it has never used), and the EC's annual budget cannot be adopted without Parliament's agreement. The *Court of Justice* is the EC's equivalent of the U.S. Supreme Court. It interprets

Community law for national courts and rules on legal questions pertaining to EC treaties that are raised by Community institutions, member countries, companies or individuals. The *Court's* rulings are binding.

Last but not least, there is a fifth EC body called the *European Council*. This body consists of the 12 heads of state of the member EC countries. The European Council meets at least twice a year to consider EC and foreign policy issues. This body can not legislate, but it goes without saying that its opinion and advice carry considerable weight.

[2]A one-currency EMU unquestionably denies individual EC governments sovereignty over monetary policy. National governments would lose their ability to set interest rates and to steer their currency up or down. Interest rates would be set by a single European central bank; exchange rates among the 12 EC countries would be fixed irrevocably. This would bring the benefit, in the absence of exchange risk, of a lower rate of return required for EC investment and a lower cost of doing business than under the existing 12 currency system.

Against these benefits, there is the fact that national governments would no longer be able to reign over their own monetary policy in a manner that cushions their cyclical ups and downs. In particular, Germany, which has a highly praised central banking tradition with a formidable record as an inflation fighter, could be expected to view such a change cautiously—insisting on the most stringent safeguards for any new European central bank.

Mistakenly, some EMU critics also fear a loss of national fiscal sovereignty. The view that a single currency must infringe on fiscal sovereignty is simply wrong. Certainly, the loss of a national monetary policy puts a limit of sorts on national budget deficits because it forbids them to be financed through the printing press—but only a dangerously reckless government could object to that constraint on its freedom. Otherwise, a one-currency EMU could and should leave governments free to tax and spend as they see fit and to run whatever budget deficits the domestic and international capital markets are willing to finance. *See*: "An Acceptable EMU," *The Economist*, October 20, 1990, pp. 12–13.

[3]A comparison of the relative rates of increase in consumer prices in the EC countries suggests that "convergence" is really a "three tier" problem. Of course, the least difficulty in achieving convergence would be among the seven countries experiencing annual inflation rates of 5% or less (see Table below). More difficult would be the problem for the three countries with annual inflation rates of 5 to 8%. Most difficult would be the two additional countries with much higher two-digit annual rates of inflation.

Relative Rates of Increase in Consumer Prices in EC Countries in 1989

	Percentage Change
Belgium	3.8
Denmark	4.8
France	3.6
Germany	3.0
Greece	14.8
Italy	6.5
Netherlands	1.3
Spain	6.9
United Kingdom	7.7
Portugal	11.6
Luxembourg	3.9
Ireland	4.7

Source: DRI

[4]This discussion of the evolution of Federal Reserve System powers to formulate and implement monetary policy is based largely on an outstanding and highly authoritative analysis of the gradual centralization of power in the Federal Reserve Board. *See*: Ellen Dykes and Michael A. Whitehouse, "The Establishment and Evolution of the Federal Reserve Board: 1913–23," *Federal Reserve Bulletin*, April, 1989, pp. 227–43. Another excellent analysis of the evolution of Federal Reserve policy making powers, especially from 1914 to 1929, can be found in Milton Friedman and Ann Jacobson Schwartz, *A Monetary History of the United States 1867–1960* (Princeton, NJ: Princeton University Press, 1963), pp. 189–298.

Chapter 11

[1]It has been observed that the Federal Reserve's official secrecy enhanced the mystique of the institution. Officials of the Federal Reserve have "unconsciously invoked the sacred aura of their institution." A former officer of the Federal Reserve Board, describing the confidential fraternity that economists entered into when they joined the Fed staff, called it "taking the veil," the expression that describes nuns entering a convent. In a similar vein, a former Chairman of the House Banking Committee sometimes referred derisively to the Fed's senior economists instead as "the monks." Another Reserve Bank officer reportedly stated that "The [Federal Reserve] System is just like the Church." He added "It's got a pope, the Chairman, and a college of cardinals, the governors and the bank presidents; and a curia, the senior staff." *See*: William Greider, *Secrets of the Temple*, p. 54.

[2]Former Fed Chairman Volcker has observed that, "I believe the recurring difficulty in acting before inflation builds momentum could be reduced if central

banking statutes in the United States and other countries stated more explicitly that the main continuing purpose of monetary policy should be the stability of the currency." *See*: Paul A. Volcker "The Triumph of Central Banking?", *The 1990 Per Jacobsson Lecture*, September 23, 1990, p. 15.

[3]*Ibid.*, p. 6.

[4]*Ibid.*, p. 18.

Appendixes

Appendix A

THE P* CONCEPT

The Greenspan Fed envisions a direct positive long-term relationship between price pressures and monetary growth. This relationship is captured in the concept of *P**. Fed Chairman Greenspan first presented this concept officially in his July 1989 Humphrey-Hawkins Congressional testimony. This concept is based on the conventional money identity or equation of exchange:

$$M \cdot \bar{V} = P^* \cdot \bar{Q} \quad \text{or}$$

$$\frac{M \cdot \bar{V}}{\bar{Q}} = P^*$$

If the income velocity of money $(\bar{V})$ follows its long-run (1955–88) trend growth rate of about 1% per year and $(\bar{Q})$

represents the Fed staff's measure of potential real GNP (estimated on the basis of longer-term trends in productivity and labor force growth to grow at about 2½% per year), then it is possible to compute the potential rate of price increase *(P^*)* for any current actual rate of money *(M)* growth. (The Fed uses the M-2 monetary aggregate in this computation.) If P^*, during any given period of time, moves above the actual prevailing rate of price increase (see Exhibit A.1), then it can be expected that inflationary pressures will, with a time lag, show increasing tendencies. Conversely, if P^* falls below the prevailing actual rate of price increase (as has recently been the case), then inflationary pressures are likely to show moderating tendencies, again with a time lag.

In Exhibit A.1, the current price level (*P*, the solid line) is the implicit GNP deflator, which is set to 100 in 1982.

The long-run equilibrium price level given current M-2 (P^*, the dashed line) is calculated as $P^* = (\text{M-2} \cdot V^*)/Q^*$, where V^* is an estimate of the long-run value of the GNP velocity of M = 2—the mean of V2 from 1955:1 to 1988:1—and Q^* is a Federal Reserve Board staff measure of potential real GNP.

The vertical lines mark the quarters when the difference between the current price level *(P)* and the long-run equilibrium price level *(P^*)* switches sign, and thus when inflation, with a lag, tends to begin accelerating or decelerating.

Unquestionably, the P^* concept has some pitfalls. Most important, it is virtually useless in the month-to-month and quarter-to-quarter context in which Fed policy decisions are made. This is because there is short-term instability in money velocity. Therefore, about the only practical use to which the Greenspan Fed put P^* was to trot it out when the Fed sought to rationalize a policy shift made for other reasons, as was the case when this concept was used in the second half of 1989 to justify easing steps.

Another criticism of the P^* concept is that it tends to confirm price changes after the fact rather than predicting them. Thus, the P^* measure for any given date, say, June

Exhibit A.1. *P and Actual Prices**

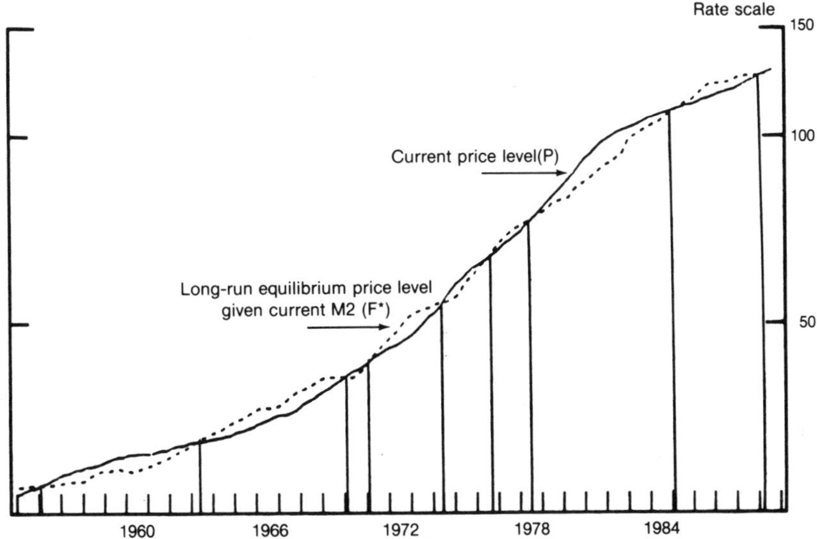

For more details, see Jeffrey J. Hallman, Richard D. Porter and David H. Small, *M2 per Unit of Potential GNP as an Anchor for the Price Level*, Staff Studies 157 (Board of Governors of the Federal Reserve System. 1989).

1979, already incorporated, in addition to the actual M-2 level at that time, the drop in productivity and the slowdown in the rate of increase of velocity in the 1980s. Of course, this is because the Fed computes the long run value of velocity *($\bar{V}$)* using data for the entire 1955–88 period, and because the Fed staff's measure of potential real GNP incorporates longer-term trends in labor force and productivity growth. (*See* Mike McNamee, "The Fed May Be Gazing at a Cracked Crystal Ball," *Business Week*, April 2, 1990, pp. 78–79).

Appendix B

Basic Policy Process and Role of Discount Rate

Through open market operations the Fed provides the lion's share of reserves necessary to support the expansion in money and credit. The immediate objective of Fed open market operations is to control the cost and availability of bank reserves; the ultimate objective of Fed open market operations is to influence economic activity. In order to increase the supply of reserves, the Fed will buy U.S. government securities or other assets, either on a temporary basis in the form of System repurchase agreements (RPs) or on a permanent basis in the form of outright purchases. Conversely, the Fed reduces the supply of reserves by selling U.S. government securities or other assets. Of course, one dollar's worth of these "high-powered" reserves created out of thin air by Fed open market purchases will produce several dollars worth of credit and deposit expansion in the banking system.

Additional reserves may be supplied temporarily through the Fed's discount window (actually each of the 12 district Reserve Banks have their own discount windows through which depository institutions in each respective district may borrow). There are three basic types of discount window borrowings: *Adjustment borrowings* represent the typical bank use of the discount window to meet temporary liquidity needs. These temporary liquidity needs might stem from unexpected deposit outflows or loan demands, from the threat of an overdraft in the bank's reserve account at the Fed, or from special circumstances such as a Fed wire breakdown. *Seasonal borrowings* are discount window borrowings for as long as several weeks by smaller banks in tourist or farming areas. Banks in tourist areas may, for example, face the reserve drain from heavy seasonal outflows of currency in circulation. Similarly, banks in farming areas face heavy seasonal loan demands for crop planting purposes. Within each year, seasonal borrowings tend to rise from a low in January to a peak in August (*see* Exhibit B.1). (Effective January 1, 1992, the Fed will charge a "market-related" rate of interest on discount credit that the Fed extends to banks under its seasonal credit program.) *Extended credit* (sometimes labeled by the Fed as special situation borrowings immediately prior to being officially classified as extended credit) are longer-term discount window borrowings by depository institutions in financial difficulty. As a result, these extended credit, or basically lender-of-last-resort borrowings should be subtracted from total discount window borrowings in measuring Fed-induced changes in reserve pressures.

When the monetary officials seek to tighten reserve pressures, they operate through open market operations to sell U.S. government securities in order to reduce the availability of bank reserves. This forces banks to temporarily increase their adjustment borrowings at the Fed discount

Exhibit B.1. Intrayear Pattern of Seasonal Borrowings (weekly 1990)

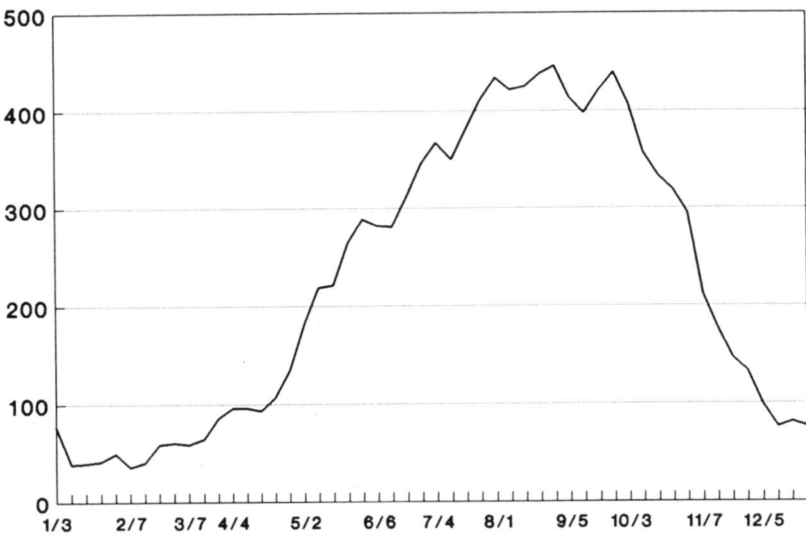

Source: Federal Reserve

window. But there is strict Fed surveillance of bank discount window borrowings (as to purpose as well as frequency and amount), and there is also a bank tradition against discount window borrowings (since repeated use of the discount window can be viewed as a sign of a bank's financial weakness). As a result of these discount window restraints, and especially Fed officials' continuous admonitions that banks should be reluctant to rely on discount window advances, banks temporarily borrowing funds at the Fed discount window will promptly try to extricate themselves by falling back on other funds sources such as Federal funds, RPs, CDs, or Eurodollars. This, in turn, will exert upward pressure on rates on these alternative sources of loanable funds. (Of course, none of these alternative sources of loanable funds represent a net addition to reserves for the banking system as a whole.)

ROLE OF DISCOUNT RATE

In a modification of its traditional confirming role, the Greenspan Fed considers discount rate adjustments (which are proposed by the Board of Directors of one or more district Reserve Banks for approval by a majority vote of the Board of Governors in Washington) as largely separate from Fed changes in reserve pressures and money market rates effected through open market operations. To a greater extent than in the past, the Greenspan Fed considers discount rate increases as a highly public exclamation point used to underscore Fed resolve to fight inflation (or in the case of discount rate declines, to fight economic weakness). (So far, the Greenspan Fed has increased the discount rate three times, posting half percentage point hikes in September 1987, August 1988 and February 1989 and has lowered it once on December 18, 1990.)

The Greenspan Fed's use of the discount rate as a separate policy tool (more as a substitute for, rather than as a complement to, open market operations) was demonstrated at the time of the February 1989 discount rate hike. Specifically, on February 23, 1989, the day before the discount rate increase, Fed policymakers tightened reserve pressures through open market operations. However, Fed officials reversed this tightening move by means of an easing step through open market operations the very next day when the substitute means of tightening in the form of the discount rate increase was agreed on. The Greenspan Fed also viewed adjustment in pressures on bank reserve positions through open market operations and discount rate adjustments as *separate* policy tools when constrasting easing steps were agreed on at the December 18, 1990, FOMC meeting. Specifically, the FOMC decided at this meeting to ease reserve pressure, consistent with a decline in the Federal funds rate to 7% from 7¼%. Separately, the Fed Board decided to cut the discount rate to 6½% from 7%. Indeed, there was some controversy at the December 18, 1990,

FOMC meeting as to whether a discount rate cut should automatically "pass through" to a partial or fully equivalent decline in the Federal funds rate, or whether, alternatively, the FOMC should formally vote on the specific decline in the Federal funds rate. In contrast, Fed policymakers have traditionally used discount rate adjustments primarily as a follow-up move to confirm changes in reserve availability and money market rates effected earlier through open market operations.

Under certain circumstances, the discount rate may entirely replace open market operations as the Federal Reserve's primary policy tool. As in 1986, for example, Fed discount rate adjustments can be used actively in easing moves to push the Federal funds rate and other money market rates lower. This active Fed of the discount rate will take place in circumstances of prolonged ease in which earlier Fed moves to ease reserve pressures through open market operations have already resulted in a decline in the Fed's target level of adjustment and seasonal discount window borrowings to frictional or minimal levels. In 1986, the Fed Board lowered the discount rate in four one-half percentage point steps, to 5½% from 7½%, and this decline was closely paralleled by a decline in the Federal funds rate to 6% from about 8%.

Appendix C

MEMBERSHIP OF THE BOARD OF GOVERNORS OF THE FEDERAL RESERVE SYSTEM, 1913–1990

APPOINTIVE MEMBERS[1]

Name	Federal Reserve District	Date of initial oath of office	Other dates and information relating to membership[2]
Charles S. Hamlin	Boston	Aug. 10, 1914	Reappointed in 1916 and 1926. Served until Feb. 3, 1936.[3]
Paul M. Warburg	New York	do	Term expired Aug. 9, 1918.
Frederic A. Delano	Chicago	do	Resigned July 21, 1918.
W.P.G. Harding	Atlanta	do	Term expired Aug. 9, 1922.
Adolph C. Miller	San Francisco	do	Reappointed in 1924. Reappointed in 1934 from the Richmond District. Served until Feb. 3, 1936.[3]
Albert Strauss	New York	Oct. 26, 1918	Resigned Mar. 15, 1920.
Henry A. Moehlenpah	Chicago	Nov. 10, 1919	Term expired Aug. 9, 1920.
Edmund Platt	New York	June 8, 1920	Reappointed in 1928. Resigned Sept. 14, 1930.
David C. Wills	Cleveland	Sept. 29, 1920	Term expired Mar. 4, 1921.
John R. Mitchell	Minneapolis	May 12, 1921	Resigned May 12, 1923.
Milo D. Campbell	Chicago	Mar. 14, 1923	Died Mar. 22, 1923.
Daniel R. Crissinger	Cleveland	May 1, 1923	Resigned Sept. 15, 1927.
George R. James	St. Louis	May 14, 1923	Reappointed in 1931. Served until Feb. 3, 1936.[4]
Edward H. Cunningham	Chicago	do	Died Nov. 28, 1930.
Roy A. Young	Minneapolis	Oct. 4, 1927	Resigned Aug. 31, 1930.

Eugene Meyer	New York	Sept. 16, 1930	Resigned May 10, 1933.
Wayland W. Magee	Kansas City	May 18, 1931	Term expired Jan. 24, 1933.
Eugene R. Black	Atlanta	May 19, 1933	Resigned Aug. 15, 1934.
M.S. Symczak	Chicago	June 14, 1933	Reappointed in 1936 and 1948. Resigned May 31, 1961.
J.J. Thomas	Kansas City	do	Served until Feb. 10, 1936.[3]
Marriner S. Eccles	San Francisco	Nov. 15, 1934	Reappointed in 1936, 1940, and 1944. Resigned July 14, 1951.
Joseph A. Broderick	New York	Feb. 3, 1936	Resigned Sept. 30, 1937.
John K. McKee	Cleveland	do	Served until Apr. 4, 1946.[3]
Ronald Ransom	Atlanta	do	Reappointed in 1942. Died Dec. 2, 1947.
Ralph W. Morrision	Dallas	Feb. 10, 1936	Resigned July 9, 1936.
Chester C. Davis	Richmond	June 25, 1936	Reappointed in 1940. Resigned Apr. 15, 1941.
Ernest G. Draper	New York	Mar. 30, 1938	Served until Sept. 1, 1950.[3]
Rudolph M. Evans	Richmond	Mar. 14, 1942	Served until Aug. 13, 1954.[3]
James K. Vardaman, Jr.	St. Louis	Apr. 4, 1946	Resigned Nov. 30, 1958.
Lawrence Clayton	Boston	Feb. 14, 1947	Died Dec. 4, 1949.
Thomas B. McCabe	Philadelphia	Apr. 15, 1948	Resigned Mar. 31, 1951.
Edward L. Norton	Atlanta	Sept. 1, 1950	Resigned Jan. 31, 1952.
Oliver S. Powell	Minneapolis	do	Resigned June 30, 1952.
Wm. McC. Martin, Jr.	New York	April 2, 1951	Reappointed in 1956. Term expired Jan. 31, 1970.
A.L. Mills, Jr.	San Francisco	Feb. 18, 1952	Reappointed in 1958. Resigned Feb. 28, 1965.

APPOINTIVE MEMBERS Continued

Name	Federal Reserve District	Date of initial oath of office	Other dates and information relating to membership[2]
J.L. Robertson	Kansas City	do	Reappointed in 1964. Resigned Apr. 30, 1973.
C. Canby Balderston	Philadelphia	Aug. 12, 1954	Served through Feb. 28, 1966.
Paul E. Miller	Minneapolis	Aug. 13, 1954	Died Oct. 21, 1954.
Chas. N. Shepardson	Dallas	Mar. 17, 1955	Retired Apr. 30, 1967.
G.H. King, Jr.	Atlanta	Mar. 25, 1959	Reappointed in 1960. Resigned Sept. 18, 1963.
George W. Mitchell	Chicago	Aug. 31, 1961	Reappointed in 1962. Served until Feb. 13, 1976.[3] [2]
J. Dewey Daane	Richmond	Nov. 29, 1963	Served until Mar. 8, 1974.[3]
Sherman J. Maisel	San Francisco	Apr. 30, 1965	Served through May 31, 1972.
Andrew F. Brimmer	Philadelphia	Mar. 9, 1966	Resigned Aug. 31, 1974.
William W. Sherrill	Dallas	May 1, 1967	Reappointed in 1968. Resigned Nov. 15, 1971.
Arthur F. Burns	New York	Jan. 1, 1970	Term began Feb. 1, 1970. Resigned Mar. 31, 1978.
John E. Sheehan	St. Louis	Jan. 4, 1972	Resigned June 1, 1975.
Jeffrey M. Bucher	San Francisco	June 5, 1972	Resigned Jan. 2, 1976.
Robert C. Holland	Kansas City	June 11, 1973	Resigned May 15, 1976.
Henry C. Wallich	Boston	Mar. 8, 1974	Resigned Dec. 15, 1986
Philip E. Coldwell	Dallas	Oct. 29, 1974	Served through Feb. 29, 1980.
Philip C. Jackson, Jr.	Atlanta	July 14, 1975	Resigned Nov. 17, 1978.

J. Charles Partee	Richmond	Jan. 5, 1976	Served until Feb. 7, 1986.[3]
Stephen S. Gardner	Philadelphia	Feb. 13, 1976	Died Nov. 19, 1978.
David M. Lilly	Minneapolis	June 1, 1976	Resigned Feb. 24, 1978.
G. William Miller	San Francisco	Mar. 8, 1978	Resigned Aug. 6, 1979.
Nancy H. Teeters	Chicago	Sept. 18, 1978	Served through June 27, 1984.
Emmett J. Rice	New York	June 20, 1979	Resigned Dec. 31, 1986.
Frederick H. Schultz	Atlanta	July 27, 1979	Served through Feb. 11, 1982.
Paul A. Volcker	Philadelphia	Aug. 6, 1979	Resigned August 11, 1987.
Lyle E. Gramley	Kansas City	May 28, 1980	Resigned Sept. 1, 1985.
Preston Martin	San Francisco	Mar. 31, 1982	Resigned April 30, 1986.
Martha R. Seger	Chicago	July 2, 1984	
Wayne D. Angell	Kansas City	Feb. 7, 1986	
Manuel H. Johnson	Richmond	Feb. 7, 1986	Resigned August 3, 1990.
H. Robert Heller	San Francisco	Aug. 19, 1986	Resigned July 31, 1989.
Edward W. Kelley, Jr.	Dallas	May 26, 1987	Reappointed in 1990.
Alan Greenspan	New York	Aug. 11, 1987	
John P. LaWare	Boston	Aug. 15, 1988	
David W. Mullins, Jr.	St. Louis	May 21, 1990	
Lawrence Lindsey		Nominated	

Chairmen[4]		*Vice Chairmen*[4]	
Charles S. Hamlin	Aug. 10, 1914–Aug. 9, 1916	Frederic A. Delano	Aug. 10, 1914–Aug. 9, 1916
W.P.G. Harding	Aug. 10, 1916–Aug. 9, 1922	Paul M. Warburg	Aug. 10, 1916–Aug. 9, 1918
Daniel R. Crissinger	May 1, 1923–Sept. 15, 1927	Albert Strauss	Oct. 26, 1918–Mar. 15, 1920

APPOINTIVE MEMBERS Continued

Name	Federal Reserve District	Date of initial oath of office	Other dates and information relating to membership[2]
Roy A. Young	Oct. 4, 1927– Aug. 31, 1930	Edmund Platt	July 23, 1920– Sept. 14, 1930
Eugene Meyer	Sept. 16, 1930– May 10, 1933	J.J. Thomas	Aug. 21, 1934– Feb. 10, 1936
Eugene R. Black	May 19, 1933– Aug. 15, 1934	Ronald Ransom	Aug. 6, 1956– Dec. 2, 1947
Marriner S. Eccles	Nov. 15, 1934– Jan. 31, 1948	C. Canby Balderston	Mar. 11, 1955– Feb. 28, 1966
Thomas B. McCabe	Apr. 15, 1948– Mar. 31, 1951	J.L. Robertson	Mar. 1, 1966– Apr. 30, 1973
Wm. McC. Martin, Jr.	Apr. 2, 1951– Jan. 31, 1970	George W. Mitchell	May 1, 1973– Feb. 13, 1976
Arther F. Burns	Feb. 1, 1970– Jan. 31, 1978	Stephen S. Gardner	Feb. 13, 1976– Nov. 19, 1978
G. William Miller	Mar. 8, 1978– Aug. 6, 1979	Frederick H. Schultz	July 27, 1979– Feb. 11, 1982
Paul A. Volcker	Aug. 6, 1979– Aug. 11, 1987	Preston Martin	Mar. 31, 1982– Mar. 31, 1986
Alan Greenspan	Aug. 11, 1987–	Manuel H. Johnson	Aug. 24, 1986– Aug. 3, 1990

EX-OFFICIO MEMBERS[1]

Secretaries of the Treasury		*Comptrollers of the Currency*	
W.G. McAdoo	Dec. 23, 1913– Dec. 15, 1918	John Skelton Williams	Feb. 2, 1914– Mar. 2, 1921
Carter Glass	Dec. 16, 1918– Feb. 1, 1920	Daniel R. Crissinger	Mar. 17, 1921– Apr. 30, 1923
David F. Houston	Feb. 2, 1920– Mar. 3, 1921	Henry M. Dawes	May 1, 1923– Dec. 17, 1924
Andrew W. Mellon	Mar. 4, 1921– Feb. 12, 1932	Joseph W. McIntosh	Dec. 20, 1924– Nov. 20, 1928
Ogden L. Mills	Feb. 12, 1932– Mar. 4, 1933	J.W. Pole	Nov. 21, 1928– Sept. 20, 1932
William H. Woodin	Mar. 4, 1933– Dec. 31, 1933	J.F.T. O'Connor	May 11, 1933– Feb. 1, 1936
Henry Morgenthau Jr.	Jan. 1, 1934– Feb. 1, 1936		

---

1. Under the provisions of the original Federal Reserve Act, the Federal Reserve Board was composed of seven members, including five appointive members, the Secretary of the Treasury, who was ex-officio chairman of the Board, and the Comptroller of the Currency. The original term of office was ten years, and the five original appointive members had terms of two, four, six, eight, and ten years respectively. In 1922 the number of appointive members was increased to six, and in 1933 the term of office was increased to twelve years. The Banking Act of 1935, approved Aug. 23, 1935, changed the name of the Federal Reserve Board to the Board of Governors of the Federal Reserve System and provided that the Board should be composed of seven appointive members; that the Secretary of the Treasury and the Comptroller of the Currency should continue to serve as members until Feb. 1, 1936, or until their successors were appointed and had qualified; and that thereafter the terms of members should be fourteen years and that the designation of Chairman and Vice Chairman of the Board should be for a term of four years.

2. Date after words "Resigned" and "Retired" denotes final day of service.

3. Successor took office on this date.

4. Chairman and Vice Chairman were designated Governor and Vice Governor before Aug. 23, 1935.

Appendix D

SCHEDULE OF RELEASE DATES FOR PRINCIPAL FEDERAL ECONOMIC INDICATORS FOR 1991

AGENCY/INDICATORS	JAN	FEB	MAR	APR	MAY	JUNE	JULY	AUG	SEPT	OCT	NOV	DEC
DEPARTMENT OF AGRICULTURE/ WORLD AGRICULTURAL OUTLOOK BOARD World Agricultural Supply and Demand Estimates	11	11	11	10	9	11	11	12	12	10	12	11
	Data are for current marketing season											
DEPARTMENT OF AGRICULTURE/ NATIONAL AGRICULTURAL STATISTICS SERVICE Agricultural Prices	31	28	29	30	31	28	31	30	30	31	27	31
	Data are for the middle of the month and previous full months											
Crop Production	11	11	11	10	9	11	11	12	12	10	12	11
	Data are for the first of the month											
Grain Stocks	11	—	28	—	—	27	—	—	30	—	—	—
	Data are for the first of the month except that the data for December are issued in January											
Cattle on Feed	25	—	—	19	—	—	23	—	—	22	—	—
	Data are for the first of the month											
Hogs and Pigs	4	—	28	—	—	28	—	—	27	—	—	—
	Data are for the first of the month except that the data for December are issued in January											
Plantings	—	—	28	—	—	27	—	—	—	—	—	—
	Data are collected during the first half of March and June											
DEPARTMENT OF AGRICULTURE/ FOREIGN AGRICULTURAL SERVICE World Agricultural Production	14	12	12	11	10	12	12	13	13	11	13	12
	Foreign data are based on the most recent information up to the time of publication											

Published by THE BUREAU OF NATIONAL AFFAIRS, INC., Washington, D.C. 20037

AGENCY/INDICATORS	JAN	FEB	MAR	APR	MAY	JUNE	JULY	AUG	SEPT	OCT	NOV	DEC
DEPARTMENT OF COMMERCE/ BUREAU OF THE CENSUS Value of New Construction Put in Place	2	1	1	1	1	3	1	1	3	1	1	2
					Data are for second month previous							
Housing Starts and Building Permits	17	20	19	16	16	18	17	15	18	18	20	17
					Data are for previous month							
New One-Family Houses Sold and For Sale	3 31	—	4 29	29	30	—	3 30	29	—	2 30	—	3
				Data generally are for previous month								
Wholesale Trade	10	7	12	8	7	7	10	7	11	8	7	11
				Data are for second month previous								
Advance Retail Sales	15	13	13	11	14	13	12	13	13	11	14	12
					Data are for previous month							
Advance Report of U.S. Merchandise Trade	18	15	20	18	17	19	18	16	19	17	19	19
				Data are for second month previous								
Manufacturing and Trade: Inventories and Sales	16	14	14	12	15	14	15	14	16	15	15	13
				Data are for second month previous								
Manufacturers' Shipments, Inventories, and Orders	4	5	5	2 30	31	—	2 31	30	—	3 31	—	5
		Releases early in month are for second month previous; others are for previous month										

Published by THE BUREAU OF NATIONAL AFFAIRS, INC., Washington, D.C. 20037

AGENCY/INDICATORS	JAN	FEB	MAR	APR	MAY	JUNE	JULY	AUG	SEPT	OCT	NOV	DEC
BUREAU OF THE CENSUS - Continued												
Advance Report on Durable Goods Manufacturers' Shipments and Orders	29	26	26	23	23	25	24	23	25	24	27	24
					Data are for previous month							
Quarterly Financial Report — Manufacturing, Mining, and Wholesale Trade	—	—	—	3 1/ (4Q '90)	—	10 (1Q '91)	—	—	9 (2Q '90)	—	—	9 (3Q '91)
					Reference period shown in parenthesis							
Quarterly Financial Report - Retail	8 (3Q '90)	—	—	3 1/ (4Q '90)	—	—	9 (1Q '91)	—	—	9 (2Q '91)	—	—
					Reference period shown in parenthesis							
Housing Vacancies	30 (4Q '90)	—	—	25 (1Q '91)	—	—	25 (2Q '91)	—	—	25 (3Q '91)	—	—
					Reference period shown in parenthesis							
Plant and Equipment Expenditures	—	—	—	10 (4Q '90)	—	6 (1Q '91)	—	—	5 (2Q '91)	—	—	18 (3Q '91)
					Reference period shown in parenthesis							
DEPARTMENT OF COMMERCE/ BUREAU OF ECONOMIC ANALYSIS												
Personal Income and Outlays	28	28	28	29	30	27	31	29	27	30	27	23
					Data are for previous month							
Composite Indexes of Leading, Coincident, and Lagging Indicators	30	—	1 29	—	1 31	28	—	2 30	—	1	1	3 31
					Data generally are for previous month							
Gross National Product	25 (4Q '90)	27 (4Q '90)	27 (4Q '90)	26 (1Q '91)	29 (1Q '91)	26 (1Q '91)	30 (2Q '91)	28 (2Q '91)	26 (2Q '91)	29 (3Q '91)	26 (3Q '91)	20 (3Q '91)
					Advance, preliminary, and final estimates are issued for each quarter							

Published by THE BUREAU OF NATIONAL AFFAIRS, INC., Washington, D.C. 20037

AGENCY/INDICATORS	JAN	FEB	MAR	APR	MAY	JUNE	JULY	AUG	SEPT	OCT	NOV	DEC
BUREAU OF ECONOMIC ANALYSIS – Continued Corporate Profits	—	—	27 (4Q '90)	26 (4Q '90)	29 (1Q '91)	26 (1Q '91)	—	28 (2Q '91)	26 (2Q '91)	—	26 (3Q '91)	20 (3Q '91)
				Reference period shown in parenthesis								
Merchandise Trade, Balance of Payments Basis	—	26 (4Q '90)	—	—	29 (1Q '91)	—	—	27 (2Q '91)	—	—	27 (3Q '91)	—
				Data are for previous quarter								
Summary of International Transactions	—	—	12 (4Q '90)	—	—	11 (1Q '91)	—	—	10 (2Q '91)	—	—	10 (3Q '91)
				Data are for previous quarter								
DEPARTMENT OF LABOR/ BUREAU OF LABOR STATISTICS The Employment Situation	4	1	8	5	3	7	5	2	6	4	1	6
					Data are for previous month							
Consumer Price Index	16	20	19	12	14	14	17	14	13	17	14	13
					Data are for previous month							
Producer Price Indexes	11	15	15	11	10	13	12	9	12	11	13	12
					Data are for previous month							
Real Earnings	16	20	19	12	14	14	17	14	13	17	14	13
					Data are for previous month							
Productivity and Costs	—	4	6	—	6	5	—	6	5	—	5	4
				Preliminary and revised estimates are issued for each quarter								

AGENCY/INDICATORS	JAN	FEB	MAR	APR	MAY	JUNE	JULY	AUG	SEPT	OCT	NOV	DEC
BUREAU OF LABOR STATISTICS – Continued Major Collective Bargaining Settlements in Private Industry	29	—	—	30	—	—	30	—	—	29	—	—
					Data are for previous quarter							
Employment Cost Index	29	—	—	30	—	—	30	—	—	29	—	—
					Data are for previous quarter							
U. S. Import and Export Price Indexes	25	28	28	25	23	27	25	22	26	24	27	27
					Data are for previous quarter or month							
FEDERAL RESERVE BOARD												
Money Stock, Liquid Assets, and Debt Measures		Data are issued every Thursday for the week ended Monday of previous week 2/										
Factors Affecting Reserves of Depository Institutions and Condition Statement of Federal Reserve Banks		Data are issued every Thursday for the week ended Wednesday, the day before 2/										
Consolidated Condition Report of Large Commercial Banks and Domestic Subsidiaries			Data are issued every Friday for Wednesday, 9 days earlier 2/									
Industrial Production and Capacity Utilization				Data are issued mid-month for previous month 3/								
Selected Interest Rates			Data are issued the first Tuesday of each month for previous month 2/									

AGENCY/INDICATORS	JAN	FEB	MAR	APR	MAY	JUNE	JULY	AUG	SEPT	OCT	NOV	DEC
FEDERAL RESERVE BOARD – Continued Consumer Installment Credit		Data are issued about the fifth working day of the month for second month previous										
DEPARTMENT OF HOUSING AND URBAN DEVELOPMENT Yields on FHA Insured New Home 30-Year Mortgages	23	25	22	22	22	24	23	22	24	23	25	23
					Data are as of the first of the month							
DEPARTMENT OF THE TREASURY/ FINANCIAL MANAGEMENT SERVICE Treasury Statement (The Monthly "Budget")	23	22	21	19	21	21	22	21	4/	22	22	20
					Data are for previous month							
DEPARTMENT OF THE TREASURY/ OFFICE OF THRIFT SUPERVISION Thrift Institution Activity		Data are issued on the fifth working day of each month for the second month previous										

1/ Quarterly Financial Report - Retail will be included in Manufacturing, Mining and Wholesale for 4th quarter 1990 (the April 1991 release).
2/ When the release date falls on a holiday, the data are released the next workday.
3/ Call (202)452-3206 for exact date.
4/ Release date subject to completion of year-end reporting requirements.

- 0 -

Published by THE BUREAU OF NATIONAL AFFAIRS, INC., Washington, D.C. 20037

Appendix E

BUSINESS CYCLE EXPANSIONS AND CONTRACTIONS IN THE UNITED STATES 1894–1990

Business Cycles Reference Dates		Duration in Months			
		Contraction (trough from previous peak)	Expansion (trough to peak)	Cycle	
Trough	Peak			Trough from Previous Trough	Peak from Previous Peak
December 1854	June 1857	. . .	30	. . .	. . .
December 1858	October 1860	18	22	48	40
June 1861	April 1865	8	46	30	54
December 1867	June 1869	32	18	78	50
December 1870	October 1873	18	34	36	52
March 1879	March 1882	65	36	99	101
May 1885	March 1887	38	22	74	60
April 1888	July 1890	13	27	35	40
May 1891	January 1893	10	20	37	30
June 1894	December 1895	17	18	37	35

Business Cycles Reference Dates		Duration in Months			
		Contraction		Cycle	
Trough	Peak	(trough from previous peak)	Expansion (trough to peak)	Trough from Previous Trough	Peak from Previous Peak
June 1897	June 1899	18	24	36	42
December 1900	September 1902	18	21	42	39
August 1904	May 1907	23	33	44	56
June 1908	January 1910	13	19	46	32
January 1912	January 1913	24	12	43	36
December 1914	August 1918	23	<u>44</u>	35	<u>67</u>
March 1919	January 1920	<u>7</u>	10	<u>51</u>	17
July 1921	May 1923	18	22	28	40
July 1924	October 1926	14	27	36	41
November 1927	August 1929	13	21	40	34
March 1933	May 1937	43	50	64	93
June 1938	February 1945	13	<u>80</u>	63	<u>93</u>
October 1945	November 1948	<u>8</u>	37	<u>88</u>	45
October 1949	July 1953	11	<u>45</u>	48	<u>56</u>
May 1954	August 1957	<u>10</u>	39	<u>55</u>	49
April 1958	April 1960	8	24	47	32
February 1961	December 1969	10	<u>106</u>	34	<u>116</u>
November 1970	November 1973	<u>11</u>	36	<u>117</u>	47
March 1975	January 1980	16	58	52	74
July 1980	July 1981	6	12	64	18
November 1982	June 1990	16	91	28	107
Average all cycles:					
1854–1982 (30 cycles)		18	33	51	'51
1854–1919 (16 cycles)		22	27	48	'49
1919–1945 (6 cycles)		18	35	53	53
1945–1982 (8 cycles)		11	45	56	55
Average peacetime cycle:					
1854–1982 (25 cycles)		19	27	46	46
1854–1919 (14 cycles)		22	24	46	47
1919–1945 (5 cycles)		20	26	46	45
1945–1982 (6 cycles)		11	34	46	44

Note: Underscored figures are the wartime expansions (Civil War, World Wars I and II, Korean War, and Vietnam War), the postwar contractions, and the run cycles that include the wartime expansions.

'29 cycles '15 cycles '24 cycles '13 cycles

Source: National Bureau of Economic Research, Inc.

Appendix F

RESERVE REQUIREMENTS OF DEPOSITORY INSTITUTIONS

Type of deposit, and deposit interval[2]	Depository institution requirements after implementation of the Monetary Control Act	
	Percent of deposits	Effective date
Net transaction accounts[3,4]		
$0 million – $41.1 million ...	3	12/18/90
More than $41.1 million	12	12/18/90
Nonpersonal time deposits[5,6] .	0	12/27/90
Eurocurrency liabilities[7]	0	12/27/90

1. Reserve requirements in effect on Dec. 31, 1990. Required reserves must be held in the form of deposits with Federal Reserve Banks or vault cash. Nonmember institutions may maintain reserve balances with a Federal Reserve Bank indirectly on a pass-through

basis with certain approved institutions. For previous reserve requirements, see earlier editions of the *Annual Report* or the *Federal Reserve Bulletin.* Under provisions of the Monetary Control Act, depository institutions include commercial banks, mutual savings banks, savings and loan associations, credit unions, agencies and branches of foreign banks, and Edge corporations.

2. The Garn–St. Germain Depository Institutions Act of 1982 (Public Law 97–320) requires that $2 million of reservable liabilities of each depository institution be subject to a zero percent reserve requirement. The Board is to adjust the amount of reservable liabilities subject to this zero percent reserve requirement each year for the succeeding calendar year by 80 percent of the percentage increase in the total reservable liabilities of all depository institutions, measured on an annual basis as of June 30. No corresponding adjustment is to be made in the event of a decrease. On Dec. 20, 1988, the exemption was raised from $3.2 million to $3.4 million. In determining the reserve requirements of depository institutions, the exemption shall apply in the following order: (1) net NOW accounts (NOW accounts less allowable deductions); and (2) net other transaction accounts. The exemption applies only to accounts that would be subject to a 3 percent reserve requirement.

3. Transaction accounts include all deposits on which the account holder is permitted to make withdrawals by negotiable or transferable instruments, payment orders of withdrawal, and telephone and preauthorized transfers in excess of three per month for the purpose of making payments to third persons or others. However, MMDAs and similar accounts subject to the rules that permit no more than six preauthorized, automatic, or other transfers per month, of which no more than three can be checks, are not transaction accounts (such accounts are savings deposits).

4. Monetary Control Act of 1980 requires that the amount of transaction accounts against which the 3 percent reserve requirement applies be modified annually by 80 percent of the percentage change in transaction accounts held by all depository institutions, determined as of June 30 each year. Effective Dec. 18, 1990 for institutions reporting quarterly and Dec. 25, 1990 for institutions reporting weekly, the amount was increased from $40.4 million to $41.1 million.

5. The reserve requirements on nonpersonal time deposits with an original maturity of less than 1½ years were reduced from 3 percent to 1½ percent on the maintenance period that began December 13, 1990, and to zero for the maintenance period that began December 27, 1990, for institutions that report weekly. The reserve requirement on nonpersonal time deposits with an original maturity of 1½ years or more has been zero since October 6, 1983.

6. For institutions that report quarterly, the reserves on nonpersonal time deposits with an original maturity of less than 1½ years will be reduced from 3 percent to zero on January 17, 1991.

7. The reserve requirements on Eurocurrency liabilities were reduced from 3 percent to zero in the same manner and on the same dates as were the reserves on nonpersonal time deposits with an original maturity of less than 1½ years (see notes 5 and 6).

Index